NEWFOUNDLAND
ISLAND INTO PROVINCE

NEWFOUNDLAND
ISLAND INTO PROVINCE

BY

ST JOHN CHADWICK

CAMBRIDGE
AT THE UNIVERSITY PRESS
1967

Published by the Syndics of the Cambridge University Press
Bentley House, 200 Euston Road, London, N.W. 1
American Branch: 32 East 57th Street, New York, N.Y. 10022

Library of Congress Catalogue Card Number: 67-12206

Printed in Great Britain
at the University Printing House, Cambridge
(Brooke Crutchley, University Printer)

DEDICATION

For grandson Patrick, who nearly ate it:
Nancy Duncan who really wrote it, and,
since there is much of France in this:
surtout pour M.

CONTENTS

APPENDICES

LIST OF MAPS

FOREWORD

BY THE RIGHT HONOURABLE LOUIS ST LAURENT

I was very pleased to learn that Mr John Chadwick had written a comprehensive and consecutive history of Newfoundland. Mr Chadwick is particularly well qualified for this task. He served the British government in Newfoundland and later at Ottawa and thereby looked at the history of Newfoundland from advantageous points of view which enabled him to give added dimensions to his work. He had the further advantage of an intimate association with the culminating event in the history he has written, the union of Newfoundland with Canada. I have always regarded that union as the most important achievement of my years in public life and I welcome Mr Chadwick's contribution to our deeper knowledge of the ancient British colony which became an integral part of Canada on 31 March 1949.

Quebec 15 November 1966

FOREWORD

BY JOSEPH R. SMALLWOOD
PREMIER OF NEWFOUNDLAND AND LABRADOR

Suddenly, quite unexpectedly, emerging from our exciting past, Mr John Chadwick appears with a carefully written account of the great events in which we were both involved. Some people were suspicious at once when the British Government announced that they were sending two of their experts, Messrs Chadwick and Jones, to assist the National Convention. Some of us were quite pleased, for we knew the need for trained minds and precise information.

When their report was presented to us at length there was no one so churlish as to deny its usefulness to all of us. And thus the names Chadwick and Jones became entrenched in the history of that time in Newfoundland.

I find it altogether captivating that twenty years later John Chadwick should take the trouble to put this useful account together, and all that we need now is to have Professor Wheare back here with us for a season.

But the situation could not be made complete without bringing some back from the dead, and even with the help of Confederation that is more than we can do.

I know that many will read Mr Chadwick's book with genuine pleasure.

St John's Newfoundland

1 November 1966

PREFACE

Why Newfoundland? Sentimentally, because this has been a long-maturing labour of love: a gesture of thanks, however modest, for hospitality repeatedly received: a tribute to a lovable, generous, often unfortunate but always friendly people.

Intellectually, because Newfoundland throughout her long and tangled history has posed some of the thorniest problems with which an imperial power has ever come to grips—annexation in defiance of colonization: settlement in the teeth of mercantile monopoly: native possession in the face of French oppression: autonomy in defiance of economy: suspended Dominion Status in the aftermath of bankruptcy: benign autocracy in search of solvency.

Historically, because in a year when Canada celebrates the centenary of confederation, it seems fitting that Newfoundland, the tenth, newest and possibly last of the Canadian provinces, and also the oldest known part of the Dominion, should have her victories and vicissitudes reviewed afresh.

In its time the Island has rung more constitutional bells than any other Colony. Fishing station; nursery for seamen; Imperial res nullius; retarded Colony; Anglo-North American aircraft carrier: bankrupt or buoyant, autonomous or acquiescent, Newfoundland has lived through and survived one crisis on another.

Much has been written of her history. Prowse, the first comprehensive local chronicler has, as often as not erratically, covered events from Cabot's day to 1895. McLintock has surveyed the period preceding and leading to self-government. The first Lord Birkenhead encapsulated Newfoundland in a study stopping short at 1920. Ten years later the present Premier of the Province enthusiastically reviewed her past and future. A Royal Commission carried the story forward to 1934. Most recently Professor R. A. MacKay, as editor and contributor to a series of most scholarly essays, has advanced the Island's history to 1946. And Newfoundland has played her part, often prominently, in many histories of the sixteenth, seventeenth and eighteenth centuries.

What lacks is a history which, in reviewing and reassessing the facts already known, carries the story further and attempts a picture in the round of Newfoundland's struggle both to obtain a place in the colonial sun and to achieve a quasi-independent status: in short a modern history of Newfoundland from discovery to federation.

The theme of this book is above all constitutional—from res nullius to effective occupation: from there to representative government and internal autonomy: on from the birth of an indigenous foreign policy to the unique surrender of Dominion Status; and through Government by Commission to the narrow sacrifice of nationhood.

Little attempt has been made to retrace in detail ground already covered. Thus, while the French fishery disputes, the Newfoundland Railway and the Labrador boundary question are dealt with at some length because of their constitutional significance, little more than summary reference is made to discovery and settlement or to Newfoundland's nineteenth-century quarrels with Canada and the United States. These and other earlier issues have been amply described by previous writers. In such necessary references as I have made, I can only hope that I have paid sufficient tribute to their work.

In brief, this is an illustrative, rather than a comprehensive history: a study in constitutional development: an attempt to explain Newfoundland to herself as well as to Britain and to Canada. At a moment when a great and growing Confederation embarks upon its second century, my hope is that in its own small way this book will make some contribution to Anglo-Canadian understanding.

London
January 1967

ACKNOWLEDGEMENTS

Many friends, on both sides of the Atlantic, have helped in the struggle to bring this book to life.

In the first place, as a civil servant detached from Whitehall but still 'on the books', I have to thank the Head of Her Majesty's Diplomatic Service, Sir Saville Garner, G.C.M.G., for authority to go to print at all. Secondly, much gratitude is due from an almost virgin author to the Syndics of the Cambridge University Press for their encouragement throughout.

In Newfoundland I owe a special debt of thanks to my old sparring partner and good friend, Mr Walter Marshall, C.B.E., as well as to Professor A. M. Fraser, for the care with which they have read and criticized my manuscript at varying stages. I am also warmly in the debt of the Premier, the Honourable J. R. Smallwood, an acquaintance of many years standing. Busy though he is, he has still found time to contribute a foreword. I have also received much helpful material from the British Trade Correspondent in St John's, Mr A. G. Ayre.

In Canada my thanks go above all to Professor R. M. MacKay, Newfoundland 'desk man' at the Department of External Affairs in the period leading up to confederation, and editor of and vital contributor to an admirable series of studies on Newfoundland, on which I have freely drawn. He too has given much of his time to constructive criticism of many of the chapters in this book. My gratitude and commiseration go also to those anonymous members of Canadian Government Departments who have read through the completed text, as well as to the British High Commissioner in Ottawa, Sir Henry Litott, K.C.M.G., and to the Counsellor on his staff, Miss Eleanor Emery. They have helped unstintingly with numerous acts of kindness and advice. My warm thanks are also due to Mr St Laurent, one of the great architects of union, for his gracious foreword.

In Britain I am in debt to many friends and colleagues. It would be difficult to mention them all by name. But Professor C. E. Carrington salvaged by his encouragement what seemed at one stage to be a foundering vessel. Mr Basil Greenhill has given much of his time and expertise to criticism of those early chapters which bear on trans-Atlantic maritime history. Sir William Dale, K.C.M.G., and Sir Charles Dixon, K.C.M.G., K.C.V.O., have guided me through the mysteries of Judicial Committee procedure. Above all Sir Alexander Clutterbuck, G.C.M.G., M.C., undoubtedly the greatest living expert outside Newfoundland on Newfoundland itself, has provided at much cost to his well-earned retirement that searching and astringent criticism that a junior would expect from his still revered superior. I am also deeply indebted to the Deputy Librarian at the Commonwealth Relations Office, Mr D. Overton, as well as to his staff and that of the Public Record Office, for his and their cheerful and expert response to the innumerable calls that I have made upon them.

Finally, but very far from last in terms of effort, I have to thank Mrs Nancy Duncan, M.B.E. Over many months she has patiently and miraculously interpreted my script: typed and retyped uncomplainingly and generally reduced this book to legible form. The results, for what they are worth—but not the blame—are due above all to her.

PRINCIPAL SOURCES

Prowse, D. W. *A History of Newfoundland*. London, 1895.

McLintock, A. H. *The Establishment of Constitutional Government in Newfoundland 1783–1832*. London, 1941.

Newfoundland Royal Commission: Report and Papers (London) 1933 Cmd. 4479.

Innis, H. A. *The Cod Fisheries*. Toronto, 1954.

Smallwood, J. R. *The New Newfoundland*. New York, 1931.

MacKay, R. A. (ed.). *Newfoundland: Economic, Political and Strategic Studies*. Toronto, 1946.

Documents in the keeping of The Public Record Office, Foreign Office, Colonial Office and Commonwealth Relations Office.

PROLOGUE

'But these Newe landes by all cosmographye from the Cane of Catous lande can not lye lytele paste a thousande myle.'

JOHN RASTELL, *A new Interlude* (London, *c.* 1519)

'We have learned in the last thirty years that man's early knowledge of the sea and willingness to venture out upon it resulted in voyages undreamt of by nineteenth century historians.'

GWYNN JONES, *The Norse Atlantic Sagas* (Oxford, 1964)

'The sea air of the late fifteenth century was laden with stories of lost or unknown lands across the ocean.'

J. A. WILLIAMSON, *The Cabot Voyages* (Cambridge, 1962)

Both east and west of the Atlantic the history primers still spoon-feed two illusions: the first of John Cabot as discoverer of Newfoundland; the second of the Island as 'Britain's Oldest Colony'. Today, as our understanding of the Norse Sagas goes deeper and fresh light is thrown on the Bristol discoveries under Henry VII, the first illusion looks ever tattier round the edges. The second was never more than a latter-day Imperial myth, born of sentimentality out of defiance of the realities of Imperial policy.

Geographers, historians and cartographers have long speculated over the Books of the Icelanders and of the Settlements, and on the Sagas of the Greenlanders, Erik the Red and Leif the Lucky. Explanations without number have been given of the position on present-day maps of the mysterious country named as Mark- or Vinland. Some experts have placed this Ultissima Thule as far north as Baffin Island: others as far south as Florida. Learned societies in Spain, aficionados of Columbus in the United States, and until recently many serious scholars in other lands, have scoffed at the very idea that ninth- and tenth-century Norsemen could have ventured to, still less succeeded in, crossing the North Atlantic in their allegedly frail craft. For them no case existed for presuming that Newfoundland was conceivably the Markland of the Vikings.

Yet in mere curachs Irishmen were risking the sea passage to Britain not later than A.D. 565. By the ninth century Irish anchorites were island-hopping via the Shetlands and Faroes to Iceland. If in turn the Norsemen could first chase the anchorites from Iceland, colonize it and then move on to Greenland, what was there in logic to prevent them from pressing westward to the coasts of Labrador? A mere glance at the map is enough to show that the distance between Reykjavik and Angmagsalik on the east coast of Greenland is no greater than that separating the Norse settlements in Western Greenland from Frobisher Bay and the northern cape of Labrador. Once that landfall had been made, there would have been little but ill-luck (or fog) to prevent a resolute Viking seaman from working his way southward along the coast, across the Strait of Belle Isle to Newfoundland, and on to Nova Scotia. That numbers of the Norsemen did so is now scarcely open to doubt. Proof of their presence in Greenland is irrefutable: that of at least one settlement—at L'Anse-aux-Meadows, near Cape Bauld in the extreme north of Newfoundland—is hardly less so. Such an authority on the sagas as Ingstad, supported by the earlier researches of Munn, Tanner and Malqgaard, has argued convincingly that ruins excavated in the area show traces not only of Eskimo but also of European habitation. Ingstad's discoveries of 1962 seem to suggest more cogently than any theories to the contrary yet advanced, that Cape Bauld was indeed the so-called Promontorium Windlandiae from which Vinland itself stretched southwards to at least New England.

Wherever the exact truth lies,[1] enough is now known or weightily adduced to put paid to those highly coloured prints of the Newfoundland landfall of John Cabot, the 'discoverer'. One used to see him in the text-books stepping ashore from the *Matthew* in Bonavista Bay one fine, bright morning in the summer of 1497. Alas! even if we discount the feats of the Viking adventurers who, by the twelfth century, had faded back into the mists whence they emerged, fresh evidence is now accumulating to challenge even Cabot's secondary claim to fame. If in fact he was the first of modern seamen to make the North Atlantic crossing, it is as likely that his landfall was at Cape Breton as in Newfoundland. But following deeper studies of the Bristol records the view has recently been advanced that Cabot's voyage may well have been preceded by that of Thomas Croft, who in 1481 sailed from the west country for the so-called Isle of Brasil.

Fascinating though these conjectures are, it matters less for the purpose of this study who first discovered Newfoundland than why. What were the motives which led men, Norsemen or English, Basques, Spaniards, French

[1] A reviewer has recently (and sagely) commented, with particular reference to the so-called 'Vinland Map': 'Perhaps a certain healthy scepticism is in order, for the discovery of America has attracted the attention of more than a fair share of cranks, zealots and charlatans' (*The Times Literary Supplement*, 20 November 1965, p. 1076; 'Westward Who?', a review of *The Vinland Map and the Tartar Relation* by Skelton, Marston and Painter. Yale, 1965). The publication of the Map, in circumstances which cannot but throw doubt on its veracity, has given rise to much controversy in the British press—see, for example, 'Is the Vinland Map a forgery?' (*Sunday Times*, 6 March 1966) and 'In the wake of the Vinland Voyagers' (J. R. L. Anderson, *The Guardian*, 7 March 1966). *The Guardian* went so far as to fit out an expedition with the aim of casting new light on the Norse voyages to Vinland. Latterly, the claims of the 12th century Welsh navigator, Madoc, have been advanced.

or Portuguese to risk their lives on so hazardous a throw? What were they after? And, when they attained it, how did this affect the new-found land?

Pace the Norsemen, the second half of the fifteenth century was, for Western European man, pre-eminently his age of exploration and discovery. Portuguese mariners who had lit on the Azores believed that more land lay somewhere to the north-west of the island group. English merchants, already trading with Iceland, were undoubtedly familiar with the earlier sagas and suspected the existence of Greenland. News of Marco Polo's eastern journeys had filtered through to western capitals and, although not all geographers believed the route to the spice islands to lie westwards through a North-West Passage, this fantasy and the challenge presented by the Treaty of Tordesillas were enough to make the English Court look kindly on any project that would buttress England at the expense of Spain and Portugal.

However thin John Cabot's claims to the discovery of Newfoundland may be, he at least was the first (naturalized) Englishman to receive in his own name and that of his heirs a charter for discovery westwards. The Letters Patent granted him by Henry VII on 5 March 1496 entitled Cabot and his sons 'with five ships...at their own proper costs and charges...to find whatsoever islands, countries...in whatsoever part of the world placed, which before this time were unknown to all Christians... acquiring for us the dominion, title and jurisdiction of the same...islands and mainlands so discovered...'[1]

Cabot may well have gone off next year in search of spices or of the North-West Passage. Today this matters little. What he discovered was land off whose coasts a rich harvest could be reaped. From the scant descriptions of the voyage which survive, it seems clear that he had lit on one or other of the shallow Banks off the shores east and south of the Gulf of the St Lawrence. On a further westward exploration of 1498, John Cabot was lost without trace. But what he had already achieved was to be a stimulus to English merchants and to the Portuguese to mount yet further expeditions. By now news of Columbus's discoveries further south had electrified the maritime states of Europe and the great trade race was on. By 1506, following the voyages of the brothers Corte Real, Portugal was importing cod from Newfoundland, soon to be followed by fishermen from the Basque country, Brittany and France. To these early voyagers, supported by merchant backers and armateurs in their home ports, the new-found island offered much—an inexhaustible supply of cod, territorial waters within which supplies of bait abounded, safe anchorages, beaches for

[1] Public Record Office, Treaty Roll 178. English translation reproduced from H. P. Biggar, *The Precursors of Jacques Cartier* (Ottawa, 1911), pp. 7–10.

drying fish and a wealth of timber for repairs and firewood. The settlement of Newfoundland was never seriously considered at this stage. Although a further charter was granted in 1501 to Cabot's son, Sebastian, England was still too underpopulated; too much in need of retaining her seamen to think in terms of colonization.[1] In short, there were at work at that time none of those social and economic forces which drove men to settle overseas. The developing European rivalry for Newfoundland turned on her waters and on the seasonal use of her harbours and beaches, not on permanent possession. Such minute settlements as may have enjoyed a fleeting existence in those early years would have been little more than staging or factory posts for the revictualling of expeditions probing further west, or for the general purposes of the fishery. National rivalries had not yet carried beyond the shoreline. If the Portuguese should be found in occupation of one stretch of coast, the English or Basques or French would move on to another anchorage. There was fish for all and to spare and King Henry was in no mood to antagonize Portugal or Spain in Europe by endeavouring, even had he had the means to secure it, a monopoly of this expanding trade.

And as the growing number of ships in Newfoundland waters testified, King Cod was to prove of cardinal importance to Europe. The oft-quoted letter of Sincino in London to the Duke of Milan, reporting on John Cabot's voyage, had affirmed that 'the sea...is swimming with fish, which can be taken not only with the net but in baskets let down with a stone'. The bait was irresistible. By 1530 close on 150 English vessels had been diverted from Icelandic waters. The Portuguese were even more fully involved, with fishermen from the northern and north-eastern ports of France not far behind. By the second half of the century Spain too had joined the lists. What underlay this concentration on Newfoundland? Why were Governments, captains and their merchant backers prepared to venture so perilously far and risk so much? In the first place fish and facilities joined happily together. Supplies of cod were inexhaustible: the cod was both easy prey and eminently 'drip-dryable'. The island offered timber for the asking and the right conditions for drying fish. Dried cod in turn was light, easily transportable and almost indestructible. There was a ready and increasing market for it. Armies marched on cod: the crews of the probing ships of the explorers above or below the Line lived partly on it. Religious observances required it. In pre-refrigeration days it was less costly than

[1] For the information in the preceding pages I am largely indebted to two recent sources: *The Cabot Voyages and Bristol Discovery under Henry VII*, J. A. Williamson (ed.), Hakluyt Society, 2nd ser., no. cxx (Cambridge, 1962)—a meticulous piece of detective work; and *The Norse Atlantic Sagas*, by Professor Gwynn Jones (Oxford, 1964)—a brilliant analysis throwing much fresh light on the earliest Atlantic voyages.

meat and game. Moreover, the prosecution of the Newfoundland fishery produced good seamen. All these were factors which led the English to take an ever-increasing share in the Newfoundland trade and which were destined to mould the Island's history.

Special protection was now afforded the industry. In 1562, for instance, Wednesdays were added to Saturdays in Lent by English Act of Parliament as fish days.[1] A further Act of 1580 banned imports of foreign cured fish by Englishmen, save for Newfoundland and Icelandic cod.[2] The fishery, whether prosecuted on the Banks or to a far lesser degree inshore, gradually took on a set routine. As McLintock describes it:

> In the spring, either in ballast or laden with goods and provisions for the season, the sack (i.e. supply) ships left Britain for Portugal or some other foreign country to secure adequate supplies of staves and the all-essential salt. On arrival at Newfoundland, they obtained in exchange cargoes of dried fish (i.e. the surplus catch which the smaller west coast fishing vessels could not carry home) for the West Indian or Mediterranean ports. Late in the autumn... these ships returned to England with wine, oil and other commodities from abroad or with the more precious bullion received in payment for the salted cod.[3]

Thus, the Newfoundland fishery proved not only a nursery for English seamen. It created a favourable balance of trade which increasingly convinced both Government and merchants that the Island should be brought more directly under English control. This in brief was the background to the annexation of 1583, which was to give Newfoundland her once proud though quite false claim to rank as 'Britain's Oldest Colony'.

On 5 August 1583 Sir Humphrey Gilbert read out to an assembled gathering on Signal Hill above St John's his commission under the Great Seal of England and took nominal possession of the Island in the right of the Crown. That same day he distributed to many English merchants present their fishing places or 'rooms' in St John's and the neighbouring harbours. His action was symbolic of the long struggle which was now to begin between those visiting merchants' agents and fishermen who wished to form permanent settlements on the Island and those in England—merchants, traders, monopolists or sea captains—who strenuously urged on the Government the need to retain Newfoundland solely as a fishing station and a training ground for seamen. The long and bitter fight for colonization, not effectively settled until the start of the nineteenth century, had been joined.

[1] 5 Eliz. c. 5.
[2] 23 Eliz. c. 7.
[3] A. H. McLintock, *The Establishment of Constitutional Government in Newfoundland 1783–1832* (Longmans Green, 1941).

For a short and indeterminate period, charters were occasionally granted under the reigns of James I and Charles I for the purposes of settlement. But the doctrine of effective occupation could hardly be said to apply to a 'Colony' which, as late as a century and a half after the so-called annexation, could boast a population of less than two thousand. And these small struggling fishing villages (or 'outports') for the most part owed their origins to fishermen absconding at the end of a season and secreting themselves inland until the last of the fleet had sailed for home. Moreover, as the sea power of France grew and threatened England, the interests of Government and merchants began ever more closely to coincide. The settlement of Newfoundland became a double threat. It was a drain on naval manpower, and it risked breaking the west country merchants' monopoly of the fishery.

Indeed, the seeds of the naval-cum-mercantile anti-settlement policy had been laid even prior to annexation. Captains of the English fishing fleet were each required to carry one 'green man' or apprentice able seaman on voyages to Newfoundland, and the first comer to each harbour at the start of every fishing season was empowered 'to seize any piece of foreshore he might select sufficient to cure and dry his cod fish'.[1] Thus began the rule of the notorious 'Fishing Admirals'—despotic, harsh and for the most part illiterate ships' masters who, having once taken their 'rooms', laid down the law and saw to it that any settler in their areas, actual or potential, was either chased inland and his miserable possessions destroyed, or re-embarked for home as autumn came. It was this growing competition for 'rooms', combined with the avoiding tactics of those few hardy souls still bent on putting down their roots, which first dictated the scattered and costly pattern of settlement that still plagues Newfoundland today.

English policy towards the Island was first spelt out in the so-called 'Western Charter' of 1634. It was designedly favourable to the 'merchants, traders and adventurers' of the west country ports and, although settlement companies were still being formed, as designedly inimical to colonization.[2] The Charter, renewed in 1661 and 1670, provided for a rudimentary system of justice—delinquents being returned to England to suffer imprisonment or worse. It laid down that no squatter might 'cut down any wood or plant within six miles of sea shore': or take up the best fishing stages before the arrival of fishermen from England. It confirmed that 'such ship as first entereth a harbour shall be admiral', and on renewal in 1670, enjoined on ships' masters that every fifth man of his crew should be a 'green' man.

[1] D. W. Prowse, *History of Newfoundland from the English, Colonial and French Records* (Macmillan, 1895), p. 61.

[2] Privy Council IV, 1723–37.

Thus, while the New England colonies were struggling painfully into existence and the white planter was making his presence felt in the West Indies, Newfoundland was to be no more than a seasonal shore line, a great ship anchored off the Banks, left each winter to its solitude save for the few bands of Indians roaming the interior. The notorious Act to Encourage the Trade to Newfoundland, passed in 1698,[1] was a further blow to the few struggling settlers, as well as to those company promoters and hopeful monopolists who encouraged them from home. Having recited the benefits to England of the trade with Newfoundland, the Act declared the fishery to be free to all and re-emphasized the penalties on settlers already contained in the 'Western Charters'

Declaratory and directory...the act had a most pernicious influence over the control of the fisheries and the growth of the colony. The amazing thing is that, until its repeal in 1824, it remained the fundamental law of Newfoundland. In fact, its presence upon the Statute book was a constant reminder of the triumph of mercantile interests over colonisation. It became the symbol of oppression and tyranny: it sanctioned obsolete and selfish customs: and it alone permitted the furtherance of a policy which was to retard the natural development of the island for over a century.[2]

In the circumstances it was scarcely surprising that Newfoundland should become a refuge for evil-doers or that such justice as the fishing admirals meted out should be both elementary and harsh—'The sacred temple of law and equity...a fish store, the judicial seat an inverted butter firkin.'[3] But despite the selfish determination of English mercantilists to brook no competition from rivals settling permanently in Newfoundland, and in face of the threat posed by continuous French efforts to establish a presence on the east coast, notably at Placentia Bay, the colonists still clung to their footholds and indeed slowly grew in number. According to a rough census taken in 1697, the male population was then in the region of 1,700, compared with the handful of 120 men estimated by Lounsbury to have wintered in the island in 1683–4.[4] For a while, indeed, England's preoccupation with the French wars, and the temporary exclusion of French fishermen from Newfoundland waters, had given an unexpected boost to settlement. By the mid-eighteenth century, upwards of two thousand people were living permanently in the St John's area alone. More and more of the fish dispatched to Europe was being caught from Newfoundland-based boats and shipped eastwards in cargo rather than

[1] 10 and 11 William III, c. 25.
[2] McLintock, p. 6.
[3] Prowse, p. 226.
[4] R. G. Lunsburg, *The British Fishery at Newfoundland 1684–1763* (New Haven, 1934), pp. 92–6.

fishing vessels. But colonization was not to be conceded without a final, long convulsive struggle on the part of the West Country merchant lobby.

As Innes has put it: 'The struggle in Newfoundland for the right of free fishing reflected the growing importance of the sea. Commercialism, built on the fishing industry, drove a wedge into monopoly control over external trade as exercised from Great Britain.'[1] But West Country merchants, who had until now provided the bulk of the vessels trading with Newfoundland continued to claim that settlement would mean, as experience with New England had already shown, that a lucrative trade would pass entirely out of English hands. As it was, boatkeepers in Newfoundland were already luring visiting seamen from their ships, and the population, both fixed and transient, was increasing so rapidly that as far back as 1602 the Government had felt obliged to appoint a Commissioner to police the fishery. He was the precursor of a long line of summer Governors who combined the role of naval commander with that of judge, jury and executor. Outstanding among these tough and generally bigoted seamen was Hugh Palliser. Deeply imbued with a sense of the Navy's importance to Britain, his appointment in 1764, at the close of the Seven Years War, marked the climax of the anti-colonial struggle. From the first Palliser showed his determination to crush the settlers. As he was later to explain in evidence before the Board of Trade, the maintenance of the fisheries under British control was essential 'because from that arises great wealth to the subjects, great revenue to the Crown, and above all, because our naval strength, consequently the security of the whole, depends more upon them than upon any other branch of trade whatever'.[2] Or, as McLintock has succinctly put it: 'The position simply resolved itself into the clear-cut alternative of preserving the trade at the sacrifice of a colony, or of permitting the inhabitants to assume control of the entire fisheries.'[3] At the time of Palliser's command, some twenty thousand English seamen were engaged in the annual fishery and the trade was worth upwards of £600,000 per annum.

At home, the political mood was in sympathy with the views so vigorously expressed by Palliser. In 1770 Lord North had taken office and an era of oppression was opening in the colonial field. Five years later Parliament sanctioned the rigorous measure destined to pass into history as 'Palliser's Act'.[4] Based on the Trade Act of 1698, it was designed to pre-

[1] H. Innis, *The Cod Fisheries* (Toronto, 1954), p. 93.
[2] Board of Trade, 6/57. Sir H. Palliser's evidence, 8 April 1784.
[3] McLintock, p. 10.
[4] 15 Geo. III, c. 31.

vent English seamen from deserting ship in Newfoundland, and generally, as a later petition from the colonists was to describe it: 'To controvert the course of nature, to keep the Island of Newfoundland a barren waste, to exterminate the inhabitants: to annihilate property, and to make sailors by preventing population.'[1] The Newfoundland historian Prowse was equally pungent. In his judgement, Palliser had 'no faiths, no hopes, no future for the colony...no ruler since the days of Charles II hated the country he was set over more bitterly'.[2]

But fortunately for the settlers, the American War of Independence blunted the edge of Lord North's repressive measures, and the sympathy aroused in liberal minds at home for the revolting colonists of New England spread out to cover Newfoundland. The Navy was for a time obliged to concentrate on the island's defences rather than on the licensing of ships' rooms and the eradication of settlements. Thus, when war ended it could be seen that the colonists had achieved a *de facto* triumph. Not only had they enriched themselves through smuggling and piracy, but their numbers had now swollen to over ten thousand. Whatever the law might say, however hard the naval Governors might labour to the contrary, colonization was at least a *fait accompli*.

But, as many eyewitnesses have recorded, it was a population wretched in the extreme. Descended from seamen who had earlier deserted from Devon or Jersey ships, with an admixture of those signed on en route at southern Irish ports, the settlers still lived in a constant state of fear of deportation. They were subject to tyrannical treatment from visiting ships' captains and naval governors alike and, as a new resident merchant class gradually established itself in and around St John's, were placed in feudal pawn to their suppliers. As human beings they represented some of the most backward and isolated areas of the British Isles. Disease, a poor diet, and chronic poverty, resulting from the erratic nature of the fishery, combined with inbreeding to debase men of fine physique. The winters were long and hard: the outports entirely cut off one from another and from the capital. Outside the Avalon peninsula communication was by sea alone. Schools there were none: no form of government existed and justice was what the summer Governors decided it to be.

Such was the background against which the settlers and their friends at home prepared for the final battle which, at long last, was to give the island the first rudiments of constitutional government.

[1] Colonial Office 194/52, encl. in 2, 'Letter to Members of Parliament' (W. Carson, 1812, pp. 14–15).
[2] Prowse, p. 319.

1

A COLONY IS BORN

Dear, delightful day of Arcadian simplicity! when we had no debt and port wine was a shilling a bottle! PROWSE, 1895

Newfoundland—the land of 'cod, dog, fog and log', the great ship anchored off the Banks, the island with six thousand miles of coastline—how could it be described now that the Norsemen had discovered and Cabot rediscovered it, and the fleets of Western Europe swarmed about it?

Slightly larger than Ireland; 42,000 square miles in area, it must have conveyed, even to the earliest voyager, the image that Ireland itself presents—'an indifferent picture in a golden frame'; the interior bleak, swampy, lake-strewn or under forest; the coastline deeply indented, rocky, studded with bays, coves, tickles and islets, and, in its northern and western reaches, grandiose in its heights of cliff and wealth of fjords. Tenth largest island in the world, Newfoundland owed its original importance to three factors: that of being the first landfall on the direct westerly Atlantic passage; of standing at the gateway to the American mainland; and of concealing off its coasts one of the world's most bounteous fisheries.

From the outset fish meant cod: fresh cod, green cod, cod salt or dried. Whether taken off the Grand Banks, inshore, or down the coast of Labrador, cod was the magnet, the ruling genius, the *raison d'être* of the struggle for settlement, the cause of rivalry between the maritime powers of Europe, and later between America and Canada, the dictator of Newfoundland's fate for centuries, the formulator of her social structure, the very arbiter of her people's daily life. A good catch meant wealth to the merchant class and something approaching comfort for the fisherman. A bad fishery could involve the imprudent merchant in ruin overnight and would certainly spell a cruel winter of discontent for the bulk of the inhabitants.

It was cod, as the Prologue to this books has briefly shown, that dictated the long fight from England against the colonists. But it was the wealth of the fishery which equally attracted settlement, provided the first slender base on which a local society grew, and enabled the struggling settlers to strike back at the mercantilist camp at home.

With the inglorious end of the American War of Independence, Britain was left with the wreckage of a primary empire. Among the semi-precious stones still set in a battered Crown was Newfoundland. At the time, in fact, the Island ranked second only to the West Indies as a source of wealth.

The protection of the fishery remained, therefore 'a fundamental tenet of England's economic creed'.[1] Or as the majority of English parliamentarians continued to proclaim: 'It was better to have no colonies at all, than not to have them subservient to the maritime strength and commercial interests of Great Britain.'[2] At all costs the new America must be barred from the Newfoundland trade and, even if France were to retain the controversial fishing rights first granted her under the Treaty of Utrecht, 1713, the Island, together with the remaining North American Colonies, must continue to be the exclusive preserve of a mercantilist Mother Country.

By 1785 the West Country merchants with their supporters in the Government and the settlers, who had the increasing sympathy of liberals at home and of public and mercantile opinion in North America, were headed on a fateful collision course. In that year English policy towards the Island was vigorously and lengthily debated before the Committee of the Privy Council for Trade. The West Countrymen now went so far as to argue that, despite current evidence of famine in Newfoundland, no foodstuffs should be imported from America. Even the local Governor at this point came to the support of the luckless settlers. By ordering the sale locally of a cargo of American flour brought to St John's in a British bottom, he drove a first nail deep into the narrow monopolistic coffin—a coffin which history had long been fashioning for this superannuated selfish merchant class.

But the battle for free trade and settlement was still not to be lightly won. For some years yet it seemed as though Parliament and Government had learnt nothing from the debacle of 1783. Towards Newfoundland English policy remained outwardly one of colonial negation. Competitors, even from other British possessions like Bermuda, continued to be excluded from the fishery. Settlement, even if now unchallengeable, was still to be hindered by all means from developing. The eighteenth century was to breathe its last before the narrow, selfish, mercantilist lobby finally persuaded itself that it and not history was out of step.

While, as has been seen, monopoly versus free competition lay at the root of the struggle to determine the Island's fate, the settlers themselves arrived at more formal recognition of their status along the less trodden path of 'law reform'. As the population grew, so increasingly there came demands for protection from the harsh and arbitrary punishments handed out by the so-called 'Admirals' and 'Governors'. A minor victory had been won in 1750 when a Governor's commission first empowered that officer to appoint commissioners for the trial of all felonies locally according

[1] See McLintock, p. 27.

[2] Extra-official State papers, Wm. Knox, vol. II, p. 53, quoted by McLintock.

to English law. The procedure was haphazard. But at least the powers-that-be had given tacit recognition to the fact that there existed Newfoundlanders to be tried. By 1790, St John's had so expanded that the need for new machinery for the hearing of civil suits had become essential and the Admiral-Governor of the day established a Court of Common Pleas. By no stretch of the imagination could this or any earlier system be deemed to have handed out impartial justice. Prowse, himself a District Judge as well as the first comprehensive historian of Newfoundland, took expert pains to emphasize 'the incongruous caricature of law and justice' presented by these early courts.[1] The magistrates were ignorant, or corrupt. They made up the law as they went along. Their greatest ingenuity was reserved for the punishments they invented. Many of them were particularly harsh on a new and growing class of settlers—Catholics from Southern Ireland. Wittingly or not they were preparing the ground for the bitter inter-denominational strife which was to plague the island for more than a century to come.

Yet out of these rough beginnings there grew, even in English mercantilist circles, the conviction that, if trade were to be adequately protected, then a properly constituted civil court, from which should lie a right of appeal to the King-in-Council, must be established in the Island. In the mercantile view, of course, the court should act in their interest alone. There was no cause for it to sit once the annual fleet withdrew. This, however, was a thesis which even George III's latter-day Ministers could not sustain. In 1791 cautiously, for one year only in the first instance, they persuaded Parliament to sanction the creation of a regular local judicature.[2] Two years later, such was the decline in strength of the anti-settler lobby, that Pitt was able with little difficulty to persuade Parliament to pass a permanent act governing the functions of such courts of judicature.[3] As another writer has commented: 'Regulations to check residency were (now) as futile as King Cnut's command to bid the waves recede.'[4] The monopolists had suffered their second political defeat.

But down though they might be, they were not yet out. The reaction to the American defeat, now combining with fears lest the excesses of the French Revolution should threaten the basis of society across the English Channel, helped to maintain an anti-reformist trend. Neither at home, nor in her remaining colonies, was Britain yet ready to think in liberal terms. Although the settlement of Newfoundland was now tacitly accepted as an unpalatable fact, the old cycle still continued. The island 'came to life

[1] Prowse. [2] 31 Geo. III, c. 29. [3] 32 Geo. III, c. 46.

[4] R. MacKay (ed.), *Newfoundland, Economic, Diplomatic and Strategic Studies* (Oxford University Press, 1946), p. 262.

with the arrival of the fishing fleet in the spring...it expired with the departure of the fleet at the close of the season, leaving the inhabitants, like the dead leaves of autumn, helpless before the blasts of legal adversity'.[1] For some thirty years in fact, stretching from the start of the American to the close of the Napoleonic Wars, Parliament purposely turned its back on colonial questions. During that period, the only colonial measures to be debated touched on the Newfoundland Judicature and the Australian penal settlement.[2]

But despite the clinging cloak of oppression, although Newfoundland might justly be described as 'The Forgotten Island', a major convulsion was now preparing. Wars, ironically, had been and were time and again to prove to be Newfoundland's blessings in disguise. Never was this truer than in the Napoleonic era. 'England's extremity became Newfoundland's opportunity, and the war which for many was a source of misery appeared to Newfoundland as an instrument of liberation.'[3] By 1812 the settlers, now numbering some thirty thousand, had in defiance of home policy built up the rudiments of an administrative system. Local merchants were firmly established in the retail and export–import business: there was a sizeable local fishing fleet and a small but increasingly dominant moneyed class. As if in grudging recognition of these developments, the Government in the year of Waterloo advised the King to appoint a full-time Governor. The long reign of the transient Fishing admiral had closed.

These political changes had their marked effect upon the fishery. It was axiomatic that, as the local population grew, it should gradually establish itself in direct competition with the English fleet. The Bank fishery was now increasingly rivalled by the 'shore' or sedentary fishery, which required far less capital outlay and in which a fisherman's family could play its part by splitting, salting and drying the cod. This development in turn was to shape the long-term social and economic life of the Colony. Just as many of the West Country adventurers had gradually established themselves as fishermen-merchants on the Island so now, as individual fishermen scattered around the coastline took to the inshore fishery in their own right, the merchants retreated to the easier role of buying fish from fellow Newfoundlanders. Gradually they came to form a closed and privileged community where the risks, though great, offered the prospect of returns still greater. Coming by degrees to serve as the fisherman's suppliers as well as the purchasers of his catch, they reflected in nineteenth-century Newfoundland the quasi-feudal economic system from which the earlier settlers had

[1] McLintock, p. 77.

[2] H. T. Manning, *British Colonial Government after the American Revolution* (London, 1933), p. 68.

[3] McLintock, p. 82.

originally escaped. To the fisherman's dependence on the price the merchant fixed for a quintal of fish or a barrel of flour, as well as to the unpredictable habits of the cod itself, was due the notorious 'Truck System'. This was to keep worker in thrall to capitalist, stamp the thinking and actions of rival political parties, retard economic development, place the burden of the cost of living where it could least well be sustained, and nurture the grievances of the underprivileged.

And the peace itself was less favourable to Newfoundland than the wars had been. Automatically, it would seem, rather than as a conscious act of policy, French—and now American—fishing privileges in the Island's territorial waters and on shore were renewed. Before long, in the face of a vacillating British Government, French masters and their supervisory commanders were asserting that under the Utrecht Settlement of 1713 they were entitled to the exercise of sovereign rights on Newfoundland's West Shore. Not until a vigorous Governor, Sir Thomas Cochrane, took issue with the French intruders in 1827 did Britain show any concern whatever. Even then this amounted to little more than an admonition to the sparsely scattered colonial officials to avoid 'unpleasant collisions' with the French. On the very eve of the colony's real birth Talleyrand, in 1831, went so far as to claim of, rather than to suggest to the British Government, that the Treaty of Utrecht had given France exclusive fishing rights along determined areas of the north-eastern and western coasts of Newfoundland. It was a sinister introduction to self-government.

The Napoleonic Wars had proved to be the first of the Island's rare golden periods. Local merchants had grown fat: the seasonal fishery had been virtually eliminated and the static population, encouraged by the absence of oversea control, had increased to fill the gap. But the 'Truck' system had already exacted its toll and, as the age of representative government dawned, the Island was sharply divided between the few privileged 'Haves' and the far more numerous fishermen 'Have Nots'. A hundred years later both the Royal Commission to Newfoundland and the great medico-missionary, Sir William Grenfell, were to describe the economic structure of the Island as 'subtle because it impoverishes and enslaves the victims, and then makes them love their chains'.[1]

But despite these handicaps the population was now in the region of 50,000. The Governor had become a permanent as opposed to a seasonal official. Palliser's inhibiting Act had been repealed, and since 1826 the Island had enjoyed the symbolic privilege of an appointed council. Further constitutional advance could now scarcely be denied. Local agitation demanded it: the spirit of reform at home at last conceded it.

[1] McLintock, p. 124.

It was in 1832 that Newfoundland effectively grew up to colonial status. By then, thousands of impoverished Irish immigrants had poured into the Island: lawlessness was rife and the western merchants were making one last convulsive effort to break the tacit policy of settlement. But this time they fought in vain. Bermuda, Upper and Lower Canada, Nova Scotia and Prince Edward Island all now enjoyed some form of local government. However rudimentary society in Newfoundland might be, however unprepared for autonomy, some concession to the petitioning settlers must be made. The form the first constitution was to take owed much to a senior Colonial Office official, James Stephens. His report of 1831 is one of the most significant of the documents relating to Newfoundland.[1]

'In every colony where the population is homogeneous', he wrote, 'a Legislative Assembly is an inestimable benefit...it either prevents discontents or gives them a safe direction...affords much innocent pleasure: and creates a subject of permanent interest in societies which would otherwise stagnate in a listless unconcern about all questions of a public character.' Far-sightedly, he continued: 'That the solemnities of such Bodies sometimes degenerate into a sort of mock heroic, and that they do not rarely become the occasion of much petty tyranny, their warmest friend would admit. But the burlesque injures no one'—(less far-sighted this)—'and the occasional injustice may be considered as the price which all human societies must pay for the advantage of civil government.' *Per contra*, Stephens argued strongly against the creation of a Legislative Council which he saw, not as a check on a lower House but as an artificially privileged body, imparting neither dignity to the Governor's position, nor weight to his authority. He urged therefore that Newfoundland should follow the original Nova Scotian pattern, the Governor ruling through a popularly elected Assembly to which *ex officio* a certain number of governmental officers should be admitted.

The Colonial Secretary of the day, Lord Goderich, accepted Stephens' report. To the Governor, Cochrane, was left the difficult task of arranging for elections among a people still largely unversed in the arts of politics: and then of endeavouring to weld his suspicious nominated Council and his other officials into a representative whole. In the autumn of 1832 fifteen elected members were returned to the youngest constituent body in America and on New Year's Day, 1833, Newfoundland's first House of Assembly was opened. It was not, commented Prowse, one whit behind any other 'in stately parliamentary pageant and grandiloquent language. H.B. [Doyle] caricatured it as the "Bow-Wow" Parliament with a big

[1] Colonial Office, 194/82, encl. to no. 21, 19 December 1831.

Newfoundland dog in wig and bands as Speaker putting the motion: "As many as are of that opinion say 'bow', of the contrary—'wow'."'[1]

'Bow-wow' or not, this small young Parliament quickly showed that it could growl. Scarcely convened, it rejected the Governor's plea that it should amalgamate with the nominated Legislative Council of officials. Suspicion on the part of the newly elected representatives that their hard-won privileges were to be curtailed by the administration was no stronger than the contempt of these same officials for the inadequacies of the Assembly itself. From the outset the two bodies were at loggerheads. The right of the Lower House to pass revenue bills was challenged. Every event was taken as an opportunity for dispute. 'Each side displayed vile temper and utter incapacity...On the whole the Council were the more cantankerous.'[2]

This sorry start to what many patriotic Newfoundlanders had dreamed of and striven for as the gateway to a golden age, had moreover to be viewed against domestic conditions of an appalling kind. The prosperity brought by war had vanished. Distress was again widespread. The Truck System had sapped all sense of thrift among the fishermen. Now, in despair, they turned to their newly elected representatives for the help that these could barely give.

For the most part illiterate, the fishermen knew nothing of the privileges of local government. To minds already poisoned by the fear of hunger and by envy of the merchant oligarchy, there was now fed by unscrupulous carpetbagging political agents and pamphleteers the bogey of religious hatred. Protestant was set against Catholic, 'have-not' against 'have'. Years of neglect from England, and the Island's long and deliberate subordination to a narrow mercantilist interest were now to bear their bitter fruits. What began as a brave if retarded experiment in democracy was to degenerate into viciousness and strife.

Between the year 1836, when following widespread rioting a first election was held invalid, and 1843 there is little worthy of serious report. Council and Assembly continued their sterile quarrels: jobbery became an accepted way of life, and religious feelings were increasingly inflamed. The Colonial Office now for the first time felt the full impact of petitioning which, as the century advanced, Newfoundlanders were to develop to the finest of the virulent arts. By the spring of 1841, passions had become so uncontrolled and law and order so inexistent that the Governor, on the authority of the Colonial Secretary, dissolved the Legislature and suspended the infant constitution. A year later it was to be replaced by one providing that Legislative Council and Lower House should henceforth sit together

[1] Prowse, p. 431. [2] *Ibid.* p. 434.

as 'the Amalgamated Legislature'—an experiment little more felicitous than the first. This Legislature's short existence witnessed the growth of the seal fishery, the advent of the steamer, a brief return to relative prosperity and the disastrous burning of the capital in 1846. Two years later the original constitution was briefly restored.

By 1848 agitation for full responsible government had reached its peak. But, unmoved by the fact that all the North American Colonies save Prince Edward Island had now attained this goal, successive British Ministries, whether Whig or Tory, refused to listen to the Colonists' pleas. To Earl Grey's judgement that 'until the wealth and population of the Colony shall have increased considerably beyond their present amount, the introduction of what is called Responsible Government will by no means prove to its advantage', his successor, Pilkington, added in 1852 that 'the wisdom and justice of these [Grey's] conclusions are confirmed by the reports since received from Newfoundland'.[1]

Yet Imperial obstruction or hesitancy was to prove short-lived. Not only was local agitation influencing Downing Street. The repeal of the Corn Laws in 1846 had brought finally to an end an eighteenth-century mercantilist Empire. In a new Empire 'founded on economic liberalism there was no point in maintaining over British peoples abroad an unacceptable political regime...After Waterloo Britain had no serious naval rival...the world of the nineteenth century was thus safe for Britain and her Colonies. In this atmosphere responsible government could flourish without prejudicing the security of colony or mother country.'[2]

Thus, paradoxical though it might seem, only three years were to pass between Pilkington's refusal to countenance Home Rule and the British Government's statement of 1855 that they had 'come to the conclusion that they ought not to withhold from Newfoundland those institutions and that civil administration which, under the popular name of Responsible Government, had been adopted in all Her Majesty's neighbouring possessions in North America...'[3] And so, with much popular rejoicing, the first House of Assembly truly responsible for the Island's internal affairs was elected on 7 May of this historic year. It consisted of 30 members, and the Legislative Council of 12. Newfoundland's first Home Rule Premier, the Honourable P. F. Little, together with his Liberal administration, were described by Prowse as an able team. 'They had the rare good luck of prosperous years, the sunshine of prosperity...beamed on the Government.'[4]

[1] Prowse, p. 463.
[2] MacKay, p. 269.
[3] See Prowse, p. 466.
[4] *Ibid.* p. 468.

Thus far, after close on three centuries of struggle and adversity had Newfoundland advanced along the road to constitutional government. Only now was her brief and quasi-independent role on the world's stage haltingly to open. How turbulent it was to be, how beset by international hindrances, how bedevilled by events both within and beyond the islanders' control, the ensuing chapters of this book will show.

The long overture had ended. The curtain now rises on a hundred years of history.

2

FEDERATE OR ISOLATE?

Three cheers for our own loved Isle Newfoundland,
No stranger shall hold an inch of her strand
Her face turns to Britain, her back to the Gulf,
Come near at your peril, you Canadian wolf.

Newfoundland–Irish Ballad, *c.* 1869

Though now equal in status with the mainland Colonies and at long last master of her own internal fate, Newfoundland had but the slimmest of bases from which to build. When all else failed, the Canadian dependencies could seek safety in numbers. Their very size was a guarantee of economic options, their populations an encouragement to the growth of local industries. Of these benefits Newfoundland had none. History had frustrated settlement and nurtured the fishery at the expense of all other forms of development. With the passing of the seasonal fleet migrations from western Europe, the island had lapsed into an isolation from which, thanks to the first Atlantic cable and the advent of steam, it was only now painfully re-emerging. Concentration on the fishery had meant above all two things: first that the whole population, now numbering roughly one hundred thousand, was at the mercy of King Cod, of his disposition to be caught and of the price that he would fetch; and, second, that the interior of Newfoundland, containing who knew what resources, lay entirely neglected and uninhabited. Not without significance was the record of a journey across the Island, made by an English visitor as late as 1856, subtitled: 'The only one ever performed by a European.'[1] While expatiating on the beauty of the country and of its prospective mineral wealth, this writer emphasized the loneliness of the great savannahs where he encountered no one save small bands of roaming Indians—'large athletic men' soon to retreat northward or to die out as civilization gradually advanced upon them. The same writer also described, briefly but accurately, how life was lived in a relatively prosperous outport at the time Home Rule came to Newfoundland. Thus:

The inhabitants of Bonavista, about a dozen families, gain their livelihood by the cod fishing. They cultivate only a few potatoes; and some other vegetables, which were of excellent quality, amongst the scanty patches of soil around their doors and obtaining all their other provisions, clothing and outfit for the fishery, from merchants in other parts of Trinity Bay, or elsewhere on the coast, not too

[1] W. E. Cormack, *Narrative of a Journey across the Island of Newfoundland.*

far distant, giving in return the produce of the fishery viz: cod fish and cod oil. They collectively catch about 1,500 quintals or 300 tons of cod fish, valued at 12*s*. per quintal, £900: and manufacture from the livers of the cod fish about twenty-one tons of oil, valued at £16 per ton, £336; which is the annual amount of their trade. The merchants import articles for the use of the fisheries from Europe and elsewhere to supply such people as these, who can actually engage in the operations of the fishery. The whole population of Newfoundland may be viewed as similarly circumstanced with those of Bonavista, together with their relations.[1]

There were by now upwards of six hundred of these fishing villages and approximately 80 per cent of the working population earned their living from the sea. It was a hard life and a precarious one. Only the suddenly expanding seal fishery, which offered out-of-season work, gave promise of quick and sometimes lucrative returns. In a good year the export value of skins and oil from a six-week season might total upward of $1 million. As many as six hundred vessels would be engaged and the return to port was celebrated annually at a banquet during which much rum would drown that rather dubious delicacy—stewed seal flipper.

St John's itself was expanding fast. Increasing political activity had given birth to the rudiments of a permanent civil service. The press, banks, lawyers' offices, insurance companies, import–export agencies and retail stores in turn were multiplying. By 1855 the population of the capital stood at close on 30,000.

But while the advent of responsible government coincided with brief years of plenty, when the fishery was bountiful, interdenominational strife reduced and the political waters relatively unruffled, the calm was not to last. The great bulk of the population, bred to adversity, drawn from the poorest quarters of the British Isles, consistently undernourished and largely illiterate, proved fertile breeding ground for rumour and sectarian passions. For their part the 'Establishment' and the merchant oligarchy were, for their own varying reasons, determined to control events. Thus, an untutored and politically uneducated majority confronted a minority in whom all wealth was concentrated and from whom jobs, credit and relief could be dispensed or withheld at whim. Add to this mixture two political parties, Conservative and Liberal, which as the years went by sought to represent 'Haves' and 'Have-nots', Protestants and Catholics, and it becomes clear that the body politic was far from healthy.

Moreover, the first administration had hardly eased itself into the saddle than it was confronted with two major policy issues ranging well beyond the narrow confines of the domestic scene. In 1857 both Government and

[1] Cormack.

people learnt with indignation of the initialling in Paris of an Anglo-French Convention designed to strengthen and perpetuate the fishing rights enjoyed by France under the Treaty of Utrecht. One year later the Newfoundland Government were invited to join with the other Canadian colonies to discuss the prospect of confederation. The fishery—or as it came to be called 'French Shore'—dispute, vital as it was to prove to both Newfoundland's economy and to her role on the international scene, will be dealt with at some length in ensuing chapters. Here it will be convenient to trace the Island's part in the making of a greater Canada, the passions to which the idea of confederation gave rise and the lessons which Newfoundland's eventual refusal to join with the Founding Fathers spelt out for the final act now to be delayed for close on one hundred years.

Viewed from the Canadian heartland, the prospects for union were far from bright. Westwards stretched territory as yet scarcely known or populated. To the east lay four colonies; Nova Scotia, New Brunswick, Prince Edward Island and Newfoundland, each of which was now enjoying the first, fiery flushes of self-government. Still British-orientated in thought and policy, the maritime colonies formed a bloc on the edge of the continent, largely cut off from the main stream of activity within the heartland. Of them all, Newfoundland remained without doubt the most isolated, parochial and independent-minded. And, as has been briefly noted, the circumstances in which the Island had at last been settled, and the socio-economic problems to which her history gave rise, were reflected in the local political machine.

The great majority of the population was so poor that the franchise, still based in theory on property, had to be very wide or extremely narrow. It had of necessity to be very wide to be representative of any but the merchants of St John's, and was a mere householder franchise. In consequence of this, the local democracies of the outports, largely Irish and Catholic, dominated the Assembly...from their popular party the Executive Council in 1857 was drawn. The opposition in the Assembly was the 'commerical party', which had its leadership among the merchants of St John's, and its rank and file support among the West country English. These incipient 'Liberal' and 'Conservative' parties were neither coherent nor principled, but were groupings of sentiment and interest. It was on their play, their formation and dissolution, that the entrance of Newfoundland into Confederation was to depend.[1]

Moreover, while the maritime colonies of the mainland were to some degree open to the pull of New England and were thus more ready to criticize any failings on the part of the Imperial power to support them in their political or commercial quarrels with Ontario and Quebec, New-

[1] W. L. Morton, *The Critical Years: The Union of British North America 1857–1873*, pp. 43–4.

foundland remained untouched by influences of this kind. The one bread and butter factor predisposing her to union was that through membership of a greater whole the Island might be in a stronger position to resist the encroachment of the French upon her shores and fishery. It mattered less to Newfoundland that the Imperial Government threatened to withdraw defence facilities. Nor was she greatly moved at the outset by London's lukewarm attitude to the very prospect of confederation. For Newfoundlanders, union was to be judged above all by local—that is by fishing, social and economic yardsticks—not by the urge of history, the pressures of a railway age or the international arguments of commerce.

Even in Upper Canada the first fumbling efforts at confederation soon foundered on the rocks of Imperial indifference. Not until 1860 was the Colonial Secretary, Lord Newcastle, brought reluctantly to concede that union between Canada and the maritime colonies might have something to offer in terms of trade and inter-communication in face of the growing military threat from America and France. The Hudson's Bay Company was in eclipse; the mainland colonies were facing marked financial difficulties; public works programmes were stretching their several resources to the limit. In short, 'federation promised to widen the credit base and thus to promote the financial strength of British North America'.[1]

The visit of the Prince of Wales, later King Edward VII, to Newfoundland in the summer of 1860 may have done something to break down Newfoundland parochialism, even though it sparked off a local quarrel between Catholics and Orangemen. But, broadly speaking, federation prior to 1864, remained 'more of an exotic plant than in the mainland colonies'.[2] It was significant that, when the Premier of Newfoundland inquired informally of the Nova Scotia Government in that year whether the Island might have any prospect of joining in a legislative union with the maritime colonies, the latter should reply that the Island's omission from the then Conference 'arose mainly from the belief that Newfoundland had no wish to be a party to it'.[3] Newfoundland was thus unrepresented at either the crucial Charlottetown Conference of 1864 or the later meetings at Halifax, Nova Scotia.

Yet the conclusions reached at Charlottetown that 'the Confederation of all the British North American Colonies would be highly advantageous to all the provinces, provided equitable terms could be agreed upon' excited growing interest in Newfoundland. There were of course many who remained either bemused by the temporary wave of prosperity that had

[1] MacKay, p. 415. [2] *Ibid.* p. 416.

[3] Sir John A. Macdonald Papers, Confederation 6, pp. 17–19 (Public Archives of Canada). Quoted by MacKay.

reached the Island or so ruggedly determined on maintaining their separate identity that nothing would induce them to consider the advantages of union. But there was an equal number both ready and eager to give the idea a run.

Thus, when Macdonald from Canada urged Newfoundland to send representatives to a third conference, to be held in Quebec in October, 1864, the Government responded favourably, if cautiously. The Island delegates would, the Prime Minister explained, have no authority to commit the Legislature since the latter had never yet debated the issues of union, whether federal or legislative. Thus, the delegation sent from St John's to Quebec was designedly non-party in status. It consisted of the leader of the Opposition, Mr (later Sir Ambrose) Shea and the Speaker of the House of Assembly, Mr F. T. B. Carter. They were strictly enjoined to reserve to the Legislature 'the fullest right and power of assenting to, dissenting from or, if advisable, of proposing modification of any terms that may be proposed to you'.[1]

The Governor of the day, Musgrave, was a keen advocate of union but, as it soon emerged, the cards were from the outset stacked against him and those who shared his views. To begin with, the status of the Newfoundland delegates was self-inhibiting. They were in practice little more than observers, empowered only to report home their personal findings and recommendations. Secondly, the mainland maritime provinces were far from unanimous in their views on the advantages of confederation. Thirdly 'Newfoundland, bound by trade to both New England and Old England, belonged wholly to the Atlantic world from which federation would have been something of a withdrawal, and was not at all attracted to those continental enterprises for which federation was a preparation'.[2] And, most important of all, there was in the Island a strong, vociferous and unscrupulous lobby which was determined at all costs to prevent the act of union.

> Remember the day
> When Carter and Shea
> crossed over the 'bay'
> to barter away
> The rights of Terra Nova.

ran one of the tuneless but telling jingles put about by what was rapidly becoming a predominantly merchant-inspired anti-Canadian platform.

The role of the Newfoundland delegation was thus a frustrating one. Not only did it have the above difficulties to contend with; it contained

[1] *Newfoundland, Journals of the House of Assembly,* 1865, Appendix, p. 848.
[2] Morton, p. 168.

no Minister, still less its Premier. The Premiers of all other provinces were present, backed by some if not all their Ministers. Neither Shea nor Carter could therefore hope to have much influence in the debates which took place at Quebec between those favouring a federal—as the maritimers did—as opposed to a thorough-going legislative Union. While the federalist view was to prevail, there was 'virtually no record of their opinion on details of the scheme' although, as each was later to proclaim: 'I (Carter) like (its) grandeur and magnitude'; and it is 'charged (Shea) with so high a mission of grandeur, whose future it was impossible for the wildest imagination to overestimate'. And, as Carter added: 'The trade of Canada would be destroyed if Newfoundland were in the hands of a foreign power. It is only necessary to look at the map to enable one to arrive at the conclusion that the stability of confederation would require Newfoundland.'[1]

It is clear that at this turning-point of her history, the Island stood to gain much from union in whatever form. Her finances were temporarily sound. She was no mendicant. Even though the Island would perforce remain in competition with the other maritime fisheries, her Government was being offered fair and adequate representation in the federal upper and lower Houses. And the proposed settlement of the thorny issue of financial terms could have raised no real grievance in dispassionate hearts. In return for assuming existing provincial debt liabilities, the central government was to have full power to levy customs and excise duties. But in compensation, it was agreed by the conference that Newfoundland should receive an annual subsidy of $115,000 in consideration of her transfer of such powers to the centre: a further annual payment, based on population, of $104,000: and a third, amounting to $150,000, in respect of her surrender of rights in mines and minerals and unoccupied Crown Land.

In fact, no other mainland colony stood to gain so much. Altogether

Newfoundland would have received for the purpose of provincial administration an aggregate annual grant of $369,376 from the general government. Estimated local revenues were $5,000 more. Furthermore, the general government would have paid for various departmental and service charges, and by doing so would have relieved Newfoundland of another $160,000 per annum. The estimated costs of government to Newfoundland under the new scheme amounted to $250,000. Newfoundland would thus be in surplus of $124,000.[2]

It was not surprising that both Shea and Carter should have believed, as the Conference ended, that they were bringing home the bacon. In the

[1] See MacKay, p. 420. [2] MacKay, p. 424.

House of Assembly, Governor Musgrave stated that the Imperial Government now regarded with favour 'a project of union which will materially strengthen each for sustaining the burden which must be borne by all'. He appealed to members 'to approach the consideration of the proposal... in a spirit of calm examination'.[1] But he reckoned without the strength of the anti-confederate lobby. A new and energetic leader was soon to emerge in the shape of Charles Fox Bennett. Although in the first stages of the great debate it was to remain dry, his powerful pamphleteering pen was eventually to prove more persuasive than a score of attractive financial arguments from across the Cabot Strait.

Playing on Irish national sentiment in the outports and on the memories of earlier French invasions, which in turn awakened resentment against Quebec, Bennett was to paint a horrifying picture of the fate that would befall Newfoundland were she ever to link her destinies with the mainland. Thousands of illiterate voters were warned that their children would be used as gun wads for Canadian cannon; that they themselves would be conscripted and that 'their bones would bleach on the desert sands [*sic*] of Canada'. The old bogey of taxation was of course well to the fore. According to the Bennett party,

> there would be taxes on everything even on the panes of glass in the windows: and in a country where coal was not mined, and wood the sole fuel supply, they were told that no man would be allowed to cut wood, with the result that many people went out, fearing this dreadful thing would befall them, and cut wood enough to last for years, and men dressed in soldiers' coats were sent about to represent Canadian press gangs.[2]

Meanwhile, in the months immediately following the return of the Newfoundland delegation from Quebec, the Legislature had acted responsibly. The proposed terms of union were examined with care and public petitions taken fully into account. Unlike certain of the mainland colonies, the Newfoundland Assembly concluded that an issue of such importance could not properly be settled without a prior test of public feeling. Thus, with Musgrave's concurrence, fresh elections were held towards the close of 1865 and, despite the propaganda put about by the Conservative party, the Liberals, led by Carter, returned to power. For a while it seemed that the Confederates would win the day. As the new government's Address in reply to the Speech from the Throne summed up the position: 'The abstract advantages of Union are so obvious as to be almost necessarily acknowledged.' However, as it went on to admit: 'On

[1] *Journals of Newfoundland House of Assembly*, 1865.

[2] Hon. Sir P. T. McGrath, 'Will Newfoundland join Canada?', *Newfoundland Pamphlets*, II, no. 46 (C.O. 1927).

the details of so grave a measure it is natural that much diversity of opinion should prevail.'[1]

It soon became clear that this 'diversity of opinion' was also rapidly developing on the mainland. While British parliamentary and press comment was now united in extolling the virtues of confederation, opposition to union was gathering strength in New Brunswick and Nova Scotia. Before 1865 was out Prince Edward Island had gone so far as to reject the conclusions of the Conference at Quebec. Although in the following year the prospects once more improved and the Nova Scotia and New Brunswick Legislatures overcame their initial hesitations, the confederate cause in Newfoundland was already doomed. The doubts had left their mark and the 'Antis', although still lacking Bennett's outright commitment to their cause, were making steady inroads into the Liberal camp. As early as March 1866 the Newfoundland Assembly had passed by a majority of seventeen to seven a resolution which was tantamount to putting the terms of union on the shelf. There was thus no authority by which a further Newfoundland delegation could be empowered to take part at the London conference in December of the same year where the basis for confederation was finally agreed. Nor, when the first Federal Parliament representing Canada, New Brunswick and Nova Scotia was ceremoniously opened in November 1867 could the Island do more than send her Governor as an honoured but powerless observer of the scene. Try though he might on his return to persuade his Government that the door to the mainland was still open, first Bennett and then the growing menace of the fisheries disputes with France were to ensure that it was firmly and finally slammed.

Musgrave, however, was nothing if not a trier. By March, 1869, he had persuaded both his Ministers and the Assembly to rebuild their bridges to the mainland. This achieved, he went so far as to express to the Canadian Prime Minister, Macdonald, his view that the prospects for Newfoundland joining the confederation were excellent. But the Government, faced with growing hostility from the Opposition, tried now to reinsure too heavily. In seeking improvements on the original terms for union, they incautiously reopened, among other contentious issues, those of taxation and customs dues on exports of fish and products to the mainland. In a week-long debate, it was only with difficulty that they defeated an amendment proposed by the anti-confederates to the terms of the report which it was eventually decided to forward to the Government of Canada. At the end of this marathon debate, they had seemingly achieved their objectives. Indeed, in the early summer of 1869 a delegation proceeded from St John's to Canada to discuss the revised arrangements. Thus, for a few brief weeks it appeared

[1] *Newfoundland, Journals of the House of Assembly*, 1866.

that Musgrave's optimism was truly justified. Macdonald and his Ministers took the generous line of statesmanship. Nearly all the Island's requests were met, full agreement was rapidly arrived at, and on 10 June 1869 the Canadian Parliament in an Address to The Queen prayed for the admission of Newfoundland into the Dominion under Section 146 of the British North America Act. Harbour was all but reached.

But with safe anchorage in sight, the long-threatening storm blew up. Elections were shortly due and it was now that Bennett threw all his weight behind the anti-confederate cause. 'A born master of the art of propaganda, he did not scruple to play on the fears and passions of the ignorant section of the electorate.'[1] Apart from the lurid threats already mentioned, Bennett frightened the fishermen with dire warnings of the taxes Canada would impose on their boats and gear: and the merchants with the bogey of competition from the mainland. By the time the campaign was over, the cause of confederation was already doomed. Carter's liberal administration was chased from office. As soon as the results were known

> the fishermen and mechanics of St John's...put together a large coffin labelled 'Confederation', which was placed on a vehicle draped in black, and this was drawn by scores of willing hands through the town, headed by a band playing the Dead March, and escorted by an immense crowd, to the head of the harbour, where a grave was dug below high-water mark and the coffin solemnly interred therein, while a local versifier of the period...delivered its funeral oration in these words:
>
> And now Confederation a shameful death has died,
> And buried up at River Head beneath the flowing tide,
> And may it never rise again to bother us, I pray,
> 'Hurrah, me boys!' for liberty, the Antis gained the day.[2]

Rise again it did, in 1887 and in 1895, but as little more than a pale, lingering, execrated ghost. For the coffin which Bennett had fashioned for it, and the folk-lore atmosphere in which he presided at its burial were to prove solid and lasting enough to create in the minds of most Newfoundlanders for close on three generations to come the acutest of suspicions and political ill-feeling towards their next-door neighbour. Those three outstanding island characteristics: superabundant faith in her own future, electoral gullibility, and rugged independence had won the day. In so doing they had caused Newfoundland to turn her back on both a generous financial bargain and an imaginative and profitable adventure. They had shaped her fortunes for close on a century to come. They had chained her rashly but tightly to a cataclysmic future. They had committed her to a

[1] MacKay, p. 438.

[2] McGrath, 'Will Newfoundland join Canada?'.

form of economic, financial and political autonomy which, through suffering alone, the Island eventually learnt that she could not endlessly sustain.

The first Lord Birkenhead's verdict was the true one.

> The politics of the colony [he wrote years later] would be braced by the ampler atmosphere of the Dominion: and the tendency towards parochialism finally arrested. As soon as the general communities which together form the Empire realise not merely their ties with the Mother Country, but also their own organic interconnection, from that moment the whole Imperial idea receives an immense accession of strength.[1]

But if the verdict rested with Birkenhead, the immediate victory lay with Bennett. The country was now in his hands and his new administration lost no time in proclaiming that:

> The subject of the Confederation of this Colony with the Dominion of Canada has been largely discussed both within and outside this House for several years past, and the result has been settled conviction in the minds of the people that such Union would not be conducive to their essential interests—a conclusion which had manifested itself at the recent General Election by the return of an overwhelming majority of representatives in opposition to that measure. Firm in their adhesion to the fortunes of the Mother Country, the people of Newfoundland shrink from the idea of linking their destinies with a dominion in the future of which they can at present see nothing to inspire hope, but much to create apprehension.[2]

Thus in the euphoria of the hour the few prophets of woe cried unheeded. A crisis nearer home was brewing and for many years to come the minds of successive governments were to be concentrated on the long-drawn fishery disputes with France. It is to these and to the growing nakedness of Newfoundland's economy that attention must now turn.

[1] (1st) Lord Birkenhead, *The Story of Newfoundland* (Horace Marshall and Son), 1920.
[2] *Newfoundland, Journals of House of Assembly*, 17 February 1870.

3

COD: BAIT AND FRANCOPHOBIA

Of late, the encroachments of the French upon Our Said Island, and Our Subjects Trade and Fishery, have been more like the Invasion of an Enemy, than becoming Friends.

The London Gazette, no. 2452, 9–13 May 1689

The Colonial authorities are very obstinate and the Members of the local Legislature are quite indifferent to the difficulties in which their attitude places H.M's Government.

Colonial Office Minute of 20 January 1888, p. 7 in C.O. 194

The cod (*Gadus callarias* Linnaeus) would win no underwater beauty prize. Nor does he rate a high I.Q. For centuries he has been jigged for with tackle of the crudest kind. Indeed, if early writers are to be believed, the cod would meekly submit to being drawn to his death in a weighted, open basket. Greed may have something to do with this fish's reckless propensity to suicide. One expert records the cod as ready to swallow scissors, oil cans, old boots, books and keys.[1] But whatever its habits, its influence on the economy of the Western Atlantic seaboard, and particularly on the very life of Newfoundland, has been profound. It was written of the Gaspé Peninsula that 'it is the land of the codfish! Your eyes and nose, your tongue and throat and ears as well soon make you realise that...the codfish forms the basis alike of food and amusements, of business and general talk, of regrets, hope, good luck, everyday life—I would almost be ready to say of existence itself.'[2] At least until a few years ago any Newfoundlander would have recognized and applied the symptoms to himself.

That supreme expert on the codfisheries, the late Harold Innis, opened his magisterial survey with the remark that 'whereas in Canada the beaver was fittingly chosen as a symbol of unity, in Newfoundland the cod was largely responsible for disunity'.[3] In so far as fish dominated Imperial policy towards the Colony for centuries and that in terms of local politics, all turned on cod, the aphorism was profoundly true. But right through into the opening years of the twentieth century, *Gadus callarias* had even wider and more disturbing consequences. His very existence embroiled Canada with Newfoundland; the United States with Canada; the State Department with both and Downing Street with all. He excited

[1] M. G. Massenet, *Technique et pratique des grandes pêches maritimes* (Paris, 1913), as quoted by H. A. Innis, p. 2.

[2] Translation from L'Abbé Ferland. *Journal d'un voyage sur les côtes de la Gaspésie* (1871), quoted by H. A. Innis, p. 2.

[3] Innis, p. 1.

Newfoundlanders to the heights of Francophobia. He involved distant islands in the Pacific as pawns in a ceaseless and increasingly futile and undignified war of *notes verbales*, *aides-mémoire*, protest and counter-protest between London and Paris, and only forewent his trouble-making role on the conclusion of the Entente Cordiale in 1904 and the Hague Court rulings of 1910. In the interim he had given harassed civil servants in the Foreign and Colonial Offices, Governors and Legislatures of Newfoundland, and the Governments of Canada, the United States and France more than a run for their money.

The seeds of these diplomatic nettles had been sown in four Treaties—those of Utrecht, 1713; Paris, 1763; Versailles, 1783; and again Paris, 1815. All first blossomed from Article XIII of the Treaty of Utrecht.[1] There the French King conceded that 'the Island called Newfoundland, with the adjacent islands shall, from this time forward, belong of right wholly to Britain'. But the same notorious Article went on to concede the privilege 'to the subjects of France to catch fish and to dry them on land in that part only, and in no other besides that, of the said Island of Newfoundland, which stretches from the place called Cape Bonavista to the northern point of the said island, and from thence running down by the Western side, reaches as far as the place called Point Riche'. Little could the draftsmen, on the British side at least, have conceived of the trouble they were willing to their successors.

Article V of the Treaty of Paris, 1763,[2] confirmed French subjects in their fishing rights. But twenty years later the Treaty of Versailles was already reflecting the quarrels which had arisen between the two nations in respect of the Newfoundland fishery. Article V of that Treaty records the King of France, already fortified by the acquisition from Britain of the neighbouring islands of St Pierre and Miquelon, as consenting

> in order to prevent the quarrels which have hitherto arisen between the two nations of England and France...to renounce the right of fishing which belongs to him...from Cape Bonavista to Cape St John, situated on the eastern coast of Newfoundland, in 50° north latitude: and His Majesty The King of Great Britain consents on his part, that the fishery assigned to the subjects of His Most Christian Majesty, beginning at the said Cape John, passing to the north and descending by the western coast of the island of Newfoundland, shall extend to the place called Cape Ray, situated in 47° 50′ latitude.

A separate Declaration from the British side gratuitously rubbed in at the expense of the luckless Newfoundland settlers the advantages which a defeated France had gained in what the French Kings had long since come to accept as wholly British territory. 'In order that the fishermen of the

[1] *A General Collection of Treatys of Peace and Commerce*, vol. III, for J. J. Knapton, etc. (London 1732), p. 431. [2] Foreign Office State Papers, Treaties, vol. 123, P.R.O.

two nations', ran this Declaration, 'may not give cause for daily quarrels, His Britannic Majesty will take the most positive measures for preventing his subjects from interrupting in any manner, by their competition, the fishery of the French during the temporary exercise of it which is granted to them...and he will, for this purpose, cause the fixed settlements which shall be formed there [fateful words] to be removed.' French fishermen, the Declaration continued, were not to winter on the coasts and when there, must confine their activities to 'building only their scaffolds' (for drying fish) and to repairing their vessels. British subjects were to be prevented from molesting the French or from injuring their property.

Although, under the Treaty of Paris, 1814, France was to lose further possessions in the western hemisphere, notably Tobago and St Lucia, the Napoleonic era ended with the doubly defeated French still confirmed by the second Treaty of Paris, 1815, in their fishing privileges along extensive stretches of the Newfoundland coastline.

What was to become known as the Treaty or 'French Shore' question was an immediate millstone round the necks of the Island's first responsible Governments: a provocation to patriotic Newfoundlanders: a running sore on the corpus of relationships between the Colony and the Imperial power and, because of the ambiguity of language of the various Treaties, a means of keeping the Law Officers steadily employed.

Between 1846 and 1886 no less than eight Anglo-French Commissions were appointed in fruitless endeavours to resolve differences of interpretation and to remove grievances. Although the substance of the quarrels became increasingly localized, their repercussions spread far wider, and British civil servants found themselves cast ever more frequently in the all too familiar role of balancing their responsibilities to a small, relatively uninfluential, but exceedingly irate oversea community against the need to placate a powerful European neighbour and potential foe.

It would be wearisome to recount in detail the fruitless labours of these early Commissions. But if Newfoundland's struggle to achieve a personality is to be understood, some account must be given of the background to the negotiations leading up to the initialling in Paris of the first and (though ultimately unratified) crucial Anglo-French 'Arrangements' of April 1884 and November 1885.

In a dispatch to the Governor, dated 12 June 1884, the then Colonial Secretary, Lord Derby, gave a summary, if purposely biased account of all that had passed on the fisheries question between France and Britain since 1844.[1] The basis of the quarrel, he wrote, had from the outset been that the

[1] No. 1 in Cmd. 4641 of 1886, 'Correspondence relating to an Arrangement between Great Britain and France respecting the Newfoundland Fishery Question'.

French claimed exclusive rights to the fishery in certain of the areas covered by the Treaties and argued that all British fixed settlements, of whatever nature, were contrary to treaty. The British for their part maintained that their subjects had the right to fish concurrently with the French and that fixed settlements, other than fishing settlements in these areas, were in no wise illegal. The British challenged a further French contention that they were entitled to fish the rivers. Most important of all in national and psychological terms, 'the colonists have for some years past been desirous of developing the resources of their country as regards mines, agriculture and other industries, but have constantly been met with the objections of the French Government to their doing so, and the development of the Colony on the part of the coast of Newfoundland where the French enjoy treaty rights has been practically at a standstill...'[1]

To all intents and purposes, long stretches of the littoral of western and north-eastern Newfoundland were a *de facto* condominium. With naval vessels from both sides patrolling the coastal waters to protect their citizens and their establishments, the situation was potentially an explosive one.

As far back indeed as 1838 the British Foreign Secretary, Lord Palmerston, had referred to 'acts of collision' between British and French fishermen in Newfoundland and had refuted the contention of the French Ambassador, Count Sebastiani, that France was entitled by treaty to any exclusive fishing rights. Such French claims, Lord Palmerston asserted, were 'founded simply upon inference, and upon an assumed interpretation of words'.[2]

The first positive attempt to reach an overall settlement of the fishery dispute, lasting from 1844–7, proved abortive, the French not only maintaining their claims but seeking in addition concurrent rights of fishery on the coast of Labrador. More hopeful talks were held in Paris in 1851. These, after much hard bargaining, led to the negotiation of an Anglo-French Convention, which was finally ratified by both Governments on 14 January 1857.

But, as the Colonial Secretary, Mr Labouchere, emphasized in pressing the merits of the Convention on the Governor and his now responsible Ministers:

> Deeply anxious as they are to effect the settlement of questions so complicated and so pregnant with possible mischief...Her Majesty's Government have... not thought themselves justified in departing from that rule of Colonial Government which is now so firmly established in British North America. They have

[1] Cmd. 4641, p. 4.

[2] Lord Palmerston to French Ambassador, note of 10 July 1838. Appendix to *Journals of Newfoundland House of Assembly*, 1857, pp. 175–6.

thought that in matters affecting the soil and the population of Newfoundland, the concurrence of the Legislature of Newfoundland itself should be sought before any Treaty stipulations could be put into execution, and that the aid of Parliament (notwithstanding its paramount constitutional power in questions of Treaty, affecting as these do, directly or indirectly, the Empire at large) ought, except in an extreme case, to be reserved for the purpose of completing whatever the Local Legislature may not have strict legal power to effect.[1]

The new Arrangements, which Mr Labouchere then so earnestly recommended to the Colonial Government, admittedly sought to limit the coastal areas within which French fishermen were to enjoy exclusive or concurrent rights. But to Newfoundlanders they represented a further hindrance to full internal autonomy. For not only was the doctrine of limited French exclusivity upheld, France was now to secure concurrent rights along considerable stretches of the Labrador. In addition she stood to obtain an undertaking that 'no British buildings or enclosures' should be 'erected or maintained on the strand reserved for exclusive French use'. Furthermore, a limited right of jurisdiction was to be conceded to the French, and French naval officers were to have the power to enforce French rights to the point of expelling from the Treaty Shore vessels attempting concurrent fishing.

It is astonishing in retrospect that an Imperial authority should have been prepared to offer such concessions to a foreign power in a colony to which it had so recently conceded autonomy. Clearly the British Government of the day sadly miscalculated both the character and reactions of the people of Newfoundland. No wonder that Lord Derby skated hastily over this difficult stretch of his historical review, commenting only that 'this convention [of 1857] did not come into force owing to the objections of the Government of Newfoundland'.[2]

These 'objections' were perhaps more correctly described by Prowse—himself a witness of much that passed on the French Shore question—as a 'wild outburst of popular indignation...the Newfoundlanders held indignation meetings as hot and fiery as the Tea Riots of Boston'.[3] Patriotic, francophobic, choleric Judge Prowse—'A most injudicious individual, and a strong partisan' a later Governor was to term him[4]—must like fresh cod, be taken with a pinch of salt; but on this issue there is no doubting his accuracy as a mirror of local feeling. The principal British negotiator of the

[1] Dispatch from the Rt Hon. H. Labouchere to Governor Darling 16 January 1857, 'Correspondence on the subject of the Rights of Fishery on the Coast of Newfoundland, 1857', pp. 1–4.

[2] Cmd. 4641, p. 6.

[3] Prowse, p. 471.

[4] Sir T. O'Brien to Marquis of Ripon, dispatch of 30 June 1894, no. 213 in North American (hereafter N.A.), no. 169.

ill-fated 1857 Convention he dismisses as 'either a French tool or thoroughly incapable official': the French themselves as 'so over-reaching and covetous of territory that even Perrier (the luckless official described above) could not concede all their demands'.[1] Throughout the Island, in short, tempers were up. '...The British flag was hoisted half mast; other excited citizens flew American flags: everywhere there was burning indignation over this proposal to sell our birthright for a mess of pottage.'[2]

Although Lord Derby's dispatch diplomatically veiled the fact, the colonists were now on the way to a notable victory over the Imperial Government. In the excitement of the hour sectarian and political rivalries were forgotten and the Legislature hastily passed a resolution to the effect that:

We deem it our duty, most respectfully, to protest in the most solemn manner against any attempt to alienate any portion of our fisheries or our soil to any foreign power, without the consent of the local legislature. As our fishery and territorial rights constitute the basis of our commerce and of our social and political existence, as they are our birthright and the legal inheritance of our children, we cannot under any circumstances, assent to the terms of the convention: we therefore earnestly entreat that the Imperial Government will take no steps to bring this Treaty into operation, but will permit the trifling privileges that remain to us to continue unimpaired.[3]

The Legislature was in turn fortified by the weight of written evidence against the Convention. From the pens of Anglican and Roman Catholic archbishops, from merchants, schooner captains and humble fishermen, from Carbonear, Harbour Grace, Brigus, New Perlican, Trinity, Bonavista and other outports poured letters protesting against the new proposals. 'What', wrote one supplying merchant, 'is the value to the people of Newfoundland...of the Treaty...? Answer. In my humble opinion not worth the paper on which I am writing.'[4] It was an opinion overwhelmingly shared by his compatriots of all walks of life.

The sole credit which the British Government could salve from this episode was their readiness, of which Newfoundland herself showed appreciation, to uphold the Island's constitutional right to accept or to reject the Convention. Thus, when the Governor reported home the strength of local feeling, the Colonial Secretary in a reply which has gone down in Newfoundland history as the 'Labouchere Letter' gracefully conceded that: 'The proposals contained in the Convention having been now unequivocably refused by the Colony, they will of course fall to the

[1] Prowse, p. 471. [2] *Ibid.* p. 473.
[3] *Newfoundland, Journals of the House of Assembly*, 1857, p. 18.
[4] Appendix to *Journals of Newfoundland House of Assembly*, p. 309.

ground, and you are authorised to give such assurance as you may think proper that the consent of the community of Newfoundland is regarded by Her Majesty's Government as the essential preliminary to any modification of their territorial or maritime rights.'[1]

Governor Darling, himself no out-and-out exponent of the Colonists' cause, had summed up the situation some months earlier in a general dispatch to London on the fishery problem.

A glance at the map [he commented] shows the position which the Island occupies in the Territorial expanse of the British Empire—lying considerably nearer to the Mother Country than any other of her Transatlantic Possessions—distant in fact, at the present rate of locomotion, only about 104 hours' steaming from the nearest point of the British Islands—commanding by its situation the ocean approaches to those splendid Provinces whose resources and spirit of enterprize are rapidly bringing them up to a level with States dignified with the name of 'Nations'. The effort about to be made—and there is just ground for hoping—made, too, with success, to place it by means of Electric communication within a few minutes' reach of the Instructions of the Imperial Government; its shores abounding with fine harbors, and its surrounding seas with the sources of wealth, while its inhabitants are a manly and energetic race, derived for the most part from those portions of the United Kingdom which are nearest to the colony itself; it may fairly be regarded as being, for all political and commercial purposes, in as close connexion with the Parent State, as Ireland and the Channel Islands were at the close of last century. Yet, the political position of a Dependency thus favoured is such that a Foreign State enjoys—and cherishes with a full appreciation of its value and importance—a right to the use of at least one half its line of coast, and avails itself of the right in such a manner as effectually to close that portion of the coast, for all practical purposes against the people of the State to which the soil of the colony belongs.

England possesses an abundance of wealth, which she seems never reluctant to pour out for a truly national object, and the object of redeeming this valuable Possession from its present unnatural position, might not be deemed altogether unworthy of the consideration of the Imperial Government and Parliament; while such a consummation would, without violating any principle of Commercial Freedom, assuredly augment to an incalculable extent the profits of the National capital employed in this quarter of Her Majesty's Dominions.[2]

Given the significance of Mr Labouchere's statement for Imperial relationships generally and for Newfoundland in particular, it is noteworthy that it finds no mention in Lord Derby's review. But that Minister's dispatch was of course primarily concerned to present in the best possible light the further understandings on the fishery question at which Britain and France had arrived in 1885. Thus it may well not have suited him to

[1] Rt Hon. H. Labouchere to Governor Darling, dispatch of 26 March 1857, printed in *The Royal Gazette Extraordinary* (St John's, Newfoundland), 14 April 1857.

[2] Governor Darling to Mr Labouchere, dispatch of 23 July 1856, Appendix to *Journals of Newfoundland House of Assembly*, 1857, pp. 229–33.

remind the colonists too forcibly of their earlier triumphs. And so, passing lightly over the events of 1857 his review went on to record that further Anglo-French negotiations were attempted in 1860 and again between 1874–6. In each case the result was failure. It was not in fact until 1881 that a fresh joint Commission, composed of Admirals on either side and assisted from time to time by the then Premier of Newfoundland, Sir William Whiteway, showed some signs of making progress. By now, the archives of the Quai d'Orsay and of the Foreign and Colonial Offices were choked with protests and the *Journals of the Newfoundland House of Assembly* bespattered with indignant Motions. Friction between settlers and foreign fishermen often reached flash point. The presence of rival fishery protection vessels, combined with the increasingly independent attitude of Newfoundland Ministers, now forced the Imperial Government at one and the same time to concede less to France and to pay greater attention to the Island's plaints.

The *raison d'être* of Lord Derby's long dispatch, carried by hand of one of his senior officials, was in short to 'sell' to the Newfoundland Government the terms of the fresh 'Arrangement' at which France and Britain eventually arrived in April 1884. One can detect in his presentation of the British case not only an anxiety to be rid of a troublesome problem but an eagerness, amounting almost to humility, to carry the Colonial Government with him. The Secretary of State went out of his way to emphasize that the final decision whether or not to accept the 'Arrangement' rested with St John's. But he 'would be gratified if your Ministers should find it in their power to convene a special meeting of the Legislature as soon as may be possible, in order that the necessary Acts may be passed to give effect to those portions of the Arrangement which require legislative action'.[1] The harshness of the Imperial voice was strangely softened.

Lord Derby was at pains to persuade the Newfoundland Government that the Arrangement had marked advantages over any other previously attempted. Thus, French claims to exclusive fishery rights and to the right to fish rivers beyond the tidal limits were to be withdrawn. Fixed settlements, fishing or otherwise, along the Treaty Shore, would no longer be disturbed. In return, Her Majesty's Government proposed to

> recognise little more than the de facto state of things existing as regards the acts of authority exercised every fishing season by the French cruizers [*sic*] in the matters over which the French Treaty rights extend, and the exercise of these acts on the part of French cruizers would only take place in case of infraction of the very reasonable provisions of this Arrangement, and then only in the absence of any of Her Majesty's Cruizers.[2]

[1] Cmd. 4641, p. 9. [2] Cmd. 4641, p. 9.

It was now contemplated, Lord Derby hastened to add, that two British ships should in future 'Cruize more especially off the northern portion of the coast, where the French are in the habit of carrying on their principal fisheries'.[1]

The omens for the special emissary from the Colonial Office were scarcely bright. Not only was Newfoundland in the emotional throes of youthful nationhood. The previous year had seen violent and bloody outbreaks of denominational fighting, resulting in several deaths. Thus the Executive Council, meeting on 16 July 1884 to consider the Imperial plea for early acceptance of their proposals, concluded that: 'the present circumstances of the Colony are very unfavourable to the holding of a special session of the Legislature...sectarian feeling is active and widespread. In this stage of things it is exceedingly improbable that the very important matter now in question would receive dispassionate consideration.[2] The Council had, however, the day previous considered in detail the text of the 'Arrangement'. While regretting that the Imperial Government had been unable to fulfil all their hopes, they were prepared to accept the Anglo-French proposals subject to certain modifications. These included the right to erect wharves and buildings in a few prohibited areas which were thought to be rich in minerals: and the redrafting of one Article of the 'Arrangement' so as to expunge any suggestion that the French had acquired the right to permanent settlement on the Treaty Shore. If these concessions could be obtained, the Executive Council were moderately confident that the 'Arrangement' would commend itself to both Houses of the Legislature. In regard to all of which, Lord Derby in turn promised to use his best endeavours with the French.

Not without difficulty both sides were brought to a large measure of compromise on these outstanding points, and the long-suffering British negotiators, Sir Clare Ford of the Foreign Office and Mr Pennell of the Colonial Office, were able on 14 November 1885 to initial a modified version of the 'Arrangement'. Their reward, in contradistinction to the cavalier treatment which their subsequent claims for travelling expenses and subsistence received at the hands of Their Lordships at the Treasury—plus ça change...—was a personal letter of thanks from the Foreign Secretary. The Marquis of Salisbury expressed his warm approval of the manner in which the two officials had carried out their task; congratulated them on their tact and ability, and expressed the hope that the new Arrangement would both 'satisfy the legitimate needs of the inhabitants of the coast of Newfoundland' and 'provide a satisfactory means of settlement

[1] *Ibid.*

[2] *Ibid.*, encl. in no. 3, p. 16.

for the constantly recurring disagreements between British and French subjects in Newfoundland'.[1]

Alas! for such high hopes. Though the French Government might, on instructions, be congratulated by the British Ambassador on the conciliatory spirit they had shown, the Newfoundlanders, on whose final agreement all still turned, were again to prove a painful thorn in Britain's side. In January 1886 Lord Derby's successor, Colonel Stanley, commended the revised Arrangement warmly to the Officer then administering the Government of Newfoundland, instructing him to lay it before his Ministers in the hopes that they in turn would forthwith commend it to the Legislature.[2] It then soon became apparent that all was far from solved.

The Senior Naval Officer on the Newfoundland Station in 1886 might well report to the Admiralty on his summer cruise that 'perfect harmony exists between the settlers and the French and the former speak of the good the latter do them, both in the way of protection and food'.[3] Such euphoria was short lived. The French still continued to poach salmon in the rivers: build weirs across their mouth: pull cod traps and protest at the erection of the smallest fixed installation on the Treaty Shore. A disastrous fishery in the following year further poisoned the atmosphere and heightened the resentment which Newfoundland fishermen and merchants already felt at the unfair competitive advantage which their rivals gained through the French Government's policy of granting substantial fishing bounties. It was thus that the issue of the sale of bait to foreign vessels now ballooned into a new major crisis in Anglo-French relations.

The bait controversy first came to prominence—ludicrous though the whole episode may now seem—when a member of the French Embassy called at the Colonial Office on 17 July 1885 to protest that according to information reaching Paris from St John's 'the Newfoundland Parliament had passed a law prohibiting Newfoundlanders to fish for bait for sale to French fishermen, also that the authorities at St John's would place obstacles to bait being supplied'. This was news to the official concerned. After consulting the Governor, Sir John Glover, who happened to be in London he was, however, able to assure the French Embassy that while a Bill had indeed been introduced in the Newfoundland Assembly, it was

[1] Marquis of Salisbury to Sir Clare Ford and Mr Pennell, 12 December 1885, encl. to no. 1 in Cmd. 4641.

[2] Col. The Rt. Hon. F. A. Stanley to O.A.G. of Newfoundland, dispatch of 26 January 1886, no. 14, Cmd. 4641.

[3] Commander Drummond to Admiralty, report of Cruise, Newfoundland Fisheries 19 August 1886, Colonial Office (hereafter C.O.) no. 194, no. 209.

framed in general terms, was not specifically directed against French interests, and had not in fact proceeded to a second reading.[1] But this was far from the last that was to be heard of the bait dispute. Meanwhile in both London and Paris, the Newfoundland fisheries question was gradually becoming entangled in a web of further Anglo-French grievances involving the treatment of British trade and shipping in the Pacific; the threat to the Australian colonists resulting from an alleged French intention to turn the Society Islands into a convict settlement; the future of Fiji and the New Hebrides, and the strategic importance of Raiatea.

The Entente Cordiale was still well over the horizon. Anglo-French relations were to undergo far graver strains before amity at last broke out. It was small wonder that the harassed officials in Downing Steet should view with increasing alarm and irritation each sign from Newfoundland of the colonists' determination to keep the French Shore issue boiling. And this, despite the finest feats of equilibrium on the British side, was precisely what they did. Hardly had the ink dried on the revised 'Arrangement' of 1885, than fresh difficulties arose. For it now emerged that the Newfoundland Legislature was going to fight tooth and nail against the so-called 'Bait Clause'—Article 17 of the Arrangement—which provided that: 'French fishermen shall have the right to purchase bait, both herring and capelin, on shore or at sea, on the shores of Newfoundland, free from all duty or restrictions, subsequent to the 5th of April of each year and up to the close of the fishing season'.[2] The importance of this Article can be realized from one gleeful if sadly unsubstantiated comment by Judge Prowse. 'Without a certainty of the supply', he wrote, 'the fishery is unremunerative: every French fisherman thoroughly understands and appreciates this great fact. This supply is entirely in our hands: we can at any moment paralyse the movements of the whole French fishing fleet by stopping their supplies of bait.'[3]

Newfoundland appeared to hold a trump card and she was going to use it if the need arose. Suspicions grew that the then Acting Governor was not pressing the 'Arrangement' on his Ministers with sufficient vigour. By April 1886 a high French official was warning the British Ambassador in Paris that if Newfoundland rejected the 'Arrangement' at this eleventh hour, the French Government 'would be thrown back upon her strict Treaty Rights, and no cause could be given either for surprise or complaint if she [France] insisted, as she undoubtedly must do, upon exercising those

[1] Colonial Office minute of 25 July 1885, 256/7 in C.O. no. 194.

[2] Arrangement signed at Paris, 14 November 1885, relating to the Newfoundland Fisheries Question, encl. 1 in no. 14, Cmd. 4641.

[3] Prowse, p. 478.

rights in their entireness without any further consideration for the wishes or interests of the colonists'.[1]

Not for the last time in Anglo-French relationships, rigidity paid off. Within two weeks, the Foreign Office were proposing to the Colonial Secretary that if the colonists persisted in blocking the 'Arrangement' on the bait issue, then the British Ambassador should be instructed to inform the French that Her Majesty's Government would be ready to take the extreme constitutional step of 'offering to guarantee the refusal of Her Majesty's Government to sanction any measure that might be passed in the Colony for prohibiting the sale of bait to other than Fishermen of the Colony'.[2] Meanwhile Colonial Office officials were toying with, only to reject, the idea of inviting Newfoundland representatives over to discuss the crisis. 'Even supposing that we overpersuaded the delegates', ran one minute, 'they would recant as soon as they returned. They have their constituents to bear in mind. The true remedy now seems to me to be to let the Colony stew in its own juice for a while and let the French have plenty of licence. The unpleasantness of the situation might then bring the Newfoundlanders to reason.'[3] But thanks largely to a fresh counter-irritant injected by the increasingly threatening tone of *aides-mémoires* from the French Ambassador in London, this 'stew in their own juice' policy was not wholly approved in higher quarters at the Colonial Office. On second thoughts the Permanent Secretary now reached the conclusion that the 'Arrangement'

> would leave Newfoundland under such grave commercial disadvantage that H.M. Government could not press the Newfoundland Government and Legislature to adopt it on its present lines...the French Government will not fail to perceive that it would be altogether unreasonable to expect the Colony to sanction the sale of bait to French fishermen who by the use of it, and subsidised by liberal bounties, are enabled to carry Newfoundland fish to distant parts of the world and sell it at such prices as the Newfoundland fishermen cannot compete with.

As a temporary way out of the impasse, he could think of no more than an agreement to disagree, coupled with the maximum of forbearance on all sides during the next fishing season. The new Colonial Secretary, Lord Knutsford, concurred, adding that the French Ambassador's unconciliatory language should not be allowed to pass without remark and that, as to his use of the term 'French Shore', he should be told that 'we in no way

[1] British Ambassador to the Earl of Rosebery, dispatch of 19 April 1886, no. 395 in C.O. 194.
[2] Foreign Office to Colonial Office, letter of 30 April 1886, no. 400 *ibid.*
[3] Colonial Office minute of 7 June 1886, no. 403 *ibid.*

admit that any part of Newfoundland can be so designated'.[1] The upshot of this particular round of altercation was the dispatch of a tart Foreign Office Note to the French Ambassador.[2] It is too long to quote here in full but, in view of its tone and substance, it is reproduced *in extenso* at Appendix I as an illustration of the extent to which the affairs of Newfoundland were now bedevilling Anglo-French relations. Briefly the British Government expressed their 'surprise and regret' at the attitude which France was now adopting. They emphatically protested at the French interpretation of the privileges they enjoyed in the Island: rejected their claim to exclusive fishing rights on any part of the coast, adding for good measure that they could 'hardly believe that the French Government could intend to apply to them [i.e. to Newfoundland fishermen], the term "foreigners" or to question the right of the colonists to procure the means of subsistence by fishing on their own coast'. Thus, temporarily at least, but at root only because the French had overplayed their hand, British sympathies veered back towards the colonists.

It was now the turn of the latter to overreach themselves. Late in 1886, in conscious defiance of known Imperial views, the Newfoundland Legislature unanimously passed through both Houses a Bill—this time deliberately aimed at France—for the preservation of bait. With the revised 'Arrangement' still in suspense and the area of Anglo-French discord constantly broadening, this action placed the British Government in a serious dilemma. Expediency now tilted them in the direction of placating France. To a newly arrived Governor, Sir William des Voeux, was left the unenviable task of informing the colonists of London's response to their defiance. Opening the Legislature on 17 February 1887 he stated

I had earnestly hoped to be able to inform you of Her Majesty's gracious allowance and confirmation of the (Bait) Bill...which...was generally regarded as the sole available means of relieving the trade of the Colony from its existing depression. It is therefore with profound regret that I announce the receipt, a few days ago, of a telegraphic message from the Secretary of State for the Colonies conveying the intimation of the inability of Her Majesty's Government to allow the Bill for this year owing...to the fact that foreign capital has already been expended in connection with the season's operations. But [he went on] my Ministers, inferring from the above message that a similar measure will be permitted to take effect after the coming season, will forthwith submit to you another Bill with the same objects.[3]

[1] Colonial Office minutes of 29 and 30 June 1886, nos. 406–7 in C.O. 194.

[2] Earl of Rosebery to Mr Waddington, 24 July 1886, encl. to no. 106 in N.A. 122. See Appendix I.

[3] *The Royal Gazette Extraordinary* (St John's, Newfoundland), 18 February 1887.

To judge from the editorials of the day, a further wave of righteous indignation swept the Island. Leaving aside the slight in principle of disallowing a measure passed by a responsible Legislature (although in this case the British Government as custodians of the Island's external policies were strictly within their rights) the fact was not lost on the local press that London had raised no such objections when a similar Bill was submitted from Canada for allowance. 'What a tender regard', fulminated one paper, 'we have here evinced by our Imperial rulers for French susceptibilities and French commerce; what an utter disregard for British Colonial interests does this episode in our Colonial History afford.'[1]

And so, with no overall solution even remotely in view, the dispute dragged wearily along. The burning issues of cod traps and lobster factories, of liquor smuggling and the marking of fishing vessels were now to be thrown in for good measure as the following pages show.

[1] *Evening Mercury* (St John's), 7 February 1887.

4

LOBSTER DIPLOMACY

> 'Fish' s'applique à tous les produits de la mer et le verbe 'to fish', qui est employé dans la rédaction du Traité de Paris de 1763 à la place du substantif, possède encore dans la langue courante de notre époque une valeur générale qui exclut toute restriction... La France a non seulement le droit de pêcher du homard mais encore celui de le préparer industriellement sur place.
>
> MONSIEUR WADDINGTON to the Marquis of Salisbury, 15 December 1888

> Lord Knutsford is of opinion that Her Majesty's Government could not admit that crustacea are fish...
>
> Colonial Office to Foreign Office, 12 February 1889

With the 1885 'Arrangement' lapsing, like the Convention of 1857 into limbo, the scene was now set for even tenser episodes. By comparison the concurrent quarrels which Newfoundland was enjoying with Canada and the United States pale into insignificance.

Events, as they unrolled, offer a curious parallel with those of the present post-war era. As in 1945, so after 1870, France was emerging from a period of profound national humiliation. At both times others sought to profit from her temporary weaknesses. Fashoda and Diem-Bien-Phu helped in turn to create an emotional climate of 'What we have, we hold'. Against this background, to which was now added a spreading spirit of Anglophobia, it is not surprising that successive governments of the Third Republic should have adopted an increasingly hostile attitude towards the Newfoundland question, nor that they should stand on the strict letter of their Treaty rights. Whether deliberately or not, they ignored the fact that, when the Treaty of Utrecht had been negotiated, the so-called 'French Shore' had been a barren littoral. It was no fault of theirs if upward of twelve thousand Newfoundlanders had since chosen to settle there. Moreover, the passage of the Bait Bill through the Newfoundland Legislature and its eventual allowance by the Queen were seen in Paris as deliberate provocation.

The French Ambassador to the Court of St James, the indefatigable Monsieur Waddington, could now give free rein to his official penchant for indignant *notes-verbale*. In the next few years, the Foreign Office was to suffer a surfeit of them and the pipelines between that department, the Colonial Office and the Admiralty, the Law Officers of the Crown, the Treasury, the Boards of Customs and Excise and of Trade, the British Embassy in Paris and Government House, St John's, were to be choked with correspondence, arising more often than not from the most frivolous complaints.

By 1889 the broad issues in dispute, to which that arising from the expansion of the lobster fishery now added a new dimension, were briefly these. The French still claimed that the earlier Treaties gave them on certain stretches of the Newfoundland coast an exclusive right of fishery, and this to the permanent prohibition of both settlement and fixed establishments. Further, the French now sought to claim a limited right of jurisdiction over their own citizens on the coast; exemption from customs dues in the treaty areas and the counter privilege of constructing fixed establishments themselves—notably lobster canning factories—on the 'French Shore'. To all this, the British reply was that the rights of fishery conferred on France by the Treaty of Utrecht did not take away, but only restricted during the annual fishing season, the British right of fishery inherent in the sovereignty of the Island. Moreover, the right of British subjects to fish concurrently with French citizens had never been surrendered. At most the Declaration accompanying the Treaty of Versailles had debarred the British from interrupting in any manner by their competition the fishery of the French during their temporary exercise of it. In short, whatever arguments France might advance in defence of exclusivity, it had never been contemplated either that the French Government's administrative or jurisdictional writ should run on Newfoundland soil: nor that Newfoundlanders should be debarred from settling and developing their own territory. This latter was a point of increasing importance given the agricultural potential of certain stretches of the Treaty Coast and the growing expectation that coal and other minerals were to be found there in quantity.

The lobster controversy did nothing to improve the atmosphere. *Homardus americanus* had provided a staple industry for the north-eastern Atlantic seaboard from as early as the 1840s. Though he had come late to the economic notice of Newfoundlanders, they by 1880 were discovering that lobster canning offered profitable returns. But it was an industry demanding a sizeable capital outlay. At the same time while offering new openings for employment, it also required the setting of traps which interfered with the inshore cod fishery, as well as fixed installations on or near the shore. It was on these two latter counts that the French Government now became increasingly vociferous in their complaints, insisting, so far as their areas of privilege were concerned, both that the traps set by Newfoundlanders should be removed and their factories destroyed. The issue which at once arose was whether, in the sense of the Treaties, *Homardus* was a fish at all.

As a Foreign Office letter to the Colonial Office currently admitted:

The question involves arguments of much nicety as to the exact verbal construction of the treaties and as to the intentions of the statesmen who negotiated those instruments, more than a century ago. Such arguments, however sound they may be, are not generally of a nature to preclude at least a plausible reply, or to carry absolute and immediate conviction to the opposite party interested.[1]

The French claimed that for Treaty purposes it ranked *pari passu* with the cod. The British Government denied that lobsters had been in the minds of the statesmen and lawyers gathered at Utrecht. As to the people of Newfoundland, they found in France's attempts to have dismantled factories on their own territory which had now stood for some years unchallenged, a more than usually intolerable grievance. Nor, when appealed to, did the highest experts in the land provide much comfort to the British Government. Asked for an authoritative definition, Professor Flowers of the Natural History Museum returned an equilibrist's reply which might equally well have been constructed by the Whitehall draftsmen.

Scientifically [he wrote] lobsters are certainly not fish in the sense in which the term is now used by all zoologists, but belong to a totally different division of the animal kingdom. Fish, or animals belonging to the class 'Pisces', a division adopted by naturalists of all nations, are capable of distinct definition. As a primary distinction from lobsters, they belong to the great division of vertebrated or backboned animals, whereas the class 'Crustacea', to which lobsters belong, are members of a totally distinct main division, the Arthropoda, and they are really more akin to beetles and spiders than they are to fishes.

So far, so good.

But [he went on] as to ordinary language, before the knowledge of the classification of animals according to their real structure and affinities had been attained, popular usage had taken the true fishes, the best known of aquatic animals, as the type of all or almost all others which resemble them in one of their most obvious attributes, i.e. living in the water, and consequently as falling under the Johnsonian definition of a fish as 'an animal that inhabits the water'.[2]

It was a case of 'You pays your money...' Faced with the dilemma and in the realization that the gap between the parties was now virtually unbridgeable, Lord Salisbury tentatively threw out the suggestion that Britain, France and Newfoundland should remit this new lobster issue to impartial arbitration.

[1] Foreign Office to Colonial Office, letter of 10 May 1889, no. 124 in N.A. no. 132.

[2] Professor Flowers to Colonial Office, 15 August 1891, no. 125 in N.A. no. 155.

Meanwhile the passage of the Bait Act had further fanned the flames of the dispute, not only with France, but as between Newfoundlanders themselves. While all shades of opinion in the Island were united in condemning France's now anachronistic privileges and the allegedly unfair operation of her bounty system, approval of the policy underlying the Bait Bill was not unanimous. Even in the Conservative-dominated Legislature, which overwhelmingly reflected the interests of the merchant community, a future and distinguished Premier, Mr (later Sir Robert) Bond, had raised a solitary voice in protest, emphasizing the economic harm which the measure would cause to the many fishermen who made a livelihood from selling bait to foreign vessels. The local distress likely to be caused was underlined in a memorial from the Catholic Prefect Apostolic on the Treaty Shore. While deploring in the name of all Newfoundlanders the continuing existence of French privileges in his area, Father Howley went on to refer to the alternative arrangements which the French fishing fleet would now undoubtedly make to secure supplies of bait, emphasizing that they would henceforth not only refuse to buy it from Newfoundlanders but would also try to prevent the latter from taking it for their own use. The Acting Governor, before whom this appeal was laid, commented that the Prefect Apostolic was clearly not exaggerating the extent of the 'mischief' of which the French would now be capable and that if their threats to fish the Treaty Shore themselves for bait were carried out, 'it will seriously affect, if not altogether destroy, the chief resource for subsistence there'.[1]

Thanks, moreover, to the original delay in bringing the Bait Bill into operation, French armateurs had gained a full year in which to make alternative arrangements for fitting out their fleets. Despite Prowse's optimistic comment that Newfoundland would bring the whole French fishery to a standstill, he had reckoned without the ordinary Frenchman's flair for improvisation. Ship's masters now brought across the Atlantic on ice supplies of bait taken in the North Sea, or tempted the cod, with varying degrees of success, on a diet of winkles and limpets. The leading French newspaper *Le Temps*, which at the time far more closely reflected the thinking of the Quai d'Orsay than its brother from Printing House Square does that of Downing Street, had some comments on the subject. Even allowing for a certain smug xenophobia, they struck close to the bone. If Newfoundlanders were entirely masters of their fate, commented the paper, they would long since have torn up the Treaty of Utrecht. But since they knew that the Imperial power was obliged to honour its international commitments, it was the aim of the Islanders to play a double

[1] Administrator Sir F. B. T. Carter to Rt Hon. Sir Henry Holland, Bt., dispatch of 13 July 1887, no. 124 in N.A. no. 126.

game: '"Puisque nous ne pouvons chasser les Français par la force", se dirent-ils, "nous allons leur rendre impossible l'exercice de la pêche".' Such had been the view of the merchants and, under their impulse, the local Parliament had acted. No question of course of consulting the luckless Newfoundland fisherman although it was he, not the French, who was now to shoulder the economic consequences. France would not suffer. All her fishermen needed to do was to fish for bait themselves, thus obviating the need to pay an annual tribute of a million francs to Newfoundland suppliers. The article concluded with a caustic comment on the 'Truck System':

Ce sont ces mêmes capitalistes qui siègent au Parlement de Terre-Neuve et font la loi; juges et parties dans l'affaire, n'écoutant que leur amour du lucre, ils se soucient fort peu des souffrances des autres, et il fault connaître le système commercial de Saint-Jean-de-Terre Neuve pour se rendre compte de l'odieux du procédé. Les pêcheurs sont entièrement dans la main des armateurs, ceux-ci les tiennent par les avances qu'ils leur font et ont pour eux les égards de créanciers à débiteurs. Ce sont ces armateurs qui fixent les cours de la morue, que seuls ils peuvent acheter, et, en retour, ils vendent à des prix exhorbitants tout ce dont le pêcheur et sa famille ont besoin, de telle sorte que nombre de marins de Terre-Neuve vivent et meurent uniquement pour engraisser les gros marchands de Saint-Jean. On se croirait en Irlande! Seuls, les marins qui venaient à Saint-Pierre échappaient à cette tyrannie: de par la volonté de leurs représentants il n'y aura plus d'exceptions.[1]

The temper of the Palais Bourbon was no less warm than that of the French Government's mouthpiece. By 1888 a spokesman for the fishing interests of Fécamp and Cherbourg, Admiral Véron, was urging his front bench to 'reconquer' French rights in Newfoundland. If, he added, to warm applause, we chase out the British from areas 'qui ne leur appartiennent pas', the French fishing industry would go from strength to strength. Even then some 15,000–20,000 fishermen were involved. Replying in the same spirit the Foreign Minister, Monsier Goblet, maintained France's claim to exclusive fishing rights not only for cod but for all other fish and shell-fish 'particulièrement...le homard'. Even the right to take salmon, which France had previously been ready to renounce, would now again be claimed. The Bait Act the Minister contemptuously dismissed with the remark that, thanks to French enterprise, all obstacles had been rapidly overcome. As to the lobster industry, Monsier Goblet was even more uncompromising. French interests, he emphasized, could not be upset by British incursions into the treaty area. He concluded with an assurance to fishermen preparing for the coming Newfoundland season that

[1] *Le Temps* (Paris), 1 November 1887.

the French Government would extend to them all the protection in its power.[1]

Such outbursts of jingoism did nothing to ease the sisyphean task of those still in search of an honourable and lasting settlement. Indeed, as France and Britain each augmented the strength of their naval patrols in Newfoundland waters, piling more and more complicated instructions upon their luckless commanders and more and more White, Blue and Yellow Books and Treaties into their ships' lockers, Newfoundland Ministers began to express anxiety about the Island's virtually defenceless state and the increasingly restless temper of the people. In March 1889 a newly arrived Governor, Sir Terence O'Brien, was reporting home that

> Should Her Majesty's Government unfortunately not be in a position to give any assurances as to the existing state of things, then I regret to have to inform your Lordship that, without a definite idea of their position and urged on by a scurrilous press, and local demagogues who wish to make political capital, as well as by ill-judged, would-be friends, I fear our ignorant population away from the centres of control will most probably actively resent any French interference, when possibly bloodshed may ensue, followed by results which will be fully appreciated by Her Majesty's Government, and on which it would be presumption on my part to offer any opinion, except to point out, in case of hostilities breaking out between the two nations, our utterly unprotected and powerless state...the French, though the nominal garrison of St Pierre is but some 20 gens d'armes, keep there a disciplinary company (military convicts) of about 150 men, old soldiers, who are regularly drilled and armed, also seven to eight guns, about 30-pounders and two carronades, this being in contravention of the treaties under which they assert their claims.[2]

But the colonists having at that very moment sparked off fresh difficulties for Downing Street by refusing to pass legislation making the marking of fishing boats compulsory for international identification purposes, were once more out of favour. 'You should tell your Government', replied the Colonial Secretary a little later that

> Her Majesty's Government are responsible—and their responsibility may even in an extreme case involve war—for the acts and omissions of the Colony towards foreign nations: yet, judging by the experience of recent years in regard to the question of treaty obligations with France, the Colony appears to pay little more deference to the views and policy of Her Majesty's Government on critical questions than if Newfoundland were an independent country.[3]

[1] *Journal Officiel* (Paris), 25 December 1888.

[2] Sir Terence O'Brien to Lord Knutsford, dispatch of 16 March 1889, no. 77 in N.A. no. 132.

[3] Lord Knutsford to Sir Terence O'Brien, dispatch of 31 May 1889, no. 139 in N.A. no. 132.

The carronades and thirty-pounders of St Pierre clearly failed to carry into Downing Street. The Colonial Office was, however, more visibly shaken by the influence of public feeling on the Island elections in the autumn of 1889. Contrary to local predictions that the existing Tory Government would be returned with a reduced majority, the Liberal opposition led by Sir William Whiteway secured a crushing victory, winning 28 of the 38 seats in the Lower House. All members of the Executive Council were handsomely defeated. Interpreting the omens aright, the British Government at once invited the new Premier to London for discussions on all aspects of the fisheries dispute.

Whiteway and his advisers reached London in May of the following year. His first proposal to British Ministers was that the dispute should be submitted for final settlement to five arbitrators, two to be nominated by France, one each by Britain and Newfoundland and the fifth by a method unspecified. A majority award should be accepted in advance as binding on all parties. The arbitrators would then determine the compensation due to France for full surrender of her treaty rights.

The presumption that arbitration would automatically favour Newfoundland put this proposal smartly out of court. Instead the French were offered, but declined, a formula under which in return for the withdrawal of their rights, the Colony would either guarantee full facilities for the supply of bait or make a reasonable money payment in consideration of the value of the advantages surrendered. The French Government in turn indicated a readiness to resolve the generality of the dispute either by arbitration or on the basis of the 'Arrangement' of 1885. This latter suggestion Whiteway at once rejected. But following his return to St John's his Ministers expressed just prior to Christmas 1890 a readiness to proceed by arbitration provided first that this presupposed total French withdrawal from the Treaty Shore: and secondly that agreement to guarantee supplies of bait was linked directly to a modification of the French bounty system.

Thus, the deadlock still persisted. As a memorandum to the British Cabinet had put it in March of the same year the French continued to maintain that under the previous Treaties and Declarations 'no permanent buildings of any kind may be erected, no mines opened, no magistrates appointed, in short that the whole coast for several hundred miles is to be closed to the colonists, and consequently the resources of the country behind left undeveloped, in order that no French fisherman shall be prevented from hauling his net or drying his fish in any spot which takes his fancy'.[1]

[1] Newfoundland Fishery Question, memorandum to Cabinet, March 1890, N.A. no. 144.

Whatever French rights might be on a strict, legal interpretation of the relevant documents, it had at least dawned on Downing Street that their maintenance on the eve of the twentieth century was not only a monstrous anachronism and a constitutional paradox, but at the same time a flagrant injustice in human terms. 'It is impossible', ran a Foreign Office letter of January 1891, 'not to sympathise with the Colonists in their impatience at the burden of stipulations which seriously interfere both with the economical development of the island and with the prosecution of its most important industry.' But while the 'Colonial Government have taken up an argumentative position...never so frankly avowed until now, the honour of England'[1] was still committed to acceptance of the Treaties. Attempts to negotiate were not assisted by the belligerence of Newfoundland Ministers and of the press and local opinion which, as the Governor now reported, was daily becoming more hostile to England. The newspapers Sir Terence O'Brien could dismiss with the judgement that 'here the press is at its lowest ebb, and is used mainly as the vehicle of personal abuse, or of vindictive political recriminations'. But the combination of a bad fishery in 1890; of 'the strong sympathy existing between the Irish priesthood and their flocks here with the agitators in Ireland and elsewhere'; and the influence on the Colony of those who had migrated in steadily increasing numbers to happier conditions in the United States, was clearly creating disturbed conditions. Furthermore, Newfoundland was now suffering the onset of a severe financial crisis. 'The Government has reached the limit of its borrowing powers...the public accounts from past extravagance, or want of control if not worse, seem to be in great confusion'.[2] In the circumstances the quest for some basis on which at least the lobster controversy could be resolved was now pursued from Downing Street with increased urgency.

Thus, before January was out, Lord Salisbury had proposed to the French Ambassador that the following principal questions should be jointly submitted for arbitration:

1. Do the words 'permis de pêcher et de sécher le poisson', employed in the XIIIth Article of the Treaty of Utrecht, apply to all kinds of animals found in the sea; if not, to which kinds is the application limited?

2. Whether Great Britain, by granting to France the right of drying fish and cutting wood along a portion of the shore of Newfoundland, and by promising the removal of 'établissements sédentaires', has engaged to prohibit her subjects from erecting any kind of building on that part of the shore, or only those buildings which are concerned with the fishery; and, if so, whether lobster factories are included in the prohibition?

[1] Foreign Office to Colonial Office, letter of 16 January 1891, no. 35 in N.A. no. 146.
[2] Sir Terence O'Brien to Lord Knutsford, dispatch of 6 January 1891, no. 40 *idem*.

3. Do the treaties, by prohibiting French subjects from any construction on the shore beyond 'échafauds et cabanes nécessaires et usines pour sécher le poisson', prohibit them from erecting removable lobster factories?

4. To what depth inland do the prohibitions against building on the part of British subjects, whatever they may be, extend?

5. Whether, under the true interpretation of the treaties, Great Britain, in virtue of her sovereignty over Newfoundland, possesses on that part of the coast rights of fishery concurrent with those of France, and equal to them; or only rights which must be so exercised as not to disturb the fishery of France.[1]

The reply from Paris was this time less grudging. The French Government were prepared, M. Waddington told Lord Salisbury on February 16th, to accept the general principle of arbitration. Within a matter of weeks France and Britain had agreed upon the names of three neutral arbiters, and the Newfoundland Government was invited to appoint a jurist to join them. Once more, however, local Ministers dug in their toes. 'My Government', telegraphed Sir Terence O'Brien in March, 'contend that the only arbitration, if such a course be necessary, should be on the whole of the Fisheries Clauses and Declarations, and this view has been repeatedly expressed...'

To this Lord Knutsford curtly replied that an Agreement for Arbitration had been signed between France and Britain on 11 March: that the arbitrators would deal first solely with the lobster controversy but could later 'take cognizance of other subsidiary questions relative to the fisheries'. The Commission of Arbitration was to consist of the three foreign jurists already mentioned and of two delegates each from Britain and France.[2]

But at this point even more serious difficulties arose. A case designed to test the right of British naval officers to enforce the Treaty obligations on land or in Newfoundland territorial waters was taken to the local Supreme Court where it was ruled that such rights were *ultra vires* earlier Colonial Acts. This meant that a recently arrived at *modus vivendi* over lobsters could not be enforced unless the Legislature agreed—which they showed no signs of doing—to pass corrective legislation confirming naval officers in their powers. After consulting the Law Officers, Lord Knutsford felt obliged to tell Newfoundland Ministers that, in this new situation, Parliament at Westminster would *in extremis* have to exercise its ultimate authority, legislating over the heads of the Colonists in order to ensure the continued honouring of its international commitments. The threat was not lost on the Legislature which promptly petitioned the Lord Chancellor and Mr Speaker not to allow any Bill to be introduced into the British Parliament

[1] Lord Salisbury to M. Waddington, 20 January 1891, encl. to no. 46 in N.A. no. 146.
[2] Lord Knutsford to Sir Terence O'Brien, telegram of 16 March 1891, no. 152 in N.A. no. 146.

until the Newfoundland Government could send a fresh delegation to London for discussions. The constitutional controversy now threatening seemed likely to reduce Anglo-Newfoundland relations to the same low level as those between the Colony and France, But, as had occurred before:

In nearly all cases where meetings have been held and resolutions passed... they have been convened or instigated either by members of the House of Assembly or by other residents in St John's...this state of things...shows how little real public opinion generally exists and how easily our ignorant population can be influenced by those who may wish to lead or mislead them for party or other interested motives.[1]

Yet the petition to Parliament which preceded the Newfoundland delegation to London was enough to stir men's hearts. It reminded the Mother of Parliaments that the measure, which she was being asked to introduce, would in a now enlightened age confer on British naval officers 'powers of summary adjudication independent of all the restrictions and safe-guards which British law has devised for the defence of the inherent rights of British subjects'. Glossing over the fact that these powers were as often as not used to protect Newfoundland fishermen against their French rivals, the petition went on somewhat injudiciously to say that they had been (and by inference would again be) exercised by persons unacquainted with legal procedure and whose peculiar training and habits of thought and action dictated unquestioning submission to their decrees...' A harsh judgement indeed on the Royal Navy to whose officers much credit was due for the tact and patience with which they had handled Newfoundlanders and French alike and on whom, year after weary year, had fallen the unenviable task of dousing a succession of potentially damaging political fires. It was on turning to broader issues that the petitioners reached safer if by now all too familiar ground.

We submit [they wrote] that this law could not now possibly be rendered applicable to the circumstances which it is designed to meet. All social and general conditions in Newfoundland, and particularly on those parts of the coasts affected by the treaties, have undergone a radical and complete change in the many years that have elapsed since the law under consideration was enacted. There was then no resident population in these localities. Population has long since settled there in considerable numbers, and trade and various sources of employment have been developed and yield their contributions to our Customs Revenue. Several years ago Her Majesty's Government confirmed the occupation of the coast by acceding to the desire of residents for representation in the House of Assembly and for the appointment of Magistrates and police.

[1] Sir Terence O'Brien to Lord Knutsford, dispatch of 28 March 1891, no. 263 in N.A. no. 146.

They are periodically visited by the Supreme Court on circuit; they have regular communication with the rest of the country, and with Canada, by mail and passenger steamers; in a word all the ordinary institutions of civil life to the extent to which the means of the Colony enable it to provide them. The permanence of their position being thus conclusively assured and recognized, it can hardly be necessary to point out with what cruel severity, with what destructive effect the proposed law would operate upon the trade, the industries, and every other appreciable interest of this section of our people. It must be clear beyond reach of doubt that to recall this instrument of coercion in their case would be to outrage the feelings and the rights of the law-abiding and loyal inhabitants of this whole [?old] dependency of the British Crown.

We would therefore most earnestly implore your Honourable House, by all your honoured and revered traditions, to desist from inflicting upon the people of this country the calamity of such an enactment as that which is now in contemplation.[1]

By the time the Newfoundland delegation had taken up its quarters at the Hotel Metropole the skies had further darkened. A little previously, the Legislature had passed an amendment to the Bait Act, designed to place Canadian fishermen in as invidious a position as Frenchmen, but retaining a privileged position for Americans. This clumsy action, which the Imperial Government felt powerless to disallow, was Newfoundland's riposte to earlier Canadian objections (described elsewhere) to a commercial treaty which the Colonial Government had sought to negotiate with the United States—and which, on grounds of imperial policy, Britain had felt obliged to hinder. Now, in quick succession, a number of events occurred, which clearly shook the delegation's faith in their tactics, if not their cause. First, the Canadian Government protested in the most vigorous terms against the new Bait Act. Secondly, the French carried out a number of seizures and expulsions on the Treaty Shore. Thirdly, and even more significant, some 600 Newfoundland west coast fishermen defied their Government's policy and ran cargoes of bait to St Pierre. That defiance did not lead to actual fighting was due solely to the tact of the Royal Navy in coping with an explosive situation. To add insult to injury a British Commissioner, who had been appointed to inquire into the practical operation of the Bait Act, now reported in terms quite contrary to the merchants' expectations. Summarized in a Colonial Office minute, the Commissioner's report was described as bearing out earlier conclusions about the 'impotency of the Bait legislation', and as showing that 'the folly of its authors is equalled if not surpassed by that of their successors who have granted licences to Americans while denying them to Canadians

[1] Petition from the Legislature of Newfoundland to the Honourable the Commons of the United Kingdom enclosed with Governor's dispatch to Lord Knutsford of 4 April 1891, encl. to no. 267 in N.A. no. 146.

and Frenchmen'. The general tenor of the report, moreover, was that the practical effect and the costly administration of the Act had been 'more or less of a failure throughout'. Its one immediate consequence had been to impoverish the west coast fishermen.[1]

Facing these unpalatable truths, the Newfoundland delegation also found themselves confronted with a British Government which, for a time at least, had established far more cordial relations with France and with a new found Anglo-French determination to proceed at all costs to a settlement of the lobster controversy. It was in vain that the delegation pleaded for arbitration across the board. Whiteway was heard at length at the Bar of the House of Lords. But despite the sympathy which the Island's cause aroused, the Colonial Secretary moved in the Upper House on 27 April the second reading of an Imperial Bill to secure the maintenance of Britain's treaty obligations.

There were, of course, pleas from the Opposition benches that the Newfoundland Legislature should be allowed time to get out of a mess of its own making and calls for the immediate withdrawal of all French privileges. But constitutionally the Government's case was strong. As Lord Knutsford explained, 'the Colonists received the grant of a representative legislature, subject to (the honouring of) such treaties and obligations. If the Newfoundland Courts now held that British naval officers had no power to enforce those treaties and if the Legislature refused to legislate to put the required authority of these officers beyond all doubt, then it was incumbent on the Imperial Government to act. Failing this, Britain could rightly be accused of breaking faith with France; anarchy would reign on the Treaty Shore and the basis for successful arbitration would never be constructed. The Bill was not coercive against the Colony. It sought solely to guarantee international obligations. Moreover, as the Colonial Secretary emphasized, if even now the Newfoundland Government were to have second thoughts and agreed to pass an Act 'which in the opinion of Her Majesty's Government, sufficiently secures the observance and execution, first, of the modus vivendi for 1891: secondly, of the decisions of the arbitrators upon the lobster question: and thirdly of the treaties and declarations, Her Majesty's Government will not go forward with this Bill'.[2] On this understanding The Lords passed the measure through its second reading by a large majority. Whether it was to be presented to the Commons would depend on how the Newfoundland Government reacted. And react they did in the way of men who feel the chill of

[1] Colonial Office minute of 25 April 1891, encl. to no. 356 in N.A. no. 146.

[2] Debate on Newfoundland Fisheries Bill reported in *The Times* (London), for 28 April 1891.

the stone wall at their backs. Slowly retreating through a maze of misunderstanding and of Notes exchanged with Downing Street, they finally persuaded their Legislature to pass a Bill so framed as to secure all that the Imperial measure sought to do but with a saving clause restricting its operation to three years. This seemed to British officials fair enough.

Not so to France. Although the Foreign Minister, Monsieur Ribot, had on 12 May piloted through the Senate in defiance of his own fishing lobby a law providing for arbitration, he was shocked at the news that the Newfoundland legislation was to be so limited in time. On learning that the Imperial Bill was in consequence withdrawn, M. Ribot expressed himself in vigorous terms to the British Ambassador, Lord Lytton. France, he asserted, now faced even more embarrassing uncertainties. He did not impugn the good intentions of the British Government, 'but on the good faith of the Newfoundland Government no reliance could be placed. If the Government was acting in good faith towards France why did it object to a permanent measure? Only...because it was resolved that, so far as in it lay, nothing in the nature of French rights should have permanent protection or existence in Newfoundland.' Moreover, within the time limit of the Newfoundland Bill a government more friendly to the Colonists' cause might have settled into Downing Street. In such circumstances he could not possibly hope to obtain the assent of the French Parliament to the arbitration Agreement.[1] Dismayed but resolute Lord Salisbury asked the French Ambassador to call. France, he said, seemed now to be entering on a field of controversy which was in no wise relevant to the international problems at stake. 'England had undertaken to execute the award of the arbitrators...France had no right to investigate the municipal arrangements by which the performance of that international duty was secured... One right, and one right only, France had acquired...and that was a right to the substantial and honest performance of the award.'[2]

By now the Foreign and Colonial Secretaries must have wished that someone would rid them of this turbulent Island. For it seemed axiomatic that as soon as France and Britain achieved an understanding, Newfoundland was there to upset the applecart. And, on the rare occasions that St John's and London saw eye to eye, Paris could be guaranteed to turn its back. It must be remembered too that in parallel to all these long-drawn diplomatic wranglings, ran a ceaseless stream of activity on the Treaty Shore itself. Naval ships were constantly on the move, fishing gear was seized, factories dismantled, innumerable reports and protests were pre-

[1] Lord Lytton to Lord Salisbury, letter of 4 June 1891, encl. in no. 469 in N.A. no. 146.

[2] Marquis of Salisbury to the Earl of Lytton, dispatch of 10 June 1891, encl. 2 in no. 502 *ibid.*

sented. More serious still, thanks to the anti-mercantile interest which the Whiteway government represented and to its almost pathological concern with the fisheries dispute, the financial situation was going from bad to worse. The Imperial Government was now urged at one and the same time to guarantee a large, new Loan, to send out a general Commission of Inquiry and to compensate the many west coast fishermen for the losses they had suffered as the result of the dismantling of lobster factories which their own Government had irresponsibly encouraged them to set up in defiance of French rights.

It was the growing financial crisis which provided Britain with a fresh card of entry. After rebuking Whiteway personally for having encouraged his lobster-canning compatriots to embark on such a disastrous path to indigence, Lord Knutsford made it clear that Her Majesty's Government would consent to review the financial situation only if the Newfoundland Legislature would now pass permanent as opposed to short-term legislation for the upholding of Treaty rights. At the same time he conceded that under any such new law, the British Government would be prepared to see established, for the interpretation of such rights and for the settlement of disputes arising from them, a Judicial Commission which would take over the functions currently exercised by British naval officers. These conditions the Premier of Newfoundland readily, but as it proved rashly, saw fit to accept.

The turn which events now took can be followed in this terse exchange of telegrams:

Governor to Colonial Secretary, 20 April 1892:

Three delegates (i.e. members of earlier Delegation to London] endeavoured to prevent Whiteway proceeding with Act: he states that he will do so next week: has grave doubts whether he will succeed.

Governor to Colonial Secretary, 29 April 1892:

...Premier has much opposition arising from the popularity of the cry against coercion influencing members. Would there be any objection to postponement of Bill until next session, as the temporary Act extends to 1893?

Governor to Colonial Secretary, 6 May 1892:

Whiteway...anxious to know whether, if Bill does not pass, H.M.G. will at once pass Act of Parliament...

Colonial Secretary to Governor, 11 May 1892:

You will remember that the £2 m. loan guarantee is contingent on your Ministers securing the passing of the Treaties Bill...No statement can be made as to what action H.M.G. will think it their duty to take in event of postponement...

Governor to Colonial Secretary, 14 May 1892:

Treaties Bill rejected last night by 23 to 8.[1]

Sir Terence O'Brien, who had already had a brush with the retiring British naval officer on the Newfoundland Station ('From a somewhat varied experience in the sister Service, I am well aware of the fact that it is almost the rule that the more a naval officer is clothed with the brief arbitrary authority of his quarter-deck—the more he is impatient and resents the acknowledgement of any authority from outside...')[2] now vented his military wrath upon his Ministers. The Premier, he said, had done his best: the enlightened classes deplored the conduct of the House, but the short-sighted and selfish mass of the people, not least the Opposition and the Irish Section of the Roman Catholic clergy who still smarted from their defeat at the polls in 1889, rejoiced at the government's defeat. What counted in the eyes of the average Newfoundland politician was the discovery of loop-holes through which he might evade his duty as a loyal British subject. The Governor in short despaired of ever being able to persuade a Newfoundland Government of whatever complexion to pass a permanent Treaties Enforcement Bill. 'The Uses of Responsible Government,' he concluded, 'in this Colony at all events, do not seem so evident as the abuses.'[3]

An interesting sidelight on this sorry episode was thrown by two of the dissenting delegates to the London talks. Writing to one of the local newspapers, they explained the reasons for their opposition to the Bill.

The leverage upon a Liberal Government [they wrote] which the Colony would sometimes possess could the Liberal Party in opposition be induced to champion our cause, greatly impressed us as delegates, and largely moulded our action when in London in 1891...We now think the time ripe to test the value of that leverage...the delegates...consented to the continuance of the temporary Act till the end of 1893 for the purpose of affording ample time to arrive at an arrangement with a Gladstonian Cabinet, if it were found impossible to agree with the Salisbury Government. It was so found impossible, but there is yet time to come to an arrangement with the Gladstonian Government.[4]

But it mattered little at this stage what political complexion the Imperial Government wore. Ministers still had international obligations to

[1] Nos. 147, 154, 160, 166, 169 and 171 in N.A. no. 156.

[2] Sir Terence O'Brien to Lord Knutsford, dispatch of 27 October 1891, no. 238 in N.A. no. 155.

[3] Sir Terence O'Brien to Marquis of Ripon, dispatch of 15 December 1892, no. 320 in N.A. no. 156.

[4] Mr Monroe and A. B. Morine, letter to *Evening Herald* (Newfoundland), 1 December 1892.

honour, the French to pacify and feelings outside St John's to reckon with. Above all, the present administration in the Colony had but a short life ahead of it. Fresh elections were due within a twelvemonth. In the circumstances all that could be done was once more to extend the modus vivendi into 1893. The lobster might be overfished, but his impact on diplomacy was undiminished. Before tracing his and his cousin cod's activities to their close, it will be convenient to review the progress of the Colony against a purely domestic backcloth. Storm signals, distantly perceived at the start of Whiteway's term of office, were now to prove that their economic early warning system could not be with impunity ignored. In fact little short of a catastrophe was pending.

5

FIRE AND ICE: QUEER STREET AND CORRUPTION

The members (of the Legislature) in a great measure were chosen only as the representative beggars of a set of paupers, and he who could get most flour was the best member. The whole system was one of robbery and demoralisation on all sides, for the distribution of poor relief among the idle and improvident, and for political purposes, is the worst species of political robbery, for it not only debases the distributors (if anything could do that), but debases and demoralizes the recipients nearly to the level of their corruptors.

THE RT REV. DR MULLOCK, Roman Catholic Bishop of St John's, May 1861

The question, as Your Lordship perceives, does not rest on the Governor's individual judgement: it is one dependent on the conditions of the ice on the coast.

SIR TERENCE O'BRIEN, 24 April 1894

Although Newfoundland was to carry off several 'firsts' in the communications field—Heart's Content as the terminal point of the first Atlantic cable (1866), Marconi's successful radio exchange with Cornwall from Signal Hill above St John's (1901): and the triumphant trans-Atlantic flight of Alcock and Brown, whose flimsy aircraft left Pleasantville, St John's, for Connemara (in June 1919), the Island, towards the close of the nineteenth century, remained both isolated and inward-looking.

Admittedly, the wealthy sent their sons to leading English public schools and took their holidays abroad, while the poor or adventurous migrated to the mainland. But those who remained—and by now the population was steadily increasing—had little inclination and scant opportunity for broadening their horizons. No trans-insular highway existed. By 1890 the ambitious and costly trunk railway, with its extravagant branch lines, had pushed north and westwards only to Grand Falls. Above all, the long struggle for colonization, the fears aroused by the authoritarian habits of the Fishing Admirals had dictated a pattern of settlement which, however praiseworthy in terms of rugged individualism, was to prove an expensive headache to any government. Apart from a concentration of population in the capital and upon the Avalon Peninsula, the bulk of the people lived strung out in hundreds of tiny outports dotted around six thousand miles of coastline. With few exceptions the north-eastern, north and south-western shores and the whole of the southern coast were inaccessible except by sea. In the long winter months, therefore, thousands of Newfoundlanders might be entirely cut off from the outside world. Radio did not yet exist: newspapers did not reach them. The fishermen fed on rumour and memory—and memories were long.

It was a situation which led to the nursing of grievances, imaginary or real: to the exaggeration of the Island's role on the international stage: to that spirit of defiance which previous chapters have described, and to a bitter cleavage between the mercantile and poorer classes. The failure of communication between the more sophisticated inhabitants of St John's and the west coast fishermen has already been mentioned. So greatly did it deepen in the course of the fisheries dispute with France that the west coasters frequently petitioned to be detached from Newfoundland and absorbed in Canada. It was a schism which was to have a significant bearing on the struggle for confederation. In addition to these social and demographic factors, the intensity of denominational feeling, although now somewhat on the decline, had also to be reckoned with, as had the economics of the fishery. The whole Island was at the mercy of the world demand for cod. The Truck system still placed the fishermen in pawn to the supplying merchants. The merchant himself depended on the out-turn of the annual fishery.

In such circumstances, the opportunities for jobbery and consequent extravagance were great. To the isolated Newfoundlander, wharves, feeder roads, schools and hospitals or the prospect of the railway or Government steamer coming his way were matters of life and death. To the politician, the provision of or the promise to provide these assets were the short-cut to securing office. Any government, however honest, would have found the Island expensive to administer. Concentration of population would have been the planner's answer to the Island's ills. But no Newfoundland Premier of those days was bold or far-sighted enough to propose so radical a remedy. And so, hundreds of minute communities cried out for the continuous duplication of expensive social services. Uneconomic roads and piers were built: expensive steamer services maintained, while the churches, in competition one with another, and with morally enforced subscriptions from their flocks, built schools in numbers quite unrealistic. The erratic nature of the fishery: the effects of the Bait Act and the uncertainty of external markets also created conditions in which thousands of Newfoundlanders might suddenly have to clamour for relief. And the granting of relief was a matter which the politicians of St John's had firmly in their hands.

From jobbery, it was but a short step to corruption and the neighbourhood of Queer Street. One might hardly expect Prowse as a contemporary writer to mention such unpalatable truths, although he did record his abhorrence of Truck as a 'dishonest system...demoralising to the people and disastrous to the merchant...there could be no genuine prosperity while [it] existed...'.[1] On the other hand, official records and events themselves spoke clearly enough of the perils in the Island's path.

The blame for the disasters which now piled upon the people of Newfoundland could not be laid at the door of one particular man or party. The political and merchant classes must be held responsible in large measure for the atmosphere of tension built up around the fisheries dispute and the churches for their partisan excursions into politics. In practice the rival political groupings represented little more than the 'ins and the outs'. It so happened that when disaster struck it was Whiteway and his colleagues who were 'in'.

Sir Terence O'Brien, who on his various tours of the Island, repeatedly drew attention to the striking difference of atmosphere as between the outports and the capital, was by the start of 1891 reporting that the fisheries dispute had so disturbed conditions locally that 'unless temporary relief is at once afforded, serious financial difficulties are inevitable'. His Ministers now appealed through him to Her Majesty's Government to guarantee a loan on the London and Westminster Bank for £150,000.[2] From such relatively small beginnings did the crisis grow. It was in no wise lessened by the general incompetence and extravagance which accompanied the continued extension of the railway system. By the end of the year, but without revealing the gravity of the situation to the electorate, the Whiteway Government had stepped up their requests. They now sought of London a guarantee on a Colonial loan of £2 million, a demand which, as already stated, the British Government were only prepared to consider provided that the Colony agreed to receive a Commission of Inquiry to look into both the financial situation and the general problems arising from the fisheries dispute. But even when the Governor opened the sixteenth Assembly of Newfoundland at the end of February 1892 the Speech from the Throne reflected nothing of the Colony's current ills. There were references to the expansion of the railway, the purchase of further steamers and to participation in the coming Chicago World Fair. As Sir Terence reported home: 'Notwithstanding the high colouring given by the Government to my speech, I fear that it will be found that along with the increased revenue, good fisheries and Co., has gone hand in hand increased expenditure without any provision being made, not only for a bad year, but even for meeting the necessary charge on the cost of the

[1] Prowse, pp. 536–7.

[2] Sir Terence O'Brien to Lord Knutsford, telegram of 5 February 1891, no. 67 in N.A. no. 146.

railway extension which must be, at all events for years, a most unremunerative undertaking...'[1]

Having already made temporary enemies of Canada and the United States through their handling of the bait issue and the proposed commercial treaty with Washington, and having simultaneously driven the French and Imperial Governments to the verge of distraction over the fisheries dispute, the Whiteway Government now faced fresh trouble from an unexpected quarter.

In the evening of 8 July 1892, and throughout the following day, St John's was ravaged by the most disastrous fire of its history. A graphic description, later recorded at length in the local press, concluded with these words:

> About 5.30 a.m. of the ninth the fire had completed its work of destruction, fully three-fourths of the city lay in ruins. $20 m. worth of property had been destroyed only covered by an insurance of $4·8 m.—nearly eleven thousand people were homeless, some two thousand houses and stores had been destroyed and the following public buildings [here followed a lengthy list including Gilbert Scott's recently completed Anglican Cathedral, a variety of other churches and chapels, four hotels, numerous printing presses, every lawyer's office]...were among the principal ones burnt.[2]

Miraculously, a minimum of lives was lost. Had the fire, as was the case in earlier disasters, occurred in mid-winter, there is no knowing how many would have died. As it was, a tented camp was quickly set up for the homeless and cash and supplies poured in from overseas.

The capital was only beginning to recover from these wounds when the Island was plunged into perhaps the strangest elections of its history. Putting the finest possible interpretation on events, Prowse reported that both sides—in November 1893—

> entered into the contest with the greatest enthusiasm: the utmost vigour and energy was displayed...it was the most stubbornly contested party fight in our annals. Both the Whiteway party and the opposition everywhere had good candidates, the Conservatives being largely composed of the mercantile party, with a powerful wing of the Catholic or old Liberal Party...The merchants used their influence to the full, and the Whiteway party employed the machinery of Government to the very utmost extent.[3]

Outside the newspaper world, this perhaps was as close to the law of libel as a contemporary chronicler, and a judge to boot, dare sail. But that

[1] Sir Terence O'Brien to Lord Knutsford, dispatch of 25 February 1892, no. 97 in N.A. no. 156.

[2] *Evening Herald* (St John's), 10 September 1892.

[3] Prowse, pp. 529–30.

Prowse was shocked by what he witnessed is clear from a later passage in which he recorded that:

The men who stir up strife between capital and labour in the Colony are no true friends of Newfoundland: what we require is more money introduced into the Colony, more patriotism, and less politics. The election campaign of 1893 was marked by a remarkable outburst of personal abuse: both the political parties vied with each other in keeping up this indecent carnival of scurrility. There was not even a stray gleam of coarse humour to palliate the nauseous dose...[1]

Bad though the campaign itself had been, worse still was to follow. The Whiteway administration retained power by a majority of 23–11, two independent members being also returned. But the Governor was soon reporting not only on the labour and class unrest which the elections had stirred up, with the threat of strikes to come, and on the markedly lower calibre of the new House, but also the fact that the Opposition contemplated filing petitions for corrupt practices against seventeen members of the Government, including the whole Cabinet. While at first this looked like a typical Newfoundland nineteenth-century political manoeuvre the Opposition were this time in earnest. Playing their cards cleverly, they left the presentation of their petitions until the last lawful moment. But an embarrassed Supreme Court still had to hear them.

Outwardly, it was business as usual. The Governor opened the new Houses of Legislature on 16 February 1894 and fought gamely but vainly on to induce his Ministers to introduce a Fisheries Treaties Bill. At the same time, looking uneasily ahead to the Supreme Court action he reported home. 'I have not the least doubt but that the Judge...will carry out his duties impartially and strictly: yet it is a curious fact that four years ago...he...had followed a similar course of giving out so-called public works for a few days at the time of the contest.'[2]

Whatever his past peccadilloes and despite the social ostracism he risked in so small a community, the Judge did in fact act fearlessly. On 27 March, after hearing the first petitions, he found against two members of the Government, who were consequently unseated. Thus was precipitated a constitutional crisis which for its complications, must be without parallel in Imperial history. The immediate and understandable inference drawn by Premier Whiteway was that, if the first petitions had succeeded, so would the rest. He therefore pressed the Governor to grant a dissolution. This the latter refused first because the expense could not be justified, and secondly for the significant but somewhat astonishing reason that under

[1] *Ibid.* pp. 530–1.

[2] Sir Terence O'Brien to Marquess of Ripon, dispatch of 26 February 1894, no. 60 in N.A. no. 169.

Newfoundland law the effect of a dissolution would have been to quash the judgements against the members already given and to nullify those yet to be heard. The Opposition, in no mood to allow the Government front bench to return to the polls as untriable martyrs, naturally urged the Governor to stand firm in refusing a dissolution, pointing out that in due course they would be able to form a majority of the unaccused. By now parliamentary business was at a standstill: government members purposely absented themselves from the House and Whiteway refused to pass Supply and Revenue Bills. The only way out of the dilemma that the Governor could see was to summon the Opposition to form a Ministry. At this point, however, their leader asked for a short prorogation, pointing out that he could not at the moment hope to obtain a majority to vote an adjournment of the House. Sir Terence, now thoroughly in the toils, called on London not only for advice, but for 'the presence of a man-of-war expedient to calm anxiety'.[1]

The man-of-war was unavailable. But advice there came in plenty. He should (if he could) form a new Ministry, the Governor was told. Thereafter, if his Ministers so urged, having regard to the state of supply, he would be within his rights in granting a prorogation—pending the fate of the remaining petitions before the Supreme Court. This advice the Governor followed through, but when the new (Tory) Premier, Goodridge announced the prorogation, Whiteway promptly moved a vote of want of confidence and 'also by a second motion kept the Usher of the Black Rod outside until the motion was passed, thereby delaying the prorogation for thirty-five minutes after the time named.' Must this' inquired the Governor, 'be considered as a vote of want of confidence, and does it necessitate another change of Ministry before a dissolution?'[2]

The first replies from London threw little light on the murk. Sir Terence himself, faced with a most unenviable task, now found each horn of his dilemma increasingly sharp to the touch. On the one hand the Revenue Act expired in mid-June and it was essential to make some provision before then for its continuance. On the other an early dissolution 'would send back to the constituents they have endeavoured to corrupt... both the men who have already been condemned and those who are now on trial...an election campaign now would be a mere appeal to prejudice and passion—its seeds creating discord for many a month'.[3] Meanwhile

1 Sir Terence O'Brien to Marquess of Ripon, telegram of 12 April 1894, no. 102 in N.A. no. 169.

2 Sir Terence O'Brien to Marquess of Ripon, telegram of 16 April 1894, no. 110 *ibid.*

3 Sir Terence O'Brien to Marquess of Ripon, telegram of 18 April 1894, no. 113 in N.A. no. 169.

the movement, or rather the unusual lack of movement of the ice along the coast, added its own complications to the tangled scene. While the latest safe date for a dissolution in relation to the voting of supply by a new House lay some time before the end of April, an experienced sealing captain advised the Governor that there was no hope of the ice packs breaking up by then. The choice therefore was to hold elections at which a number of constituencies would be disenfranchised by nature herself, or to delay matters, thus risking a later vacuum in supply. With some faint hopes of inducing the warring factions to form—at least temporarily—a coalition, the Governor now compromised by proroguing the Legislature until the latter half of May.

Sir Terence was understandably depressed.

I do not believe—[he reported] that any temporary government would stand. As then dissolution becomes inevitable and the return to power of the Whiteway party most probable, the Governor would then have as his Ministers those whose acts involved dismissal and who are self-convicted of corruption, a case so unprecedented as to give grounds for serious reflection if taken in connection with the following figures showing the position of the Colony ten years ago, when it was on the eve of the accession to power of Sir W. Whiteway, and what it is now, exclusive of the payments in the near future for the railways—

	Public Debt
	$
1883	1,549,313
1884	4,133,202
1892	6,439,367.

The situation was further complicated, the Governor complained, by the fact that those to whom he had a right to look for unbiased counsel 'on points of law—the Attorney-General and the sole other lawyer in the Whiteway Government—had both been implicated in the Supreme Court trials.'[1] 'I have', added the Governor a few days later, 'endeavoured to steer clear of these difficulties by means of what is I believe a recognised standard authority on this subject viz:—Todd's Parliamentary Government of England and the Colonies...He, however, I find, never contemplated a case of a Governor being bereft of the support of his Cabinet by their being with one exception defendants in actions for bribery and corruption.' The general feeling in the Colony, he added, could be summarized in a dictum he had overheard; namely that while the Whiteway party gave the people their share of the money, the others put it in their own pockets, the general belief being that the money itself was 'sent out by The Queen'.[2]

[1] Sir Terence O'Brien to Marquess of Ripon, dispatch of 21 April 1894, no. 131 in N.A. no. 169.

[2] *Ibid.*

The question whether or not to dissolve was left temporarily in abeyance while both parties fought a by-election caused by the disqualification of a further member of the Whiteway group. This awakened dormant sectarian feeling, one of the candidates, the Grand Master of the Orange Fraternity, being roughly handled by a Roman Catholic mob. While the Whiteway-controlled press, under threat of legal action, had temporarily called off its attacks on the judiciary, 'its Billingsgate amenities',[1] as Sir Terence wryly reported, were now transferred to him. The Colony presented a sorry spectacle indeed. The Whiteway faction not only refused to co-operate over supply failing fresh elections: they deliberately sought to create a loss of confidence in the banking world and to import large quantities of goods in the expectation that these would enter the Colony duty-free once the Revenue Act had lapsed in June. Standards of morality dropped to an alarming degree, the Chairman of a Local Road Board to whom the Whiteway faction had entrusted sizeable sums of money by way of local 'douceurs' being found leading a group of wreckers against a large steamer thrown on the rocks in his area: and even worse, the Speaker of the Assembly breaking into the Customs House, assaulting the police and illegally carrying off a parcel.

By now, with more and more Ministers and backbenchers being unseated or disqualified by successive Supreme Court rulings, it became increasingly difficult to understand who was 'in' and who was 'out'. The Governor himself adopted the technique of describing the Whiteway party as 'my Government' and the Opposition as 'my Ministers'. Though he might modestly add that he had perhaps 'had to deal with more peculiar constitutional points than most Colonial Governors, still it would be presumptuous in an old soldier to pose as a parliamentary lawyer',[2] he had undoubtedly steered his way through the maze not only with skill but without losing the personal affection of his feuding advisers who eventually petitioned the Colonial Secretary to extend his normal term of office for a further year.

Not that the press spared its own rivals.

The Tory 'Premier', Goodridge [cried the Whiteway *Evening Telegram* on 30 May] can spare time from his political duties to prowl about lonely roads at night and make himself highly objectionable to unprotected pedestriennes... While a lady and one of her female friends were walking out Rennie's Mill Road, this man Goodridge not only approached the lady and insolently stared her in the face, but afterwards turned round and followed her some distance...

[1] Sir Terence O'Brien to Marquess of Ripon, dispatch of 26 April 1894, no. 145 *ibid.*
[2] Sir Terence O'Brien to Marquess of Ripon, dispatch of 11 June 1894, no. 203 in N.A. no. 169.

What a character to occupy the position of Premier of the Colony! Any person desirous of ascertaining particulars of the affair can be accommodated on application at the *Telegram* office.

But anything the *Telegram* could do, the *Evening Herald* claimed to do far better. 'Scathing exposure of a Base Plot by Whiteway and Bond to frighten the electors', screamed its headlines of 4 June, 'the scheme outlined in all its hideousness'. There followed blood-curdling details of an alleged scheme by Whiteway to link an unwilling Newfoundland with Canada once he had been returned to power. 'We do not deal in forged letters nor stolen telegraph despatches like the *Telegram*', claimed its rival, 'but publish straight facts.'

Such was the atmosphere in which the constitutional crisis reached its climax. The Speaker of the Lower House might for all one knew have had 'diabolical motives' in relation to his purloined parcel. But the 'Herald' was wrong later in June to accuse him of gross exaggeration when he claimed that the Colony was in a disturbed state, with public credit greatly shaken and trade almost at a standstill. By now even the Premier, Whiteway, if he still qualified for that title, had been unseated and by early July the Legislature was reduced to thirteen members. Of these, five were for the Government, five for the Opposition, two were absent and the thirteenth 'unfortunately weak-minded and does whatever the last person may tell him'.[1] Somehow, with an eye to a minor general election later in the year to fill the seats now vacated by so many disqualified Whiteway supporters, the Governor managed to get the rump of the Assembly together and to persuade them to pass all essential legislation. The crisis, he then reported, was over: 'the law has been vindicated, the Judges upheld and the delinquents punished'.[2]

But in the wider sense, the crisis had yet to break. The 'little elections' of the autumn once more reversed the party balance in the Lower House giving Whiteway's faction 22 seats against the 14 held by Goodridge. Only now did the dammed-up consequences of shaken confidence, of class warfare, improvidence, peculation and gross mismanagement of the public pursestrings burst over the Colony with monsoon-like ferocity.

The fisherman, paying only indirect taxation, saw in any increase in the cost of living the evil hand of the merchant to whom he was tied by truck. World trade was stagnant. This not only affected the price of Newfoundland fish; the season itself had been poor all round. Worse still, retrenchment at home seemed impossible in view of the way in which successive govern-

[1] Sir Terence O'Brien to Marquess of Ripon, dispatch of 9 July 1894, no. 218 in N.A. no. 169.

[2] Sir Terence O'Brien to Marquess of Ripon, dispatch of 20 August 1894, no. 246 *ibid.*

ments had created and multiplied posts by way of reward to their supporters. And who would dare to cut back on poor relief which in the aftermath of a bad fishery was essential in both human and vote-catching terms? Given these facts, plus the mounting debts to the railway contractors, Mr Goodridge, still nominally Premier despite the out-turn of the latest by-elections, lost no time in seeking to be relieved of his responsibilities. Before doing so, however, he asked the Governor to report home the following despairing news:

The Commercial Bank has failed; the Union Bank cannot possibly keep open much longer. The interest payable in London next January upon the Colony's bonds, which the Union Bank was to pay for the Colony to the London and Westminster Bank, cannot be provided and the Colony therefore will be a defaulter unless aid is afforded. The disaster, which involves the whole trade of the Colony, has been long impending, but has been precipitated by the suspension of a London firm of agents. Nearly $1,500,000 is due by the two banks to the Government Savings Bank, forming a preferential claim on their assets. About an equal amount of the deposits in the Savings Bank is invested in bonds of the Colony. Therefore the Savings Bank has no available funds to pay depositors who, by the closing of the other banks, will be forced to draw upon deposits or suffer for the necessaries of life. Fish to the value of £1,600,000, now in stock, needs to be shipped to be realised, but there will actually not be funds enough in the Colony to pay shipping expenses unless help can be afforded. On the loan authorised last Session of the Legislature, nearly $700,000 is for debt due London and Westminster Bank. Against the balance, say, $800,000, and the Colony's bonds owned by Saving Bank, say, $1,400,000, as collateral, a temporary advance to Savings Bank of $1,000,000 at least must be procured in London or the utmost misery and loss be the result. Will the Imperial Government aid in obtaining this? The utmost haste is needed in order to avoid the worst results.

The services of a war-ship to prevent possible disturbances and attacks upon property are called for, and it will serve to allay panic if directions are immediately sent to order a ship.

A Royal Commission to inquire into the whole political and commercial position of the Colony is absolutely essential, and Her Majesty's Government cannot decline to send such a Commission forthwith without serious and far-reaching results.[1]

For once, the Admiralty drummed up a ship from the West Indian Station. On 21 December her captain signalled 'All quiet at St John's'. Meanwhile Goodridge had finally resigned and the Governor reluctantly summoned Whiteway to form a new administration. Thus ended one of the darkest hours of Newfoundland's tormented history. To Prowse the dubious honour of this epitaph:

Merchants and politicians on both sides [he wrote] have helped to bring the unfortunate Colony into disrepute by the fierce rancour and bitter personal

[1] Premier Goodridge to Marquess of Ripon, telegram of 10 December 1894.

hate which characterised their party struggles: in their mad desire for revenge on each other true patriotism disappeared...The spoils system lies at the root of all political corruption...It is only therefore by the reform of the Civil Service on the English model that elections can be carried out in a fairly decent and honourable way...How any set of politicians aware of the condition of the Colonial finances, and, as directors of the banks, cognisant of the state of the trade, could have ventured on this wild career and rushed the Island down headlong to ruin, seems utterly unintelligible...The real interests of the Colony were never considered...The misery caused by the failure of banks and mercantile houses was as disastrous...within our border as the bursting of the South Sea Bubble was in the United Kingdom.[1]

Morally and financially the Colony could sink no lower. But the people, bred to disaster from their daily struggle with the sea, drew courage from adversity. Nearly four centuries had rolled by since Cabot's landing and a new century was beckoning ahead. The see-saw fortunes of the Islanders at least convinced them that what had come down must in time invariably go up. And yet, if 1894 was a year to recall with shame, that still to come was a year best forgotten.

[1] Prowse, pp. 534–6.

6

A YEAR BEST FORGOTTEN

Here may I remark the curious fact that what elsewhere is an evil, would here be welcomed as a blessing i.e. the existence of a pawnbroker in our midst, to enable those now thrown out of employ to get rid of their superfluities. GOVERNOR O'BRIEN, 9 March 1895

'There can be no doubt', ran a Colonial Office memorandum prepared at the turn of the year 1894, 'that the Colony is at the present moment hopelessly insolvent.' One-fifth of the revenues, derived solely from heavy import duties, was now having to be disbursed on poor relief. No government could hope to remain in power without agreeing to serve as 'the conduit pipe' through which such moneys were distributed. The Civil Service was miserably underpaid: 'the politicians on both sides, recruited largely from the superabundant bar at St John's hopelessly corrupt, and with but few exceptions as ignorant and incapable as those who elect them'.[1] For years the colony had covered its deficits by borrowing, and the annual charge on the debt now amounted to about half the yearly revenue.

It was a sorry situation. Even allowing for the fact that minds in Downing Street had been prejudiced by the increasingly bitter nature of the Governor's reports, and that Newfoundland laboured beneath the economic incubus of French treaty rights, the Colonial Office assessment was as true as it was scathing. What a *laissez-faire* Liberal administration at home might be prepared to do about it was another matter. The uncharitable principle of the day—one indeed which persisted well into the coming century—was that the boon of responsible government carried with it the bane of conducting one's own affairs without assistance. Thus, as seen from London, there was no onus on Her Majesty's Government to rescue from 'their own credulity and folly those who had lent to Newfoundland. The debt obligation could be discharged only from the Colony's own resources, the Imperial Government, in fact, administering it as receiver in bankruptcy'.[2] The ultimate solution, should law and order utterly collapse, would be for Newfoundland, as Jamaica had once done, to surrender her constitution, leaving Britain a free hand to clear up the mess. Meanwhile, it would have to be brought home to the British public in an unmistakable way 'that a Colonial security is not British Consols'.[3]

[1] Colonial Office memorandum of 17 December 1894, printed as N.A. no. 173.
[2] *Ibid.* [3] *Ibid.*

The finances of the Island were by now as involved as they were parlous. At the turn of the year, the Commercial Bank had failed: the Union Bank was heading for disaster. And both banks, of which many leading politicians were directors, were in turn indebted to the Savings Bank to the tune of some $1½ million. An equal amount of the deposits in the Savings Bank was invested in the bonds of the Colony. There was thus no liquid cash with which to meet the claims of depositors. These, for the most part were rentiers, fishermen or members of the small middle class. Failing an advance from some source to this Bank of at least £1 million, the Colony would have to default on its loans, and thousands of depositors would be reduced to abject misery—and this with long winter months ahead.

The cry went up locally for a Royal Commission. Meanwhile the minority Goodridge administration had resigned and the Liberal faction returned to power, though for tactical reasons, not at once under Whiteway's leadership. They seemed, oblivious of facts, to be bent on maintaining their previous policies, turning a deaf ear to pleas from their opponents that while the crisis lasted a policy of retrenchment should be pursued—a policy, the latter added, which could be enforced only 'by union upon the part of leading men in both parties...and with a solemn pledge by them, neither to oppose nor to assist anybody else in opposing the Government which shall undertake such a policy'.[1]

Before the New Year opened, the Governor reviewed the Island's desperate straits. It was a report even gloomier than usual. The majority of the directors of the Commercial Bank, he wrote, would soon face criminal charges. Through their actions, people of every rank were now reduced to destitution. There was a mounting campaign for union with the United States. The sole ray of hope was that the Bank of Montreal and other Canadian banks might step in and, temporarily at least, avert wholesale national bankruptcy. This hope in fact materialized. In January 1895 the Bank of Montreal opened a branch in St John's and advanced to the Government the sum of $400,000.[2] This was enough to meet the half-yearly interest due on Government debentures and to cover the Government's immediate liabilities to its employees. If courageous, this was also a shrewd and far-sighted move on the Bank's part, for at one stroke they became the Colony's official agents and brought the Island firmly within the Canadian currency system.

The attitude of the British Government was less imaginative. In response to the numerous petitions which they were now receiving through the

[1] Letter (undated) of December 1894 from Mr Goodridge and others to leaders of the Liberal Party, encl. 2 in no. 23 in N.A. no. 174.

[2] Sir Terence O'Brien to Marquess of Ripon, telegram of 4 January 1895, no. 41 *ibid.*

Governor for the urgent appointment of a Royal Commission—petitions which reflected the broad anxieties of those in the Island with no political axe to grind—their cautious response was that they could not act unless requested to do so by the Colonial Legislature. Nor could they bind themselves in advance to accept such financial proposals as a Commission might eventually put forward. Moreover, while the Opposition gave its backing to the Royal Commission campaign, the attitude of the Government was curiously ambivalent. Many of the petitions flooding in from the outports were mutilated before reaching Government House and their lists of signatories truncated. While the Legislature was busy passing Bills for the liquidation of the Commercial Bank and to make the Canadian dollar legal tender in the Island, the temper of the unemployed—now numbering close on 40,000—was growing ugly and wild rumours circulated in the local press and in pamphlets of an American take-over bid. If, commented a senior Colonial Office official, 'Canada makes difficulties, Sir W. Whiteway and his creatures will certainly, having nothing to lose, play for annexation to the States which his newspaper has for some time been paving the way for'.[1] The *Evening Telegram* had in fact for some weeks past been serializing extracts from the New York and Boston newspapers, whose leader writers were expatiating on the advantages to Newfoundland of seeking safety under America's rather than Canada's wing.

This was by no means the way the Governor saw things. While his wife was energetically organizing soup kitchens and relief committees, he was pleading with London that 'England—whose role is ever to be a parent to her offspring, might now be induced to take her sadly stricken child under her wing, when by the temporary aid necessary to restore strength, and by a stringent regime in the future, a healthier state of things could be restored'.[2]

But by now Whiteway had himself once more accepted office. One of his first acts was to ask the Governor to communicate with the Governor-General of Canada with a view to discussions being opened on the subject of confederation. This was followed rapidly by an adjournment of the Legislature. Whiteway's motives were not far to seek. He and his colleagues were opposed to a Royal Commission from Britain for fear of what its report might reveal of their past mismanagement. The press campaign for union with the United States served conveniently to confuse the issues and to bring home Britain's basic indifference to the Island's plight. Discussions with Canada would at the worst gain time. If by some miracle they should

[1] Colonial Office minute of 22 February 1895, no. 206 in C.O. no. 194.

[2] Sir Terence O'Brien to Marquess of Ripon, dispatch of 28 January 1895, no. 91 in N.A. no. 174.

lead to a firm basis for confederation, then the Imperial Government could at least be depicted as having forced Newfoundland to join Canada through its own unwillingness to help.

While the Colonial Office had provided a modest sum of money to relieve immediate distress and was preparing to send out a Special Commissioner—Sir Herbert Murray, later to succeed Sir Terence O'Brien as Governor—to administer it, their general attitude was frankly negative. In response to suggestions that the British Government might guarantee the Newfoundland bonds, the Colonial Secretary telegraphed belatedly and coldly in mid-February that this

> would create a precedent of wide application which would involve His Majesty's Government in responsibilities which they could not undertake with justice to the taxpayers of the United Kingdom...it is a necessary consequence of the self government enjoyed by colonies having responsible government that such colonies should not look to the Imperial Government to aid them in their financial affairs: such aid would require constant supervision inconsistent with self-government.[1]

Tempora mutantur!

Viewed from London, there was of course every advantage to be gained from Newfoundland's final absorption into Canada. 'The complete consolidation of Her Majesty's Dominions in North America', wrote the Colonial Secretary to the Governor-General of Canada not without irony, 'is, I need not say, an object favourably regarded by Her Majesty's Government, and the present circumstances of the colony of Newfoundland appear to present a suitable opportunity for accomplishing that object on satisfactory terms.'[2] Lord Ripon went on to warn the Governor-General of the problems which his Canadian Ministers might inherit by way of treaty obligations and of the need to ensure that France should have no cause to complain that these were in the process disregarded. The British Government, he concluded, stood ready to assist the negotiations in any way they could. Not so Sir Terence, although little heed was then paid to his views. For him confederation would mean forcing an unpopular decision on the Colony, depriving Britain of a source of trade and of her traditional nursery for seamen, and inflicting a death blow to local industry.

> I have been but little in Canada [he confided to Lord Ripon] so can speak with no authority in the matter; moreover I have no desire to impugn the loudly expressed loyalty of its people, though its very loudness is to me suspicious, as is the great desire to hamper itself with a bankrupt province...notwithstanding

[1] Marquess of Ripon to Sir Terence O'Brien, telegram of 19 February 1895, no. 264 in C.O. no. 174.

[2] Marquess of Ripon to Earl of Aberdeen, letter of 23 February 1895, no. 95 *ibid.*

these loyal expressions, during the three weeks I was there, I heard rank treason uttered by two or three most distinguished men...it will be a wise man indeed who can predict what the position of Canada towards England may be two generations hence...[1]

Yet, to do the Governor justice, he was little enough supported at home or locally. Press attacks upon him were probing new depths of scurrility and the 'annexation to America lobby', sedulously fomented by the Whiteway interests, was making headway. The large number of Newfoundland immigrants in the Boston area, said by now to number close on 30,000, was particularly active in the anti-Canada campaign. What Sir Terence described as the danger of avoiding 'the political Scylla on the Treaty Shore' only to fall on 'a future American Charybdis'[2] was high-lighted by the arrival from Boston of a widely circulated pamphlet prepared by the leader of the Newfoundland community in that city.

You know [ran this document] what the effect of confederation with Canada has been and means to the other maritime provinces. Nova Scotia was treacherously handed over to the Confederacy against the will of the majority of her people. The pledges made by Canada to the politicians who gave away the province's rights have never been redeemed. The people of New Brunswick curse the day they entered the scheme. Do not allow yourselves, then, to become simply an adjunct to a country the entrance to whose waters you control.

As a Newfoundlander by birth I ask you in the name of common liberty and the best interests of yourselves and your children, to resist any attempt that may be made by politicians, irrespective of party, to legislate away the privileges of free government that you now have in your hands. As you overwhelmingly defeated the measure in 1869, defeat it now, and forever, in 1895.

The United States has always shown toward you the feelings of brother to brother. At the time of every disaster, past or present, the people of this free country have opened their purses, without regard to creed or caste.

They are ready to do it now. Yes, they are going to, and will see you through the time of distress between now and the opening of the fishing season rather than permit your rights to be starved away from you through the machinations of a Home ministry that would sacrifice your liberty only to fatten on your labor. Once more, in the name of God, Liberty, and Country, vote NO.[3]

The 'Join America' movement was to have its pale counterpart during the penultimate national heart-searchings of 1946–9. But even at this earlier time of stress, it never developed into a serious campaign. Before March 1895 was out, the Whiteway Government had nominated its delegates to the talks in Ottawa—'three attorneys and a speculator', as a

[1] Sir Terence O'Brien to Marquess of Ripon, dispatch of 4 March 1895, no. 345 in C.O. no. 194.

[2] Sir Terence O'Brien to Marquess of Ripon, dispatch of 9 April 1895, no. 496 *ibid.*

[3] Letter to the People of Newfoundland, William Whittle, Boston, 30 March 1895.

Colonial Office minute sourly described them.[1] They left on their assignment by the mail boat conveying one of the Governor's more than usually scathing dispatches via Halifax to Tilbury. 'It is difficult', he wrote, 'to obtain a correct appreciation of the feeling in this matter (of confederation) from the press as the editors of our three papers are confederates and, I am told, have declined to publish a number of letters in opposition to it'. However, matters seemed to go forward locally much as heretofore since, before their departure, the members of the delegation to Canada helped their colleagues to make a number of new appointments. Their value may be guessed at from the drift of Sir Terence's increasingly convoluted prose.

I mention to show you, My Lord, how party services are alone regarded irrespective of all other considerations. First; as physician to the Lunatic Asylum a medical man, one of the late disqualified members, has been nominated who has been turned out of the Medical Society for unprofessional conduct; secondly, as Head of the Police, the Governor of the Gaol, succeeds Colonel Fawcett the former having when previously in the Force been ordered by one of my predecessors to be dismissed for insubordination, a sentence which I however must say was subsequently condoned, his place being taken by another of the disqualified members, of whom all I know is that only last year he was had up for obstructing the police in the execution of their duty while he some years ago was the guest of my late drunken butler and was entertained in my servants hall by him with my wine which he must have known was stolen and lastly in face of the protest of the Chief Medical Officer in charge of our Hospital they have removed his present Assistant (a political opponent) and replaced him by one of their unsuccessful candidates who if formerly known for his intemperence, is now stated by Dr Shea to be addicted to opium and morphia.[2]

That Confederation was not wholeheartedly welcomed was clear from the manner of the Delegation's going. They were preceded to the wharfside by a large crowd bearing banners swathed in crepe and their ship sailed to an unnatural silence. Their departure in short was very different from that of their predecessors. Those who had left for Canada in 1888 were negotiating from a position of relative strength. Whiteway was en route to Canossa *in forma pauperis*. Moreover, he was due to confront a Canadian Government which was itself on its last electoral legs.

Since the earlier delegation had returned empty handed, there was indeed little to suggest that either side was enthusiastic for union. Certain groups on the west coast of the island had admittedly petitioned to be detached from the authority of St John's because of their *animus* against the Bait policy of the merchants. But most of them would have been as ready to revert to Crown Colony government by way of partition as to seek their

[1] C.O. minute of 27 March 1895, no. 434 in C.O. no. 194.

[2] Sir Terence O'Brien to Marquess of Ripon, dispatch of 26 March 1895, no. 448 *ibid.*

fortunes through confederation. Nor had the British Government lent their support to such fanciful notions. In their view the eventual completion of the trans-insular railway would put paid to the antagonisms between the east and west coast factions. In any case, the Imperial Parliament could hardly be expected to condone the constitutional backsliding of one half of a Colony which had now enjoyed a generation's worth of responsible government. Furthermore, Canadian–Newfoundland relations had been exacerbated by the fisheries dispute and by Newfoundland attempts to sign a commercial treaty with the United States in alleged defiance of Canadian interests. As early as 1891 the Newfoundland Executive Council had drawn up a list of complaints designed to prove the 'hostile action of the Canadian Government towards the Colony'. Grievances included the efforts of Canada to obstruct the passage of the Bait Act, Canadian support for French interests in the Island based on the Dominion Government's need to placate the Province of Quebec, and the imposition of a protective tax on Newfoundland fishery imports. In their own words:

> The Committee fails to see any ground for believing that the action of the Canadian Government is in any way influenced by a desire to foster a friendly relationship conducive to the advancement of this Colony, or for the interest and advantage of the Empire: but upon the other hand, the Committee is most unwillingly obliged to arrive at the conclusion that the Canadian Government is solely actuated by selfish motives in the course it is following...The Committee cannot recede from the position it has taken viz:—to yield no point so long as the Canadian Government maintains its present attitude towards this Colony.[1]

When one considers that Canadian Ministers were equally convinced of Newfoundland's unfriendly attitude to the Dominion, that the French-Canadian press was deeply suspicious of any move to bring the Island into confederation and that Canadians generally were doubtful of the wisdom of saddling themselves with the double incubus of Newfoundland's treaty obligations and her public debt, it becomes clear that the omens for this third essay at union were far from bright.

In the upshot the Newfoundland delegation spent less than three weeks in Ottawa, returning before April was out—disheartened, as Lord Aberdeen reported, at having nothing to bring home. Terms of union were admittedly discussed in depth[2] and a broad measure of agreement was reached on the island services which the Dominion would be ready to assume in the event of union. But, as always, the bogey of Dominion–

[1] Minute of Newfoundland Committee of the Executive Council 24 December 1891, encl. in no. 24 in N.A. no. 156.

[2] For a more detailed analysis of the financial issues at stake, the reader should see MacKay, pp. 451–8.

Provincial relations loomed over the conference table, and the issue of responsibility for Newfoundland's public debt finally brought the discussions to their negative conclusion. Both sides agreed that the Island's total indebtedness and other obligations amounted at the time to $15·82 million. For the Dominion, the Prime Minister, Sir Mackenzie Bowell, offered to assume $10·35 million. This, calculated on the basis of $50 per head of population, was the highest figure to which the Canadians felt able to go without reopening the question of terms with every other province—a departure which, on the eve of fresh elections, was politically unthinkable. How was the gap to be bridged? The Newfoundland delegates made clear at once that they would find it impossible to provide for the balance of $5·48 million, while at the same time maintaining their local services with such other resources as might become available to the Island under confederation. Lord Aberdeen placed the dilemma firmly in the lap of the Imperial Government.

Your Lordship will observe [he wrote] that there is a considerable gap between what Canada is prepared to offer and what Newfoundland claims as necessary for the accomplishment of the desired union.

Under the circumstances, I have to convey and express the earnest hope that Her Majesty's Government may be prepared to take such action as would enable this gap to be bridged over.

It is unnecessary for me to allude to the many serious considerations which, especially at the present time, point to the importance of getting Newfoundland incorporated with the Dominion, as these will doubtless be fully present to your Lordship's mind. I may state, however, that at a meeting of the Conference, when I was present, the Newfoundland delegates gave an undertaking that, in the event of an agreement as to the financial terms of union being arrived at, the Government of Newfoundland would at once pass as a permanent Act the Bill relating to the French shore rights, in the form already suggested by Her Majesty's Government, in place of the temporary Act which was proposed as a sort of modus vivendi. Mr Bond, the leader of the Newfoundland delegates, further stated, in reply to a question, that they were fully empowered by their Government to give an undertaking to the above effect, and that their Government have now a two-thirds majority in the Legislature of Newfoundland.

I may add that the present Leader of the Opposition in that House is a strong advocate of Confederation.[1]

That Britain might find a modest act of statesmanship beyond her means became apparent only too soon after Lord Aberdeen's appeal, for as Prowse wrote privately to Lord Ripon on 1 May:

I understand there is a hitch in the settlement of terms of union between Canada and Newfoundland: I suppose it wants no wizard to divine that the difficulty is

[1] Earl of Aberdeen to Marquess of Ripon, dispatch of 16 April 1895, no. 197 in N.A. no. 174.

financial. When [he went on] I had my very pleasant interview with your Lordship, I said that the mother country would have to behave like a benevolent parent at a wedding, in Yorkshire phrase she would have to put down 'some brass' for the young couple and smooth the way for them...The Dominion is incomplete without Newfoundland: as Sir John A. Macdonald said to me, 'Newfoundland holds the key to our door, the gate of our field'. A dissatisfied annexionist Newfoundland would be a constant danger to Canada.[1]

Britain's attitude was indeed an ambivalent one for on the very day that Lord Aberdeen was urging on London that 'the further amount required to enable Canada to accomplish union is a lump sum of one million sterling',[2] Lord Ripon was assuring the Governor of Newfoundland that the policy of Her Majesty's Government remained distinctly in favour of Confederation—but not, it would seem, at a price. The Colonial Secretary was clearly intent on a bargain. As he replied to Lord Aberdeen, the Canadian Government seemed to be doing less for Newfoundland on a *per capita* basis than they had done for Prince Edward Island. Moreover, bearing in mind that the Newfoundland railway would on completion become the property of the Dominion, it seemed to him only reasonable that Canada should assume the totality of the Island's debt. These suggestions the Canadian Government brushed aside, the Governor-General on 8 May telegraphing to Downing Street that 'unless the $5 million are provided for, there is no possibility of confederation'. He added, from his own knowledge of the growing anti-confederate feeling on both sides of the Cabot Strait; 'Whiteway telegraphs that any further delay in favourable reply would be fatal to the project.' And delay there was—from a quarter which had so often wrecked the hopes of visionaries and seers. Ponderously the Lords Commissioners of the Treasury ruled that a condition precedent to any financial help to Newfoundland must be the appointment of a Royal Commission of Inquiry. Knowing the earlier reluctance of the Whiteway Government to admit any such machinery to the Island and presumably well aware of the political need for an early settlement, the British Government were now quickly strangling the bride whom it had been their professed intention to drag before the altar. The Governor, himself no champion of the confederate cause, at least saw matters clearly. On 16 May, he reported, the Legislature had reconvened after a short adjournment while waiting on further news from London. The proposed terms of union were then laid on the Table of the House. 'From all I can hear I believe Confederation, unless those terms be

[1] D. W. Prowse to Marquess of Ripon, letter of 1 May 1895.

[2] Earl of Aberdeen to Marquess of Ripon, telegram of 4 May 1895, no. 204 in N.A. no. 174.

greatly modified, so as to include the assumption of the entire debt is dead.'[1]

And dead it was. On the British side the contention was that Parliament could not be asked to vote funds on Newfoundland's behalf at least until a Royal Commission had reported. The Canadian excuse was party and provincial politics.

The negotiations were indeed a commentary on British and Canadian statesmanship of the day. The terms requested by Newfoundland, if out of line in some respects with those granted other provinces, were not unreasonable in view of the necessitous condition of the Colony's finances. Moreover the formula of debt allowances and subsidies embodied in the British North America Act had in fact been applied with great elasticity, especially in the case of the provinces which had entered since 1867, namely British Columbia, Prince Edward Island and Manitoba. On Bowell's behalf it should be noted that his hold on parliament was becoming precarious, that the Dominion treasury had just managed to scrape through many lean years, and that the hungry provinces were continually pressing for increased subsidies. Yet Bowell's Government cannot escape the charge, not only of political ineptitude in dealing with the Newfoundland issue, but of singular lack of vision as well. The refusal of the Imperial government of aid without first a royal commission of enquiry was equally unimaginative and inept. The vision of the 1860's of Canada as a great North American nation under the Crown seemed indeed to have faded on both sides of the Atlantic.[2]

If few tears were shed in Ottawa, joy in St John's was scarce confined. Even before certain failure had been announced, the Whiteway Government were actively embarked on an alternative quest for funds. For, whatever the political Schadenfreude to be extracted from the failure of the talks, nothing could hide the stark facts of the financial crisis.

Early in April, and again in mid-May, the government had had to resort to the Bank of Montreal for further loans of $200,000 in all to keep the Savings Bank afloat. The Special Relief Commissioner was busy organizing soup kitchens and interviewing applicants for emergency assistance, limiting the dole to the unemployed, from the exiguous fund available to him, to 50 cents a day as against the national average rate of wage to the unskilled of $1 *per diem*. The directors of the Commercial Bank were now on trial. Against this background, the Government decided to send a senior Minister, Mr Bond, the so styled 'Colonial Secretary', on a mission to 'the money markets for the purpose of effecting a loan upon the credit of the Colony',[3] the sum not to exceed $2½ million. For the first time mention was made of the need to establish a sinking

[1] Sir Terence O'Brien to Marquess of Ripon, dispatch of 18 May 1895, no. 246 in N.A. no. 174.
[2] MacKay, p. 458.
[3] Minutes of the Newfoundland Executive Council, 11 May 1895.

fund. At all costs Whiteway remained determined to avoid the Royal Commission of Inquiry for which the Opposition and middle classes pressed in vain and failing which the Imperial Government professed their inability to help the Colony.

To the general surprise, Bond's mission proved successful. Although he met blank faces at the counters of the two Canadian banks established in St John's and even colder stares at the financial houses at which he called in New York and Montreal, he managed first, by pledging his personal credit, to obtain a short-term loan of $150,000 from a firm of Montreal brokers—a move which in the nick of time averted disaster for the Savings Bank—and second to place a long-term loan on the London market of £550,000 at 4 per cent. Finally, to round out his triumph, he obtained a third short-term loan of $850,000 which put the Savings Bank out of all immediate difficulties.

Fortified by this success: with a prosperous seal fishery behind them and the prospect of an abundant cod fishery to come, the Government now for the first time embarked upon a policy of retrenchment. Seen through the Governor's eyes, this was less a broad and statesmanlike act than a means of settling old political scores. For the first targets were Sir Terence himself, who was to lose not only his A.D.C. but £650 in salary to boot, and the judges of the Supreme Court. Both victims reacted vigorously, the judges protesting that the independence of the judiciary was now at risk and Sir Terence that the desire of the Government to lower the Governor's position to the utmost was to his mind beyond doubt.

After an unusually long spell of office, lasting over six years, Sir Terence O'Brien was now on the eve of departure from the Colony. An embittered and disillusioned man, he was obliged before leaving to suffer the mortification of assenting to the Act reducing his and other salaries. Yet in addressing the Legislature for the last time on 4 July he was able, with some conviction, to proclaim his Ministers' view that 'the dark cloud which has hung like a pall over this colony for a short time is gradually passing away...The prospect is favourable for an abundant cod fishery, and agricultural operations exhibit every indication of yielding plentiful returns. The present brightening outlook should inspire our people with new hopes and new aspirations'.[1]

There was, however, little brightness in the Governor's own passing. As he reported in one of his last dispatches, he was now ending

perhaps the most unprecedented and unpleasant tour of service that it has fallen to the lot of any Governor of Her Majesty's Colonies to deal with. I certainly

[1] Sir Terence O'Brien, speech to the Legislature, 4 July 1895, *Newfoundland Journals of the House of Assembly*, pp. 894–5, pp. 126–7.

thought [he added] that the discredit brought on this unfortunate Colony by its politicians had last year reached its climax, when 17 out of 36 representatives were had up for gross bribery and corruption, but I now fancy 1895 will beat this record as, out of 15 members of the Legislative Council, 3, and 1 member of the House of Assembly, have been arrested for fraud: as were one ex-member of the former and 2 of the latter body, exclusive of one who would have been in the same category had he been alive.[1]

Nor did the local press spare him in his final days. By now the Governor had become the symbol of all that divided the parties. 'They [the Tories] never should have been permitted to grasp the reins of power', wrote the Whiteway editorialist, 'nor would they if Sir Terence O'Brien possessed an adequate idea of the duties and responsibilities of a viceroy in a self governing colony...Like most military men whose experience of actual warfare is very limited, Governor O'Brien affects an inordinate fondness for pomp and glory.' There followed a long list of alleged misdeeds and the comment that 'all these things are still fresh in the people's memory, and can only be obliterated by the departure from our shore of the most incompetent and unpopular Governor that ever ruled here'.[2] This was enough to put the Tory leader writer on his mettle—'When the Governor is made the subject of a particularly abusive attack', he countered, 'it may be set down at once that Whiteway & Co. have some special reasons for insulting him...The reason for this was that last week His Excellency refused to invite any of the "white-washed" political convicts who compose his Executive.' After a swingeing attack on the Premier ranging far beyond the confines of mere libel, the newspaper vindicated its champion with the endearing comment that 'Sir Terence is every inch an Irish gentleman, and that is saying a good deal for one who knows how to display those finer traits of the Celtic character to the best possible advantage'.[3]

Small wonder that a less sensational daily paper should later carry in its columns the following:

Wanted—A Governor for Newfoundland who will keep up the hospitalities o Government House, stand unlimited abuse, and perform the duties of his office with promptness and pleasure. He will be kept busy writing despatches and looking after the erratic conduct of his ministers. As the post is so eminently desirable only a small stipend is attached, sufficient to pay the running expense only. Applicants should be furnished with

AMPLE PRIVATE MEANS.

[1] Sir Terence O'Brien to Mr Chamberlain, dispatch of 25 July 1895, no. 286 in N.A. no. 174.

[2] *Evening Telegram* (St John's), 5 July 1895.

[3] *Evening Herald* (St John's), 6 July 1895.

This is a glorious opportunity for ambitious moneyed men or susceptible millionaires. The title of 'Your Excellency' will be an additional, if not the chief, inducement. Applicant will please state the amount of their private fortunes, and enclose medical certificate, as to their ability to stand contumely, abuse and slander. Apply

J. CHAMBERLAIN,
Downing Street, London.[1]

As Sir Terence O'Brien moved out of Government House, St John's, so Mr Joseph Chamberlain moved into the Colonial Secretary's lofty room in Downing Street. But the return of a Conservative Ministry to power in Britain had scant influence on developments in Newfoundland. What the Acting Governor was soon describing as 'the mutual low invectives of party newspapers' continued unabated: the directors of the Union bank at long last joined their arrested colleagues from the Commercial Bank in the dock and trouble still smouldered on the Treaty Shore. The year had shown how bitter was the animosity between the politicians and how reckless they were of the Colony's true interests. It had killed all early hopes of union, and underlined the brittle frailty of the Newfoundland economy. If a tight financial corner had been turned and a partial recovery achieved, the Island was still a long way from stability.

[1] *Daily News* (St John's), 18 September 1895.

7

THE (ALMOST) GREAT TRAIN ROBBERY

They sowed the wind, so that it ill becomes them to put on the lion's skin.
Colonial Office minute of 1 March 1898

[Good Lord! What a metaphor! But the idea is sound.
Marginal note by MR CHAMBERLAIN]

The Railway, it must be remembered, will not for years pay for the grease to the wheels. Colonial Office minute of 1 March 1898

Practically it seems that the Ministry are going to sell the Colony to a contractor—a rather novel proceeding and a questionable result of self-government. We cannot prevent them—but we might at least wash our hands of the business. MR JOSEPH CHAMBERLAIN, 5 March 1898

It is a quaint recurrence that all parties in Newfoundland can join hands when they think these hands can be dipped into Imperial pockets.
Colonial Office minute of 12 April 1898

Terre-Neuve a trouvé dernièrement son Cecil Rhodes: c'est un Canadien qui s'appelle M. C. R. Reid. *Dépêche Coloniale*, 2 February 1899

One of the spectres consistently haunting the minds of late nineteenth-century Newfoundland ministries, and which so largely contributed to financial excess and peculation, was that of the trans-Island railway.

Newfoundland burst late into the railway age. In England the Stockton and Darlington line had been opened in 1825. Less than ten years later the French Government was encouraging railway construction as a matter of State policy. On the North American mainland the Delaware and Hudson line had begun to operate in 1832 and a quaint local railroad was running at St John's, Quebec, by 1837. Before 1869 was out it was possible to cross the United States by rail; while 1887 marked the completion of the Canadian Pacific Railway's link between Montreal and Vancouver. Not until 1881 was the first line of rail laid down in Newfoundland.

The time lag was not accidental. The habits, the economy of the Island were dictated by the fishery. Introspective and isolated, Newfoundlanders still looked upon the sea as their main road. Newfoundland was a constellation of scattered outports, 'isolated and self-contained, their people strangers to those of neighbouring villages, save as the men folk met at sea or on the Banks'. The Island faced 'eastward and southward and back upon history, not westward to a continental frontier and forward to continental growth'.[1] But when eventually the railway mania caught up with her, the Island all but died of the effects.

[1] Morton, p. 42.

As the population grew and the first tentative efforts were made to diversify the economy, the need to link east with west and to open up the interior became self-evident. What failed the country were a curb to enthusiasm and local ability to distinguish the carpetbagger from the reputable contractor. Prowse might well proclaim that 'a railway policy is always a progressive policy; like the proverbial snowball, it gathers strength [*sic*] as it rolls: when once a line is built, however short the distance, it must go forward: its benefits are so obvious, its accommodation to the public is so apparent, its advantages to the great labouring population are so striking that its extension goes forward as a matter of course'.[1] That was precisely what the Newfoundland railroad failed to do. Its progress was rather by fits and starts. Speculators came, and having burnt their fingers, left. Politicians saw in it a rich mine from which to quarry votes. The French opposed its extension to the Treaty Shore. At times of financial crisis work stopped altogether. And at one point, in its determination to see the line completed, the Government of the day all but signed away the Island in fee simple to a private company. The railway in short symbolized much of the political history of late nineteenth-century Newfoundland.

The first positive action resulted from a report presented to the Legislature in 1880 by a Joint Committee of both Houses. This argued eloquently the need to look to other resources to supplement the fishery. Fortified in advance by the favourable outcome of a preliminary survey for a trans-island line, which had been carried out five years previously, the report went on to recommend that a start at once be made with the construction of a narrow gauge line from St John's to Conception Bay. For this purpose the government should be authorized to raise loans not exceeding half a million dollars in any one year. The necessary legislation was quickly passed and the Liberal administration of the day, headed by Whiteway, granted a charter to an American concern, the Newfoundland Railway Company. The company was required to complete the railway within five years, and then to maintain and operate it, the government guaranteeing to pay an annual subsidy of $180,000 over thirty-five years and to make grants of five thousand acres of land per mile constructed. This, it may be noted, was in accord with practice on the American mainland in the early days of the railway age.

The employment generated and the money circulating once work began in August 1881 came on the whole community, if Prowse is to be believed, 'like the gentle rain from heaven: its refreshing dews descended alike on the friends and opponents of the new enterprise: its rills trickled into everybody's pocket'.[2] But it soon became clear that the iron monster was not

[1] Prowse, p. 622. [2] *Ibid.* p. 508.

universally welcome. Within two years, as the line approached the southern shore of Conception Bay, there occurred the so-called 'Battle of Fox Trap'. A St John's merchant opposed to the railway scheme spread rumours that the local farmers were about to be dispossessed. To a man they rose, stoned the engineers and drove them from their work. It took five days to restore order and to calm their fears.

Nor were the politicians slow to turn railway construction to party advantage. Whiteway having resigned in 1885 in the aftermath of serious inter-denominational rioting, his Tory successor, Thorburn, embarked on the construction of a costly branch-line to Placentia, built it was said at $250,000 a head to secure the loyalty of two local members of the legislature. Meanwhile, as this expensive side issue was building, the main Railway Company, chronically under-financed from the outset, had fallen into the hands of receivers. It was with great difficulty that work continued at all. By 1890, however, following the return of the Liberals to power, a new contract was entered into between the Government and two wealthy businessmen, Mr R. G. Reid, a well-known Scottish Canadian contractor, and Mr G. H. Middleton.

The new company was required, within five years, to continue the existing main line of rail a further 265 miles as far as Hall's Bay, to furnish rolling stock and machine shops and to operate the Placentia branch line free of charge. Three years later, Mr Middleton having dissolved the partnership, Reid entered into a further contract with the Government for the completion of the trans-insular railway with a terminus on the West Coast at Port-aux-Basques, a total distance of some 500 miles.

The terms of the contract are worth studying in some detail for they were to pave the way to a constitutional precedent unique in colonial history. To begin with Reid was to receive $15,000 per mile of line constructed. Payment was to be in sterling in the form of Newfoundland Government debentures maturing in 1947 and bearing interest at 3½ per cent. The contractor was to maintain and operate the line and to construct a telegraph system throughout its length. Subject to full performance of those engagements Reid was to be granted in fee simple no less than 2½ million acres of land running on each side of the track and throughout its length.

By the middle of 1895 the Acting Governor could report that 'the line is completed for...374 miles from St John's, the extreme point being... approximately 30 miles from the West Coast at the Bay of Islands, further there are some 20 miles under construction beyond the end of the metals now laid'.[1] But at what cost! At the abortive Ottawa Conference of 1895 on Confederation, the Newfoundland delegates were tabling documents on the financing of the railway and arguing that it was one of the Colony's

[1] Sir William Carter to Mr Chamberlain, dispatch of 25 July 1895, no. 316 in C.O. 194.

most viable assets, for which the Dominion should make appropriate payment. These papers revealed that close on $6 million had already been spent on construction, rolling stock and feeder roads: and that a further $3·62 million would be needed to complete the Reid contract and to provide terminal wharves at Port-aux-Basques. Mention was also made of commitments to construct two further branch lines at an estimated cost of $312,000. In all the debt represented by the construction of the railway system amounted to over $9½ million.[1]

As the line of rail reached the west coast and turned southwards on its way to the terminus, the bogey of French treaty rights stood haltingly across its path. Throughout 1896–7 the British naval commander had been reporting difficulties with his French colleague over the construction of piers and even as to the right of Reid to build track within a half mile of the shore. One English mining company, which had moved in in the wake of the railway and had sunk sizeable capital in the construction of a pier to ship its chromite, now found its operations frustrated. 'It is inconceivable to my Board', wrote the Secretary to Mr Chamberlain, 'that British enterprise on British territory should be crushed by subservience to a foreign nation. The grand idea of Imperial Federation, which to the minds of my Directors is personified by you, must be retarded in becoming a reality if our oldest colony is to continue to be really subject to France.'[2] The British naval commander read the answer in more measured terms, apportioning blame to both the dog-in-the-manger attitude of the French and the misleading propaganda tactics of the local Government. 'The question which the Colony pretend they suffer from', he reported to the Admiralty, 'and the sentiment which the leaders and others in this country are never tired of reiterating is "We do not admit that the French have territorial rights in Newfoundland". This is, no doubt, a splendid sentiment, calculated to bring down a house filled with British subjects, but I think it is neither fair to the French nor fair to the Colony.' But, he added, the attitude of France was itself ambivalent. In 1896 she had objected to the very construction of a railway on the Treaty Shore. A year later, while protesting that she had no desire to hinder the commercial expansion of the colony, her naval officers were demanding the demolition of railway works. And this at a time when the French presence on the west coast had dwindled almost to vanishing point.[3]

[1] Financial Statements presented at the Newfoundland Conference, Ottawa, April 1895, Appendix to *Newfoundland Journal of the House of Assembly*, 1894–5, pp. 382 ff.

[2] Newfoundland Mineral Syndicate Ltd., to Colonial Office, letter of 3 August 1897, No. 172 in N.A. no. 180.

[3] Commodore the Hon. M. Bourke to Admiralty, letter of 14 September 1897, encl. in no. 95 in N.A. no. 180.

Growing realization in France that her Treaty rights were being jeopardized through failure effectively to exercise them was vigorously expressed in an article in *Le Matin* of April 1898. After referring to renewed efforts by the armateurs of Fécamp to show the flag and listing the activities of their competitors, the paper continued: 'Et ce n'est pas tout. Un gros capitaliste anglais, Mr Reid, vient d'obtenir la construction immédiate d'un chemin de fer qui traversera l'île...Il n'y a donc pas un instant à perdre...Il faut attaquer, et sans retard, si nous voulons vaincre sur ce terrain économique où nous ne comptons plus nos défaites. En avant!'[1]

But in the previous autumn, the Whiteway party had been resoundingly defeated at the polls and a new Tory Government, led by Sir James Winter, returned to power determined to put paid to the railway controversy and if possible to the generality of disputes arising from the treaty obligations. Meeting in June 1898 the Executive Council decided to send a delegation to London in the hopes of persuading the British Government to appoint a Royal Commission, one of whose tasks should be to consider 'the objections raised by the French to the extension of the railway system of the Colony to the Treaty Coast and the deterrent effects thereby produced upon the railway and other enterprises'.[2] Following their arrival in London, the Newfoundland delegation set out their complaints in greater detail. On the railway issue they wrote:

The question of the development of the mineral and other resources of the interior and the west coast of the Colony has become crucial, by reason of the completion of the railway to Port-aux-Basques, and from other causes. The burden of the interest upon the public debt incurred to build the railway presses upon the people, and that burden can best be lightened by development of the resources referred to. By non development, therefore, the financial condition of the colony is made worse than it would otherwise be, and relief is denied to our overburdened taxpayers. Deposits of coal, iron, and copper and other minerals, and petroleum oil, have been discovered in the regions referred to, and capital awaits an opportunity for investment in their development. But this is prevented by British enforcement, in effect, and for all practical purposes, as against the Colony, not of the treaties with France, but of the French interpretation of the declaration of King George III, accompanying the treaty of Versailles. This virtual enforcement is contrary to the interpretation placed upon the treaties by a long succession of British statesmen in their official correspondence, and takes place not in the interest of justice, but to avoid trouble with France, and for Imperial consideration. It is constantly asserted, but we submit, unfairly, that the Colony refuses to consent to the enforcement of the Treaties. The Colony's complaint is, that the treaties, according to the British and the correct interpretation of them, are not enforced; but that, on the contrary, the effect and opera-

[1] *Le Matin* (Paris), 18 April 1898.

[2] Minutes of the Executive Council of Newfoundland 11 June 1898.

tion of the methods hitherto adopted for the carrying out of the treaties has been the enforcement, as against the Colonists, for all practical purposes, of the untenable claims and pretences of the French, which are continually becoming more and more obnoxious, and more and more injurious to the best interests of the Colony.[1]

Since no financial issues immediately arose, the British Government for once showed marked and early sympathy. Before August was out a two-man Royal Commission had been appointed. Its terms of reference were broadly to examine how French treaty rights were then exercised and to what degree they obstructed the Colony's industrial development. The Commissioners spent two months in the Island and their report, bearing as it does primarily on fishing rights, can more conveniently be left to an ensuing chapter.

These surface manoeuvrings, however, could not conceal that Newfoundland was again teetering on the verge of bankruptcy and that desperate remedies were once more being called in aid. As early as January 1898 the new Governor, Sir Herbert Murray, was reporting on a further loan which his Ministers had raised on the security of the railway debentures and was voicing his fears that 'at least three times the amount of the present loan [$100,000] will be required to meet the liabilities which will accrue between the present time and the 30 June'.[2] What, added the Governor a few days later, was previously only a railway project, 'is now a railway almost built, and it is the debt which has been run up in the building of the line which is now the source of difficulty to the Colony'.[3] The first hint of astonishing solutions to come could be gleaned from the Governor's further dispatch of 31 January in which, after referring to his Ministers' unprecedented action in issuing Treasury notes backed by an exiguous silver reserve, he reported that a move was afoot to sell the railway to contractors.[4] That this was no chimera became rapidly clear. Within three weeks Sir James Winter had tabled a resolution in the Legislature proposing the outright sale of the railway to Reid for $1 million. In return for his agreement to operate it for fifty years, he was also to receive grants in fee simple of a further 1·6 million acres of land. Sparse as the intelligence then was, the Colonial Office was seized with a mixture of paternal indignation and cold hostility. The effect, wrote one junior official, would be to sell the railway for a very small portion of its actual cost, leaving the Colony destitute of any valuable unrealized assets. The next official up the line was even more

[1] Sir J. S. Winter to Colonial Office, letter of 7 July 1898, no. 145 in N.A. 180.
[2] Sir Herbert Murray to Mr Chamberlain, dispatch of 11 January 1898, no. 1683 in C.O. no. 240, pt. 1.
[3] Sir H. Murray to Mr Chamberlain, dispatch of 13 January 1898, no. 1686 *ibid.*
[4] Sir H. Murray to Mr Chamberlain, dispatch of 31 January 1898, no. 1693, *ibid.*

outraged. Reid, he said, would now bring his holding of land in the Colony up to 4 million acres. The Government would be parting with 600 miles of railway for two-thirds of the price it had paid for the construction of the first 83 miles. 'The sale of Esau's birthright was a joke compared to this transaction.' The only consolation he could find was that the contractor, to whom the Island was practically being sold, might make a better job of running it than any government could do. 'I have no confidence in any party or person in Newfoundland', commented the Under Secretary. 'We must leave the Colony to reap the whirlwind. When they are on their knees, as they soon will be, we can dictate our own terms.' Mr Chamberlain himself accepted that the Imperial Government had no constitutional *locus standi* in the matter. But at the same time he issued instructions that a dispatch should be prepared pointing out 'in strong terms the apparent improvidence of this bargain and the consequences'.[1]

Meanwhile the Governor had forwarded the draft contract with Reid as introduced into the Legislature. It was an astonishing document.[2] In addition to the facts already known, it now emerged that the proposed grant of lands to the contractor carried with it the right to mine 'coal, precious metals, minerals and mineral oils of every kind'. Reid was also to obtain a large area in the interior where coal deposits had recently been discovered: to receive mail subsidies for the steamers he agreed to operate: and to purchase the St John's dry dock at the knock-down price of $325,000. Writing of the contract, one outstanding legal expert later described it as involving 'a sacrifice incalculably grave of the colony's prospects, but those who brought it forward no doubt reflected on the truism that he who has expectations, but neither assets nor credits, must reinforce the latter by drawing in some degree upon the former'.[3]

While neither the Governor nor Downing Street was under any illusions as to the ability of the Winter Government, with its strong majority, to railroad the contract through both Houses, opinion outside the Legislature was roused. Many thinking Newfoundlanders concluded that the politicians were abdicating the Island's sovereign power and binding their successors. Numerous petitions flooded into St John's. Their burden was that the electors had never been consulted about the contract: that assets worth upwards of $17 million were being absolutely disposed of for a mere $1 million; that the whole coastal carrying trade and telegraph system were to be given over to a monopoly, and that no provision was made for the development of the huge tracts of land which Reid was now to acquire.

[1] C.O. minutes of 20–25 February 1898, no. 4129 in C.O. no. 240, pt 1.
[2] Sir Herbert Murray to Mr Chamberlain, dispatch of 25 February 1898, no. 5678 *ibid.*
[3] F. E. Smith, *The Story of Newfoundland* (Horace Marshal and Son, 1920), p. 146.

One of the most curious protests came from the Roman Catholic Archbishop of St John's. On reading that a Bill legalizing the contract had been rushed through both Houses and was then awaiting the Governor's approval, he put it to Sir Herbert Murray that with all the Colony's assets now on the point of being signed away, only one source remained to which the Government could in future turn—the Savings Bank. 'You will remember', he went on, 'that some time ago Your Excellency gave me your word that you would protect the Savings Bank and on the strength of that guarantee, I wrote to the papers to calm the people.' If, however, the Governor now felt unable to resist the force of the party in power he, the Archbishop, would feel obliged, despite 'the terrible upheaval of the whole community' to make a public pronouncement 'informing the people that I had no confidence in the Savings Bank, and advising them to draw their money at once from it'.[1]

While no doubt the Archbishop's adherence to the opposition Whiteway cause underlay his unecclesiastical threats, neither they nor the overall effects of the contract could be disregarded. Powerless constitutionally though he might be, the Colonial Secretary was determined that the danger of the course on which they had now embarked should be made fully known to the people of Newfoundland. On 23 March, therefore, he addressed the following formal dispatch to the Governor, instructing him to publish it in the Colony Gazette:

SIR,—In my telegram of the 2nd instant I informed you that if your Ministers, after fully considering the objections urged to the proposed contract with Mr R. G. Reid for the sale and operation of the Government railways and other purposes, still pressed for your signature to that instrument, you would not be constitutionally justified in refusing to follow their advice, as the responsibility for the measure rested entirely with them.

2. Whatever views I may hold as to the propriety of the contract, it is essentially a question of local finance, and as Her Majesty's Government have no responsibility for the finance of self-governing colonies, it would be improper for them to interfere in such a case unless Imperial interests were directly involved. On these constitutional grounds I was unable to advise you to withhold your assent to the Bill confirming the contract.

3. I have now received your despatches as noted in the margin, giving full information as to the terms of the contract, and the grounds upon which your Government have supported it, as well as the reasons for which it was opposed by the Leader and some members of the Opposition.

4. I do not propose to enter upon a discussion of the details of the contract, or of the various arguments for and against it, but I cannot refrain from expressing my views as to the serious consequences which may result from this extraordinary measure.

[1] Archbishop Howley to Sir H. Murray, letter of 1 March 1898.

5. Under this contract, and the earlier one of 1893, for the construction of the railway, practically all the Crown lands of any value become, with full rights to all minerals, the freehold property of a single individual: the whole of the railways are transferred to him, the telegraphs, the postal service, and the local sea communications, as well as the property in the dock at St John's. Such an abdication by a Government of some of its most important functions is without parallel.

6. The colony is divested for ever of any control over or power of influencing its own development, and of any direct interest in or direct benefit from that development. It will not even have the guarantee for efficiency and improvement afforded by competition, which would tend to minimize the danger of leaving such services in the hands of private individuals.

7. Of the energy, capacity, and character of Mr Reid, in whose hands the future of the colony is thus placed, both yourself and your predecessor have always spoken in the highest terms, and his interests in the colony are already so enormous that he has every motive to work for and to stimulate its development; but he is already, I believe, advanced in years, and though the contract requires that he shall not assign or sublet it to any person or corporation without the consent of the Government, the risk of its passing into the hands of people less capable and possessing less interest in the development of the colony is by no means remote.

8. All this has been fully pointed out to your Ministers and the Legislature, and I can only conclude that they have satisfied themselves that the danger and evils resulting from the corruption which, according to the statement of the Receiver-General, has attended the administration of these services by the Government, are more serious than any evils that can result from those services being transferred unreservedly to the hands of a private individual or corporation; and that, in fact, they consider that it is beyond the means and capacity of the colony to provide for the honest and efficient maintenance of these services, and that they must, therefore, be got rid of at whatever cost.

9. That they have acted thus in what they believe to be the best interests of the colony I have no reason to doubt; but, whether or not it is the case, as they allege, that the intolerable burden of the Public Debt, and the position in which the colony was left by the contract of 1893, rendered this sacrifice inevitable, the fact that the colony, after more than forty years of self-government, should have to resort to such a step is greatly to be regretted.[1]

Quite undeterred by these strictures the House of Assembly proceeded *nemine contradicante* to pass a resolution calling for a Royal Commission to inquire into the conditions of the Colony. As one member put it in the course of debate 'the Colony was never in a better condition to approach the British Government for assistance. By the recent railway contract we had decreased our National Debt by one million dollars, and we had converted what were liabilities to be assets of the Colony'. He believed that the Imperial Government 'could float a loan for us which would save us three

[1] Mr Chamberlain to Sir H. Murray, dispatch of 23 March 1898, Cmd. 8867, Newfoundland, Correspondence relative to a contract for the Sale of the Government Railway, no. 26.

hundred thousand dollars a year in interest alone'.[1] But Mr Chamberlain was not to be taken in by such manoeuvres. 'You will be good enough to point out to your Ministers', he replied to the Governor, 'that circumstances have greatly changed since 1890 and 1891 . . . It is impossible for the Imperial Government to take any responsibility, or accord any financial assistance, in the case of a self-governing colony which has had full control of its own finances and is solely responsible for its mismanagement.'[2] Faced with this damping retort, Winter's Government had to make do with the far more restricted Royal Commission concerned with French treaty rights, to which reference has already been made.

But if the Legislature had got away in the dark winter months with little short of national *felo de se*, the effects of the contract on the Island began gradually to dawn on the people as a whole. As news filtered through to outlying areas—and despite Mr Chamberlain's injunction his major dispatch of 23 March was not in fact published in the local *Gazette* until mid-July—wholesale petitions were got up. With the advance of summer, their trickle became a flood. One paragraph may be quoted as symbolizing the general unease. Coming from the Spaniard's Bay area, the main burden of this particular petition ran:

Notwithstanding the fact that under the contract made in the year 1893, between the Newfoundland Government and Mr R. G. Reid, the latter was bound to operate the railway without further compensation until the year 1903, this gigantic scheme was hastily introduced into the Legislature and passed through the House of Assembly in all its stages in half an hour. No opportunity was given for adequate consideration or discussion of such an important measure.

The extraordinary haste with which the Railway Bill was rushed through the Legislature prevented the constituencies from learning that such a sweeping transfer of the Colony's assets was even contemplated much less accomplished by the members of that very party who a few short months before had been so loud in denouncing the far milder concessions of their predecessors. And it is only since the publication of the correspondence relative to the Railway Contract that the people had an opportunity of understanding on what grounds and by what means the Contract received the temporary assent of His Excellency the Governor. And owing to the fact that the population of Newfoundland is scattered over an extensive seaboard with comparatively few opportunities for communication with the capital, it is only at the present time that the outlying districts are becoming aware of what has been done in this matter.

In the light of that knowledge so recently acquired, your Petitioners desire most respectfully to protest against the ratification of this improvident and extraordinary Bill.[3]

[1] *Daily News* (St John's), 26 March 1898.

[2] Mr Chamberlain to Sir H. Murray, dispatch of 15 April 1898, Cmd. 8867, no. 30.

[3] Petition signed by 155 inhabitants of Spaniard's Bay, encl. to Governor's dispatch of 30 August 1898, no. 20517 in C.O. no. 241, vol. II.

By mid-September Murray was reporting that the Colony was at last waking up to the realities of the railway deal and that if elections were then held most of those who had voted for the contract would probably lose their seats.[1] Petitioning was admittedly a favourite pastime in Newfoundland and there was truth in a current Colonial Office comment that people signed because they were asked and without troubling or caring much as to the subject. But there was no doubting the genuine and widespread local indignation. In Downing Street some passing thought was given to the prospect of Newfoundland reverting to Crown Colony status, but with Reid already half-way to honouring his side of the bargain—in October he had paid over half a million dollars to the Government—the Imperial authorities could see no way of putting the clock back, still less of advising the Queen to disallow the Newfoundland Act under which the contract had been legalized. At best the Colonists would have to be told once more that responsible government carried with it obligations as well as privileges and that the Colonial Secretary could no longer be looked to as a court of appeal from their own elected representatives. It was now that Mr Chamberlain decided that the British Government's stand in the matter must be finally and unequivocally set forth. In a further published dispatch, which Lord Birkenhead later described as laying down 'the great constitutional doctrine which is the Magna Carta of Greater Britain',[2] the Colonial Secretary wrote *inter alia* as follows:

The step, which I am urged to take, is one for which there is no precedent in the history of colonial administration. The measure the disallowance of which is sought is not only one of purely local concern, but one the provisions of which are almost exclusively of a financial and administrative character.

The right to complete and unfettered control over financial policy and arrangements is essential to self-government, and has been invariably acknowledged and respected by Her Majesty's Government and jealously guarded by the Colonies. The Colonial Government and Legislature are solely responsible for the management of its finances to the people of the Colony, and unless Imperial interests of grave importance were imperilled, the intervention of Her Majesty's Government in such matters would be an unwarrantable intrusion and a breach of the Charter of the Colony.

It is nowhere alleged that the interests of any other part of the Empire are involved, or that the Act is in any way repugnant to Imperial legislation. It is asserted, indeed, that the Contract disposes of assets of the Colony over which its creditors in this country have an equitable, if not a legal, claim, but, apart from the fact that the assets in question are mainly potential, and that the security for the Colonial debt is its general revenue, not any particular property or assets, I cannot admit that the creditors of the Colony have any right to claim the

[1] Sir H. Murray to Mr Chamberlain, dispatch of 19 September 1898, no. 21997 *ibid.*
[2] Smith, p. 158.

interference of Her Majesty's Government in this matter. It is on the faith of the Colonial Government and Legislature that they have advanced their money, and it is to them that they must appeal if they consider themselves damnified.

No doubt, if it was seriously alleged that the Act involved a breach of faith or a confiscation of the rights of absent persons, Her Majesty's Government would have to examine it carefully, and consider whether the discredit which such action on the part of a Colony would entail on the rest of the Empire, rendered it necessary for them to intervene. But no such charge is made, and if Her Majesty's Government were to intervene whenever the domestic legislation of a Colony was alleged to affect the rights of non-residents, the right of self-government would be restricted to very narrow limits, and complications and confusion from the division of authority must arise.

In so far as the demand for disallowance is based on criticism of the policy and details of the Act, I have already indicated that where no Imperial interests are involved, or unless the measure was so radically vicious as to reflect discredit on the Empire of which Newfoundland forms a part, it would be improper for Her Majesty's Government to intervene in what is essentially a matter of local finance, the policy of which is a matter for the Government and Legislature of the Colony.

But it is alleged, as a further reason for intervention, that though the subject was one of far-reaching consequence to the future of the Colony, no allusion to the contract was made in the speech from the Throne at the opening of the Session of the Legislature, and that when it was brought before that Body shortly after the beginning of the Session, it was pushed hurriedly through both Houses before knowledge of the matter could have reached the voters, and without allowing due time for its consideration.

These charges have been dealt with by your Ministers in the Minute of Council already referred to. They are questions affecting the conduct of Ministers in the administration of business for which they are responsible to the Legislature, and if the members of the Legislature have failed to protect the interests and discharge the duties of their position they will have to answer for their failure to their constituents. The fact that the constituencies were not consulted on a measure of such importance might have furnished a reason for its rejection by the Upper Chamber, but would scarcely justify the Secretary of State in advising its disallowance, even if it were admitted as a general principle of constitutional government in Newfoundland that the Legislature has no right to entertain any measure of first importance without an immediate mandate from the electors.

Nor is the fact that I have been urged to advise the disallowance of the Act by petitions alleged to be signed by more than half of the registered electors of the Colony one which can be properly considered by Her Majesty's Government in this connection. The Act was passed by the Assembly, elected so recently as November, 1897, by an enormous majority, only five members out of a house of 36 voting against it, and in the Legislative Council, as I gather from the last paragraph of your despatch of 30th April, it was received with practical unanimity, only one member having spoken against it, and even he did not carry his opposition so far as to record his vote against the measure.

It is not the duty of Her Majesty's Government to attempt the task of deciding whether the action of the Legislature has been in accord with the opinion of the electorate. Even a Governor, who is to some extent in touch with local opinion, would be taking a serious step if, in response to petitions such as have been addressed to me, and against the advice of his Ministers, he refused to assent to a measure of local concern which had been duly passed by the Legislature; and if he failed to find other Ministers prepared to assume responsibility for his action, and able to secure the support of the Legislature, his position would become untenable. Any such step on the part of a Governor would have to be taken entirely on his own motion. It is essential that for every act of the Governor in local matters full responsibility should attach to a Ministry amenable to the Colonial Legislature.

In advising Her Majesty as to the exercise of her prerogative of disallowance, the Secretary of State has to consider the legislation submitted from a still more restricted point of view than the Governor.

That prerogative is a safeguard for the protection of those interests for which the Secretary of State is responsible to Her Majesty and to the Imperial Parliament. To advise its exercise in cases where only local interests are concerned would involve the Imperial Government in liability for matters of the control of which it has divested itself, and for which the Colony has accepted full responsibility.

In the present circumstances of Newfoundland there are special reasons of the greatest importance which preclude Her Majesty's Government from taking such a departure from recognized constitutional principles and usage as the memorialists desire.

You have stated in your despatch of the 30th of April last, that the language used by the responsible Finance Minister of the Colony, in the speech in support of the Contract which he delivered from his place in the Assembly, implied clearly that if the measure was rejected the Colony would be unable to meet its immediate financial obligations.

Neither in your despatches nor in the memorials is this assertion challenged, and it is obvious that if Her Majesty's Government were to annul a measure seriously declared by the person who is in the best position to know to be essential to the continued solvency of the Colony, the creditors of Newfoundland would not fail to fasten on Her Majesty's Government responsibility for the consequences of their action.

As I have already said, the debts of the Colony have been incurred solely on the credit of the Colony, and any step which would transfer responsibility for them in the slightest degree to the Imperial Government would entail consequences which would not be confined to Newfoundland, and which Her Majesty's Government would not under any circumstances be justified in contemplating.

The considerations which preclude me from advising Her Majesty to disallow the Act apply equally to the alternative request, that I should defer tendering advice to Her Majesty in regard to it until the people of the Colony have had an opportunity of expressing their views upon the measure.

The Act is already in force, and the Contract to which it gives effect has been in part already performed, and the continuing obligation of the Contractor would not be suspended until Her Majesty's pleasure was finally declared. It remains in full force till the Act is disallowed or repealed. It would be unjust therefore to the Contractor, and would only add to the already heavy liabilities of the Colony, to accede to the prayers of the petitions.

The question of the propriety of a dissolution is not one upon which I can advise: it is entirely a matter for the Governor and his advisers.

While I am unable to advise Her Majesty to grant the prayer of the petitions, this decision must not be understood as an expression of opinion on the merits of the Contract, or on the action of the Government and the Legislature in connection with it. My opinion on these points has already been made known to the inhabitants of Newfoundland by the publication of my despatch of the 3rd March, in which I commented on the extraordinary and unparalleled character of the Contract, and the serious consequences which may result from it.

My action has throughout been governed solely by constitutional principles, on which I am bound to act, and I think it desirable that it should be made quite clear that, in accepting the privilege of self-government, the Colony has accepted the full responsibilities inseparable from that privilege, and that if the machinery it has provided for the work of legislation and administration has proved defective, or the persons to whom it has entrusted its destinies have failed to discharge their trust, they cannot look to Her Majesty's Government to supplement or remedy these defects, or to judge between them and their duly chosen representatives.

I have to request that you will publish this despatch for the information of those who have signed the petitions.[1]

In the light of these weighty constitutional principles, the Queen duly signified her allowance of the Newfoundland Act. But it was with the ordinary voter, who had been left so singularly ill-informed, that the last word rested. In the first of two general elections in 1900, fought largely on the contract issue, the Winter Government was narrowly defeated and Bond for the first time took office as leader of the Liberal party. His immediate and indeed unavoidable policy was to treat the contract as a *fait accompli* but to be prepared to bargain toughly with Reid over any further concessions and amendments to the existing deal. Before the defeat of the Winter Government the contractor had in fact proposed that all his holdings be turned over to a corporation, capitalized at $25 million and consisting of his three sons and himself. To this Bond's reaction was that he would accept the proposal subject only to Reid resigning his proprietary rights in the railway; restoring the telegraph system to government ownership and modifying the grants of land made to him in the interests of settlers who could establish *de facto* ownership. In other words the Government were ready to assent to an assignment only on condition that the contractor surrender his most valuable assets. Not unnaturally he refused, and the Island for the second time in one year was plunged into a general election.

[1] Mr Chamberlain to Sir H. Murray, dispatch of 5 December 1898, no. 23 in Cmd. 9137, Further Correspondence relating to the Contract for the Sale of the Government Railway.

Reid now threw himself vigorously if rashly into the campaign, even going so far as to put up his own nominees. As the local correspondent of *The Times* reported: 'One of Mr Reid's sons has been accompanying him through his constituency, and is mooted as a candidate. Two captains of Reid's bay steamers are running for other seats. The clothier who supplies the uniforms for Reid's officials is another, and a shipmaster, who until recently was ship's husband for the Reid steamers, is another.'[1]

As Lord Birkenhead put it: 'success at the polls would have enabled Mr Reid to say, with Louis XIV—"L'état, c'est moi."'[2] But indignation against the contract had now reached fever point, it became the sole issue of the election: the Reid interests suffered a crushing defeat and Bond was returned to power with a majority this time sufficient to break the railway monopolies. He lost no time in doing so. By August 1901 he had secured the assent of the Legislature to a Bill[3] sanctioning a fresh agreement with the contractor. Under this Reid, whose interests were now to be incorporated in the Reid Newfoundland Company, agreed to surrender his rights first to own the railway in 1938: secondly to take up the further 2½ million acres of land to which the principal contract had entitled him: and thirdly his monopoly of the telegraphs. In return for these concessions, the new Company was to be compensated by Government to the tune of close on $3½ million. At the same time, while sacrificing virtual ownership, Reid and his sons were still to operate the rail, mail and steamship services of the Colony, the dry dock and the tramways of the capital and to retain their original land grants of over 2 million acres, with the timber, mineral and other rights that went with them. Not until 1923 was a Newfoundland Government to feel strong enough to repeal this Act and to take the railway and its ancillary services wholly under its control.

If this episode has been recounted at some length it is as much because of the important constitutional doctrine which it spelt forth as for the financial fecklessness which gave it birth. That a Colony with over a generation's worth of responsible government behind it could go so near to selling its birthright to a single individual—and he a 'foreigner'—and that it could do so with such scant regard for the opinions of its own electorate, was proof enough that the people had been getting the government they deserved. That matters had come to this pass at all underlined yet again the precarious nature of the economy. That the Imperial authorities refused to go further than criticize the hopelessly one-sided nature of the contract was final proof that internal autonomy now meant quite unmistakably what it said.

[1] *The Times* (London), 31 October 1900.

[2] Smith, p. 159.

[3] Railway (Amendment) Act, Ed. VII, c. 1, 1901.

At Reid himself no charges of dishonesty could possibly be levelled. The age was one to suit his drive and vision. The circumstances of the country and the calibre of the politicians with whom he dealt had enabled him to strike the hardest of hard bargains. And at least he could claim that out of it all Newfoundland had now got itself a railway.

There were in fact many, both inside and outside the Island, to defend him. Even if, as a technical journal later pointed out, Newfoundland now stood second in the North American hemisphere in its railway mileage per head of population,[1] the circuitous route followed by the trans-island line was justified by the fact that it served all the main bays en route. Even though one traveller described the interior, seen from a railway carriage, as showing 'no token of human occupancy save...vast tracts of burned woodland, gray, ghostly, silent'[2] there were others eager to justify the railway for the very reason that it would now open up this *terra incognita*. Thus the railway 'brought the lumberman and the papermaker to the forest and the miner to the buried coal and minerals. No longer is the island a mere fishing station: no longer are its people confined to the sea margin and dependent on a precarious sea harvest...between 1890 and 1900 the value of farming output doubled.'[3]

Certainly, and whatever the financial and constitutional consequences, island life would never be the same again. Gradually the railway would break down old habits: draw men away from the traditional fishery and modestly pave the way to the creation of new industries. The old century had breathed its last, unlamented at least in Newfoundland. With the new came hopes of cleaner politics, a more efficient administration, wider opportunities for employment and expanding trade. For once they were to prove well founded.

[1] *Engineering News* (New York), 2 December 1909.

[2] *Bulletin of the American Geographical Society* (New York): 'The Railway in Newfoundland', C. M. Skinner, vol. XXXVII, no. 11 (1905).

[3] *Journal of the Canadian Bankers' Association*: 'The Railway Enterprise in Newfoundland', P. T. McGrath, vol. XIX, no. 1 (October 1911).

8

FRENCH LEAVE

This island, which some of us love so dearly despite its backwardness, its isolation, its ruggedness, physical and climatic, may henceforth be hailed not only as our native land, but our own land, freed from every foreign claim, and the blasting influence of foreign oppression—ours in entirety—solely ours.

SIR ROBERT BOND, 20 April 1904

Depuis de longues années, par la force même des choses, sous la poussée des lois économiques, notre privilège n'était plus devenu qu'un principe, bien difficile à défendre, même sur le terrain des principes et nous ne renonçons plus en vérité qu'à l'ombre d'un privilège dès longtemps disparu.

M. FRANÇOIS DELONCLE, Chairman of the French Parliamentary Commission on the Convention of 1904, 21 October 1904

Between 1893 and 1900 all hopes of settling the fishery disputes with France were shelved. First Newfoundland's preoccupations with her own financial problems; then Britain's involvement in the Boer War put paid to any prospect of serious negotiation. Resignedly Paris and London continued their verbal battle. Indignantly French or Newfoundland fishermen and lobster canners chased their rivals from the beaches: destroyed each others' nets and seines: broke up or burnt each other's factories. Tactfully, the naval commanders on both sides reduced the temperature, exchanged notes more cordial and diplomatic than their civilian masters and generally policed the Treaty Shore. Year by year, the *modus vivendi* over lobsters was renewed. And with each renewal, the Imperial Government pressed, prodded or cajoled the Colonial Legislature into extending the Treaties Act itself.

Despite the mounting frustration in Newfoundland at France's negating grip on the west coast of the Island, the patriotic sentiments aroused by the South African War brought the Colony back to closer sympathy with Britain. Chastened by the experiences of the dark years from which they had just emerged; increasingly aware of a public opinion which was tiring of sordid political manoeuvres and personal vituperation, both press and government began to mend their ways. Thanks largely to the growing stature and leadership of Sir Robert Bond, a new sense of responsibility was to be detected in the acts of Ministers and of the Legislature. These changes were in turn reflected in the more dispassionate nature of the official reports from Newfoundland. Gone were the days of Sir Terence O'Brien's despairing dispatches with their accent on corruption and decay. A new spirit was abroad.

In London too the affairs of Newfoundland were being viewed with understanding rather than with mingled impatience and distrust. This change of heart was inspired not only by the better atmosphere in the Colony but by the findings of the Royal Commission which, as already mentioned, had been appointed in 1898 to inquire into the operation of the Treaties. The Commissioners had shown much sympathy for the Colonists. They urged that Britain and Newfoundland must be seen to be working in harmony if a viable solution were to be reached with France. They felt too that some assurances were due to the islanders as to their free right of access to the Treaty Shore. One of the main conclusions at which the Commissioners arrived was that the French fishery was now dwindling to vanishing point and that the troubles created by the enforcement of the Treaties were quite disproportionate to the number of French ships and men involved. Another was that opinion in Newfoundland was still divided as to the best method of arriving at a final settlement with France. The construction of the railway had helped to create one body of opinion—the 'development party'—which cared little about the bait issue but which insisted on unrestricted access to the west coast for industrial purposes. A second party represented the merchant interests. To them the question whether or not to supply bait to French fishermen was overriding. Beside it, plans for diversifying the economy took second place. The Commissioners heard much evidence as to the need for the Imperial Government to 'buy out' French rights. But they were neither prepared nor empowered to advocate any particular solution, and contented themselves with the observation that 'whatever line Her Majesty's Government may feel at liberty to take, they would find themselves supported by some portion of the inhabitants of the Colony'.[1]

Even French Ministers were by now beginning to admit, privately if not in public, that the interests of France were in the practical sense virtually extinct. But as the new Governor, Sir Henry McCallum, commented: 'It will, I am afraid be a matter of some little difficulty to persuade them that what they are entitled to is scarcely worth having, and that either they must confine themselves in the future to the vanishing remnants of a past industry and respect the rights of British sovereignty, or otherwise abandon altogether any claims or rights on the Treaty Shore in consideration of such reasonable compensation as Her Majesty's Government may think just.'[2] That there was still a long way to go was

[1] Royal Commissioners to Colonial Office, letter of 18 March 1899, no. 11 in N.A. no. 184. (Because of its possible adverse effects on negotiations with France, the report of the Royal Commission was not published.)

[2] Sir H. McCallum to Mr Chamberlain, dispatch of 27 June 1899, no. 49 in N.A. no. 184.

clear from his further report, written well over a year later. After complaining of the difficulties which he and the British naval commander continually experienced in enforcing treaty obligations, the Governor continued:

In Newfoundland...where nine-tenths of the voters are fishermen, abstract duty is almost invariably sacrificed to political expediency, anything antagonistic to the personal interest of the fishing industry is opposed either openly or passively; statutes are not enforced if political support is likely to be lost...; an innate sense of long-standing unredressed grievances embitters the community against any acts of administration connected with the Treaty Shore: and a feeling that what they have saved in the past has been mainly due to opposition amounting to virtual hostility makes it difficult for a Governor to command... that support from his Ministers which he has a right to expect.[1]

By the autumn of 1900 the Colonial Office, having fully digested the report of the Royal Commission, concluded that the time was ripe for the opening of further negotiations with France. Ministers were being pressed in Parliament to publish the Report—a development which in Mr Chamberlain's view would prejudice all hopes of an amicable settlement. And the railway had brought with it to the Treaty Shore yet further problems of interpreting the nature of fixed settlements. The Colonial Secretary suspected that France herself was now in a mood to explore some face-saving means of withdrawing from Newfoundland. It seemed to him that the hour had come to act—and speedily. As he caused his officials to put it to the Foreign Office, the French Government must now surely admit that the present state of affairs in Newfoundland 'is incompatible with modern ideas of public policy, and repugnant to that spirit of progress which characterizes the French nation. The advantage, if any, which its continuance confers on French citizens is insignificant, certainly out of all proportion to the loss it inflicts on the Colony of a Friendly Power.'[2] The Foreign Office in principle agreed but in practice gave warning that any attempt to negotiate the surrender of French rights against monetary compensation would be doomed to failure unless preceded by arbitration.

In consideration...of the feeling towards England that unfortunately exists at the present moment in France [they replied] and of the inability of any French Ministry to carry the assent of the Chamber to international arrangements unless they appear to be very obviously to the advantage of France, Lord Salisbury does not believe that a pledge could at present be obtained for the abandonment of the French rights before their nature and extent have been defined by arbitration...[3]

[1] Sir H. McCallum to Mr Chamberlain, dispatch of 20 September 1900, no. 149 in N.A. no. 184.

[2] Colonial Office to Foreign Office, letter of 27 October 1900, no. 162 *ibid.*

[3] Foreign Office to Colonial Office, letter of 9 November 1900, no. 166 *ibid.*

And, as was fully recognized in London, arbitration might well tilt in France's favour.

But weighty though the Foreign Office arguments were, the attitude of the French Ambassador to the Court of St James, Monsieur Cambon, still kept some flickering hopes alive. Speaking off the record to the new Foreign Secretary, Lord Lansdowne, in December, he threw out the thought that some arrangement might be arrived at between the two governments provided that French firms established on the Treaty Shore were compensated for withdrawing, and that French fishermen were granted equal rights of fishing and permission to buy bait freely throughout the Island. That these suggestions outpaced the mood of his own Minister seemed to worry M. Cambon not at all. Although M. Delacassé assured an impatient Senate in January 1901 that 'A Terre Neuve nos droits sont incontestables, ils sont indiscutés: rien n'empêche qu'ils soient exercés',[1] the Ambassador was simultaneously injecting the fresh thought that some final settlement might be arrived at by territorial concessions on the British side. He mentioned *en passant* the Gambia. The British Government, looking on this at the time as a diversionary tactic, decided to bring home their determination to resolve the problem by other means. On 3 January 1901 Chamberlain invited Bond to London to discuss what terms might best be put to France.[2]

At their first meeting in March, Bond outlined his Government's conditions. They were that France should withdraw from the Treaty Shore and from St Pierre and Miquelon in return for a money consideration. Failing this, the whole Treaties issue should be submitted to arbitration. The bait question might, however, be dealt with separately, the Newfoundland Government standing ready to guarantee supplies to French fisherment against an undertaking from France that the bounties paid to her fishermen, if not wholly abolished, would at least not be increased and would not apply to fishermen from the offshore islands. While doubtful of the wisdom of introducing the suggestion of territorial concessions into the preliminaries for a settlement, the British Government in June formally proposed to M. Cambon that the Newfoundland plan should be taken as a basis for negotiation.[3] The French reaction was lukewarm. It dismissed out of hand as of purely domestic concern, all idea of discussing the bounty system. But France would be ready finally to renounce her rights on the Treaty coast subject to three conditions: first that supplies of bait to

[1] M. Delcassé to M. Garreau, letter published in *Le Figaro* (Paris) on 11 January 1901.

[2] Mr Chamberlain to Sir H. MacCallum, telegram of 3 January 1901, no. 4 in N.A. no. 191.

[3] Foreign Office memorandum respecting the Newfoundland Treaty Shore, 19 June 1901, enclosure to no. 123 in N.A. no. 191.

French fishermen were guaranteed by the British Government: secondly, that French shipowners, fishermen and industrialists should be compensated for such losses as they incurred: and thirdly, that France should be compensated in territorial terms for her losses on the 'French Shore'.[1] It was the third point which stuck in British gullets. The bounty issue might well prove capable of separate settlement. But, as the Foreign Secretary wrote to the British Ambassador in Paris, parting with the Gambia, or any other possession in Africa would excite public opinion, and 'would give rise to further demands on each side for concessions and counter-concessions, demands which in my opinion would probably destroy all hopes of an arrangement'.[2] Matters were not eased by leakages to the press. On 14 August *L'Agence Havas* carried a tendentious statement to the effect that a convention had just been signed between the British authorities and a Gambian chief living in territory nominally controlled by France. There was, added the agency, no truth in rumours currently circulating that the British Government were on the point of ceding the colony in return for concessions made elsewhere. It was an unfortunate gaffe which, for the first time brought M. Delcassé, fully armed, into the lists. He had never, said the Foreign Minister, instructed M. Cambon to ask for the Gambia. Territorial compensation for the abandonment of French rights in Newfoundland was admittedly the only solution France could foresee, but his Government had made no demand for 'any specific compensation'.[3] In any case, as the French Ambassador later confided to Lord Lansdowne, the Gambian concession would be 'a petty one [mince] having regard to the great value of the interests which France was expected to surrender in Newfoundland'.[4]

Now, more than ever, the Imperial authorities felt that they were carrying a double white man's burden. The favourable outcome of any resort to arbitration seemed to them extremely doubtful. Newfoundland's case was just. But France was a power whom they could not afford to flaunt. The only recourse was to fall back on a mixture of semantics and compromise.

The liability of the inhabitants of Newfoundland to the burden of these Treaty obligations [the Colonial Secretary wrote to a new Governor, Sir Cavendish Boyle in January 1902] does not depend on any connexion of the Colony with the British Crown. If that link were severed, the inhabitants of Newfoundland

[1] M. Cambon to Foreign Office, note of 24 July 1901, encl. to no. 141 *ibid.*

[2] Marquess of Lansdowne to Sir Edmund Monson, dispatch of 31 July 1901, no. 144 *ibid.*

[3] Sir E. Monson to Marquess of Lansdowne, dispatch of 14 August 1901, no. 151 in N.A. no. 191.

[4] Marquess of Lansdowne to Sir E. Monson, dispatch of 23 October 1901, encl. to no. 164 *ibid.*

would be not one whit less under the Treaty obligations...I think it is essential this should be borne in mind...In these circumstances it is incumbent upon your Ministers and the people of the Colony to face the position squarely and to recognize that the Colony, having come into existence subject to these burdens, cannot claim relief solely at the expense of the rest of the Empire...His Majesty's Government would suggest, therefore, for your Ministers' consideration, that proposals for a settlement should be made to the French on the following basis:–

(*a*) The French to give up their right of drying fish on shore altogether, or, if this cannot be obtained, accept a right of drying on unoccupied parts of the coast.

(*b*) The French to give up the priority of their right of fishery, and accept an equal right. If this cannot be obtained, the prior right to be defined as excluding British subjects from fishing within, say, half a mile of French vessels actually engaged in fishing on the Treaty Coast.

(*c*) His Majesty's Government to compensate holders of existing French fishery establishments on the Treaty Shore, and the French to abandon their claim to catch shell-fish or lobsters.

(*d*) The Colony to pass an Act giving the French, on the conclusion of such an arrangement the right to purchase bait freely on the same terms as the inhabitants of the Colony.[1]

These revised proposals aroused scant enthusiasm in Newfoundland. For a while, indeed, Ministers were far more concerned with persuading the British Government, in the face of unrelenting pressure from Canada, to authorize them to enter into a fresh commercial treaty with the United States. It proved to be a deflection not without value for, by August, the French were themselves for the first time taking the initiative. In a conversation with the British Ambassador in Paris, M. Delcassé expressed himself as 'glad if a satisfactory solution could be found'. It was likely, the Ambassador reported, that 'M. Cambon will raise the question with Your Lordship before long'.[2]

In the short term the Ambassador's optimism proved ill-founded. M. Cambon was certainly on the Foreign Office doorstep before long, but in the guise of protestor, not conciliator. Throughout 1903, indeed, the atmosphere was increasingly soured, first because of the inability of prospective overseas investors to obtain satisfactory guarantees as to their freedom of action on the Treaty Shore; secondly, through complications arising from the whaling industry. Moreover, and as if to add to the tangle, there occurred in March 1903 a development of great potential significance to Newfoundland. Messrs Harmsworth of London, proprietors of the *Daily Mail*, sought permission of the Bond Government to establish pulp, paper

[1] Mr Chamberlain to Sir C. Boyle, dispatch of 22 January 1902, no. 219 in N.A. no. 191.

[2] Sir E. Monson to Marquess of Lansdowne, dispatch of 8 August 1902, encl. to no. 375 *ibid.*

and lumber mills over wide areas of land, some of which abutted on to the Treaty Shore. The draft contract submitted by the company included a clause providing that if they should take up land 'within the limits of what is known as the Treaty Shore, the (Newfoundland) Government will guarantee them, against any interference in the free and peaceful conduct of their operations and against any action that may be taken against them in connection with the French Treaty rights...' The value of this contract to the Island was obvious. The Government were ready and eager to close the deal. But, as the Governor reported, he had felt obliged to warn both his Ministers and the Company's representatives of Britain's continuing obligations to France, and to point out to them that the Newfoundland Government could only offer guarantees 'within the limits of their responsibility'.[1] This necessary warning was endorsed by the Colonial Secretary, who asked the Governor to inform his Ministers of the 'very serious pecuniary liability' in which they might involve the Colony 'if it should be found necessary in the execution of Treaty obligations to interfere with the operations of Messrs Harmsworth...His Majesty's Government cannot accept any responsibility whatever in regard to the liability'.[2]

Concurrently the Colonial Government was faced with demands from British applicants for licences for the construction and operation of whaling factories. The whaling industry was growing locally in importance. Thanks to improved techniques it was now possible not only to extract oil more efficiently but also to market a fertilizer which commanded a ready market. But here again the difficulty was, either that the factories were to be erected on the Treaty Coast, or that the operations themselves would interfere over wide areas with the traditional fishery. Once more the Governor had to reserve his position while seeking London's views. And these of course were that, while the fishing rights enjoyed by France did not embrace whaling, the establishment of whaling factories on the Treaty Shore would certainly be in breach of Treaty obligations. As Mr Chamberlain put it: 'I am reluctantly compelled to instruct you to refuse your sanction to any such concession.'[3]

Paradoxically, it was the whale, the latest entrant to the Treaty lists—the last and weightiest straw indeed—that was destined finally to blow the French from Newfoundland. Although the Colonial Government had, early in 1902, sought the opinion of learned counsel in England as to the likely outcome of arbitration over the Treaties and had been warned that 'an award might be unfavourable to Newfoundland on matters which are

[1] Sir C. Boyle to Mr Chamberlain, dispatch of 30 March 1903, no. 61 in N.A. no. 194.
[2] Mr Chamberlain to Sir C. Boyle, dispatch of 6 May 1903, no. 85 *ibid.*
[3] Mr Chamberlain to Sir C. Boyle, dispatch of 26 May 1903, no. 100 *ibid.*

of real importance' and further that 'the whole dispute is probably one of the class which is best dealt with by diplomatists',[1] the hardships now placed in the way of the whaling industry proved to be a blessing in disguise. The anachronistic farce could hardly last much longer. In August 1903 Bond was pointing out to the Governor that although the Newfoundland and British Government had been turning down applications for whaling licences, other applicants, taking it on themselves to approach the French naval commodore direct, had been assured that France saw no objection to such activities on the Treaty Shore. Surely, urged the Premier, it was time for Britain to take 'such immediate action as will convince the people of this Colony that it is altogether unnecessary for them to seek for the permission of a foreign power to carry on their business in any quarter'.[2] Hardly had the appeal been forwarded to London than the Governor reported that the annual renewal of the Treaties Act was in doubt. While the measure should pass the Lower House without difficulty, there was the danger of defeat in the Legislative Council. The sole way out of this risky situation was the nomination—which the Colonial Secretary subsequently approved—of further members to the Council. But it was a development which enabled the Colonial Office, before the year was out, to issue a further warning. 'Unless', they wrote to the Foreign Office in December, 'some indication as to the present position of the negotiations with France on the Fishery question can be given to the Government of the Colony... it is doubtful whether even if they are willing to bring forward the renewal of the Treaties Act, they will be able to secure its passing.'[3]

It was, tactically, the right note on which to end an exasperating year. The British Cabinet had already been reminded that the decline of the French inshore fishery in Newfoundland 'had been continuous for almost a century...Fifty years ago, France had four thousand five hundred men fishing on the Treaty Shore. In spite of the creation of a new industry in the lobster fishery...the numbers had sunk to less than a thousand ten years ago, and now are less than five hundred'.[4] Even before this, Reid and his newly formed company had referred in trenchant terms to the difficulties they were encountering in building wharves and railway sidings on the Treaty Coast. The proprietors of the picturesquely named Blow Me Down mine were in similar trouble. Every mining licence requiring the Governor's approval contained a caveat as to the insecurity in

[1] R. B. Haldane and E. H. Coles, opinion of Counsel, 11 August 1902.

[2] Sir R. Bond to Sir C. Boyle, letter of 1 September 1903, encl. in no. 154 in N.A. no. 194.

[3] Colonial Office to Foreign Office, letter of 29 December 1903, no. 219 in N.A. no. 194.

[4] 'Newfoundland Fishery', memorandum for the Cabinet, 13 November 1903, N.A. no. 196.

law of leases or grants in the Treaty zone. The Harmsworth developments were virtually estopped; the lobster canners in indignant despair; and one overseas whaling company due to appear on appeal to the Judicial Committee of the Privy Council. All this at what seemed at the time the enlightened start of an enlightened century!

Unobserved in Newfoundland enlightenment was, however, breaking on the scene. The tactfully contrived settlement with the Boers; the impact of King Edward VII's personality on France; French sympathy with him in his grave illness, the range of wider issues in dispute—all these were factors into which the Newfoundland irritant was eventually subsumed. By now the diplomatists on both sides of the Channel were concerned not merely with the Treaty Shore but with British rights in Morocco, administration in the New Hebrides and frontier problems in Tropical Africa. Despite earlier misgivings on the British side about the wisdom of compensating France territorially in return for final renouncement of her rights in Newfoundland, the complex of Anglo-French problems demanding settlement now ranged so wide that the Island was overnight no more than one pawn on an already cluttered chessboard.

The climax was as dramatic as it was swift. With scarcely an advance word of what was in the wind—beyond a secret warning to the Governor in January 1904 that Britain and France were now considering ways and means of policing a joint Fishery in Newfoundland waters—news reached the Island in April that an Anglo-French Convention, highly advantageous to Newfoundland, had been signed in London on the 8th of that month.[1] So much has been written of the significance of this document for Anglo-French relations, and for the future of Europe and Africa, that one need refer here only to its effects of Newfoundland. Briefly, in return for frontier adjustments at Britain's expense in the Gambia, off the Guinea Coast, to the east of the Niger River and on Lake Chad, the Government of France now finally relinquished its privileges in Newfoundland under Article XIII of the Treaty of Utrecht. An arbitral tribunal was to be set up to decide the monetary indemnities to be paid by Britain to French citizens still engaged in fishing on the Treaty Shore. A French Consul was to be accepted at St John's and a British Consul in St Pierre and Miquelon. And, subject to submitting themselves to the laws of Newfoundland, French fishermen were to remain free to fish in the territorial waters of the Treaty area and to purchase bait. The policing of the fishery was to be subject to regulations to be drawn up and agreed between both Governments.

[1] Convention between Great Britain and France, respecting Newfoundland and West and Central Africa, State Papers, vol. 97, 1903–4, pp. 31–6. [N.B. The Articles of direct relevance to Newfoundland are reproduced at appendix II.]

But as the events of 1857 and 1885 had proved, signature was one thing: ratification quite another. At first in St John's there was joy abounding. The capital was *en fête*. The people endorsed the view of the new Colonial Secretary that 'the advantage to Newfoundland of becoming the mistress of the whole of her coasts and of being free to devote her energies to the development of their natural resources cannot be over-estimated'.[1] But doubts were quickly raised. If, the Governor reported within days, there was any truth in a rumour which at once began to circulate in the Island that the material effect of the Convention would be to debar both French and Newfoundland fishermen from the winter fishery, thus leaving it open to American competitors, then his Ministers would feel unable to approve the arrangement. If, as the Opposition press at once began putting it about, the Colony was to be left to indemnify the French, then equally the Convention must be rejected. Not without difficulty Britain smoothed away these false doubts and fears. On 28 April, after an all night sitting in the course of which he defeated a vote of censure on the Imperial Government's handling of the negotiations with France, Bond secured the passage through the Legislature of a motion expressing confidence in the advantages accruing to Newfoundland from the Anglo-French Convention. For the Premier, it was a day of consummation. In a long, euphoric speech, he made the most of it. To his compatriots his words must have made the tastiest of banquets. But to the armateurs of France, they were bitter meat indeed. Disappointed though he had been in his efforts to secure to Newfoundland the constitutional right to ratify the Convention, and genuinely indignant though he might be at continuing Opposition criticism of the victory now at long last won, Bond was unstinting in his praise for Britain.

We have ample reason [he told the House of Assembly on 21 April] to rejoice and to be truly thankful for what has been accomplished. The French Shore Question has been settled after years and years of vain endeavour. Settled, too, without sacrifice of any interest of this Colony whatsoever. It was feared by many that a settlement would never be reached without a repeal or modification of the Bait Act, the operation of which so materially affects French interests. But the Bait Act remains unaltered, and no new baiting privileges are conveyed under the Convention. Henceforth, in the catching of bait, as well as other fish on or near our coast, the fishermen of France will be subject to our Fishery Rules and Regulations, and to such other police Rules and Regulations as shall be approved by this House.

Under this Convention, let it be remembered that the French have to abandon their fishing rooms and lobster factories on every portion of the coast. If they could not successfully conduct the codfishery while they possessed the privilege of establishments in which to dry or cure their fish, and we know they have not been able to do so for many years, we may conclude that now they are

[1] Mr Lyttleton to Sir C. Boyle, dispatch of 12 April 1904, no. 94 in N.A. no. 199.

denied that privilege they will speedily abandon the fisheries on the west and north-east coasts altogether. Their catch of cod they cannot dry on our shores, and the lobster fishery they must necessarily abandon immediately because their factories are to be moved. No other Convention ever contemplated the abandonment by the French of their establishments on the Treaty Shore. This does more, it heralds the near approach of the time when even the memory of their presence will fade like a fevered dream before the brightness of a new day. It is for us now to encourage by every legitimate means the development and settlement of what has hitherto been known as the Treaty Shore, and thus effectively blot out of remembrance that which has been a curse to this country and a stain upon British rule.

I congratulate this House, Sir, I congratulate my fellow-countrymen far and near, upon what has been accomplished, and I desire also to record an expression of my gratitude to His Majesty's Government, who, at the cost of the Empire, has purchased the release of the people of this Colony from the humiliation and suffering, which, in the interest of that Empire, they have so long and patiently borne.[1]

Bond thereafter lost no time in accepting an invitation to visit London to help in the drafting of the new fishery regulations. But the French Government, pressurized by their own fishing lobby which, like England's in the eighteenth century, was determined to die in the last ditch, still caused anxious moments. First they challenged the seasonal limitations placed on their fishermen in Newfoundland under the Convention. Next they showed signs of giving way to demands from the Central Committee of French shipowners that the Convention be ratified subject only to the Newfoundland Bait Act having been previously repealed. Before June was out M. Cambon was telling Lord Lansdowne that he had heard from Paris 'that opposition to the Newfoundland Agreement was rapidly developing. The Normandy and Brittany contractors had obtained the support of Chambers of Commerce connected with other parts of the country, and an organized attack was to be expected. M. Cambon had found M. Delcassé much preoccupied and anxious to find some means of conciliating his opponents.'[2] The French Foreign Minister himself confessed to the British Ambassador 'his incapacity to understand why a negotiation intended to remove all grievances should maintain or create some of the most annoying of them'.[3] By July the diplomatists were arguing about the right of French fishermen to use seine nets, and it was dawning on indignant Newfoundlanders that the Convention had still to take practical effect. In the same month it became clear that there was no prospect of the French Chamber

[1] *Evening Telegram* (St John's), 22 April 1904.
[2] Marquess of Lansdowne to Sir E. Monson, dispatch of 22 June 1904, encl. in no. 193 in N.A. no. 199.
[3] Sir E. Monson to Lord Lansdowne, dispatch of 17 June 1904, encl. in no. 197 *ibid.*

ratifying the Agreement prior to the summer recess. The tone of Bond's speech had violently antagonized French opinion and the Government could only wait in the hope that tempers would cool. Meanwhile, a number of Conseils-Généraux in the maritime departments were busy passing hostile resolutions. For a time the very future of the Convention seemed in doubt.

But mercifully the French Government's hand was strengthened by a report from the Parliamentary Commission for Foreign and Colonial Affairs. Tabled in October, it reviewed at length the history of the fisheries dispute and concluded optimistically that: 'Loyalement exécutée, la nouvelle Convention de Terre Neuve ne peut être que profitable aux pêcheurs français. Nous l'avons déjà dit: en fait elle ne change rien au statu quo actuel: demain comme aujourdhui, nous exerçons les mêmes droits sur le French Shore, nous n'aurons en moins qu'un principe de privilèges.'[1]

Casuistical though the conclusion might be, it served to win the day. Admittedly, there were fireworks still to come. The curiously named M. Archdeacon for instance attacked the Convention in the Chamber as 'a fresh development of the policy of the "effacement" of France before England: with violent references to Fashoda, the Irish question, the Transvaal war etc.'[2] But both indignation and interest were on the wane. On 12 November the Chamber of Deputies approved the Convention by 443 votes to 105. That M. Delcassé had as a price for victory to undertake to negotiate certain 'améliorations' is today of little consequence. On 10 December the Agreement was formally ratified in London and the long and weary battle closed.

There were many matters still to settle: fishery regulations to be tripartitely agreed: arbitration procedures to be worked out, claims heard and monies paid, a final winter of Colonial discontent to be endured before the Convention entered into force. But, as Newfoundland Ministers now telegraphed through the Governor to London, they desired to express to King Edward their 'respectful humble acknowledgement of great boon conferred on people of this Colony by Anglo-French Treaty...which they appreciate His Majesty the King was largely instrumental in initiating...'[3]

Some historians have seen in the successful outcome of this long, painful and acrimonious dispute a signal victory by colonists over imperial masters. Thus, 'Throughout her struggle with France her (Newfoundland's)

[1] Chambre des Députés. Huitième Législature, Session Extraordinaire de 1904, annexe au procès-verbal de la Séance du 21 Octobre 1904.

[2] Sir C. Monson to Marquess of Lansdowne, dispatch of 4 November 1904, no. 320 in N.A. no. 199.

[3] Governor Sir W. Macgregor to Mr Lyttleton, telegram of 8 December 1904, no. 351 *ibid.*

contributions to the development of the Empire paralleled the contribution made by Nova Scotia in her struggles with the United States. What Newfoundland accomplished in external affairs when dealing with France was paralleled by the significance in Imperial affairs of the inclusion of Nova-Scotia in the Canadian federal system.'[1] Or again: 'The struggle with France...assumed the form of a struggle with the Imperial Government because Imperial treaties were at stake...in the process of liberalizing the Empire, responsible government could not be limited to internal affairs.'[2]

Significantly both writers were Canadian. But, as documents later open to inspection suggest, their conclusions, while broadly true, do not reach to the heart of the matter. Certainly, all shades of opinion in Newfoundland looked on the Treaties as an unfair incubus. Yet at times the colonists were far from united in their opposition to them. Some wished unrealistically to revoke the Treaties unilaterally. Others blamed France for their effect rather than Britain for their existence. While the merchant lobby, the railroad enthusiasts and the industrialists wished to banish the French from Newfoundland, many west coast fishermen made a living from their presence. It was not, indeed, until Britain herself was finally converted to the conviction that the Treaty of Utrecht was in the late nineteenth-century an anachronism that public opinion in the Island became united in its determination to make Newfoundland a land fit for Newfoundlanders alone to live in.

But in bringing to a close this one among many of David's struggles against Goliaths from overseas, one cannot quarrel with MacKay's remark that: 'It was not until the nineteen twenties that autonomy in external affairs became an accepted postulate of empire. The influence of Newfoundland's long struggle against the shackles of unwelcome Imperial treaties in bringing about the new order has often been overlooked by students of the British Commonwealth of Nations, but it should not be discounted.'[3]

What the long, frustrating negotiations did show beyond a doubt was that if France could not move without Britain or Britain without France, and if Newfoundland was powerless unless the two major powers agreed, the colonial mouse could time and again break through the netting of the Imperial lions and thrust discord or amity between their massive paws.

[1] Innis, p. 417.
[2] MacKay, p. 273.
[3] *Ibid.*

9

FISH TAILS

It has to be remembered that the population, speaking generally, is not agricultural but piscatorial...It does not seem probable that there is any other country of equal size and importance that has to import from abroad practically the great mass of the necessaries of life.

Report on the Foreign Trade and Commerce of Newfoundland, 1905

Between 1905 and the end of the First World War, Newfoundland enjoyed a longer period of uninterrupted prosperity than at any previous time. The world price of fish increased: catches on the whole were good and, with the introduction of a large pulp and paper mill and fresh ventures in the mining field, the economy seemed at last to be on the road to a healthy diversification. Even in the fishing industry ideas of modernization were in the air. In St John's itself, the basis for a civil service composed of permanent rather than political or denominational appointees was being laid.

Yet, as though cod abhorred a vacuum or a fight with the men of Newfoundland alone, the long fishery dispute with France had scarcely ended than the smouldering embers of old quarrels with Washington blazed suddenly to life.

No attempt has been made in this study to trace through, in such detail as has been done in the case of the major diplomatic war with France, the disputes over Newfoundland which occasionally envenomed nineteenth-century Anglo-Canadian and Anglo-American relationships.[1] The former, as has been shown, were in themselves a contributory factor to the death of the earliest confederal dreams.

Briefly, the Treaty of Versailles, 1783, had secured to the revolting American colonists equal rights with British subjects to take fish of every kind in all the waters of British North America, including the Grand Banks and the coastal waters of Newfoundland. Yet the Treaty of Ghent, 1814, which brought to an end the war of 1812 left continuing American rights in Newfoundland in doubt. It was not until an Anglo-American Fishery Convention was signed in 1818 that matters were, for a time at least, clarified.

The Convention restricted American fishermen to defined stretches of the Newfoundland and Labrador coasts. But against this the previous ban on the drying and curing of fish on shore was to some extent removed, and

[1] For a full account of these controversies the reader should turn to A. M. Fraser's contributions (chh. VII–X and XII) in MacKay.

Americans were granted 'the liberty for ever, to dry and cure fish in any of the unsettled bays, harbours and creeks of the southern part of the coast of Newfoundland'.[1] The interpretation of the words 'unsettled' and 'bays' was to prove a painful bone of contention for many years to come as well as being, so far as the definition of 'bays' went, a pointer to the Law of the Sea controversies of the late 1950s.

By 1850 the British repeal of the Corn Laws had introduced a new element to the Northern American scene. The mainland colonies now perforce sought alternative American markets. This led the United States in turn to seek fresh fishing privileges in, *inter alia*, Newfoundland. The upshot was the Anglo-American Reciprocity Treaty, 1854, which, in July of the year following, the Newfoundland Legislature approved. While maintaining American fishermen in their right to take fish in Newfoundland waters, it provided that Newfoundland fish and fish products would henceforth enter the United States duty free, a benefit soon however to be offset by the outbreak of the Civil War, and abolished by the decision of Congress in 1868 to abrogate the Treaty unilaterally. The resulting fishery controversies were in part quietened by certain Articles of the Treaty of Washington, 1871, to which the Island Government adhered in 1874.

The upshot of these various Treaties and Conventions had been, on the admission of the U.S. Government itself, to provide greater advantages to American fishermen in Canada and Newfoundland than it gave in the reverse direction. In 1877, therefore, a Commission consisting of British and U.S. representatives and of a Belgian nominated by both parties met at Halifax, Nova Scotia, to take evidence from aggrieved parties. The Newfoundland case, based on the Island's inability to make practical use of the right to fish in American waters and on the value of the concessions they themselves had made, was ably argued and led the Commissioners to award the colony $1 million by way of compensation.

Yet euphoria in Newfoundland was short-lived. By now the dispute with France was at its height and sensitivities were strong. Soon disputes broke out over the taking of bait by American vessels. These led to an incident in 1878 in Fortune Bay where local fishermen destroyed a number of American nets. The U.S. Government reacted vigorously, demanding compensation (which Britain paid) and imposing a swingeing tax on imported Newfoundland cod-oil. At the same time they gave notice of intent to abrogate the Treaty of Washington in 1885. Once more recourse had to be had to the old device of a local *modus vivendi*. When in turn this lapsed, both Canada and Newfoundland fell back on strict enforcement of the provisions of the 1818 Convention. By now tempers on all sides were inflamed. Newfound-

[1] Herstler's *Treaties*, vol. II, p. 392, as quoted by MacKay.

land sought to negotiate separately in Washington; Canada protested to London. The British Government stepped in and a mixed Commission eventually met in Washington in 1887 to sort out the quadripartite mess. The sensible treaty that emerged failed, however, to secure ratification from the American Senate. But a *modus vivendi* was again arrived at under which U.S. vessels, on payment of an annual licence fee, were admitted to the bays and harbours of Newfoundland and Canada to purchase bait, this fee to be waived if the U.S. Government in turn admitted Newfoundland and Canadian fish and by-products duty-free. It was this mutually satisfactory arrangement which was to be so rudely shaken by the events of 1905.

'The history of the fisheries, and the numerous difficulties which have arisen upon the Treaty Coast', wrote Secretary of State Elihu Root to the British Ambassador in Washington in October of that year, 'indicate that this conflict between the orders of the Newfoundland Government and the rights of our fishermen...may lead to very serious and regrettable incidents.'[1] 'This conflict' resulted from a sudden decision of the Newfoundland Minister of Marine and Fisheries to prohibit further fishing by American vessels in the Colony's coastal waters. The State Department reaction was firm and unequivocal. 'Any American vessel', wrote Root a week later, 'is entitled to go into the waters of the Treaty Coast and take fish of any kind.'[2] He called on the British Government to recognize this elementary fact and to instruct the Newfoundland Government to remove from their Statute book their once more enacted anti-bait legislation.[3]

The skeletons of the French Shore question now tumbled noisily from cupboards so recently locked and barred. The complaints referred to, retorted Sir Edward Grey in a memorandum from Downing Street, 'appear to have been based on some misunderstanding...The Convention (of 1818) confers no rights on American vessels as such. It enures for the benefit only of inhabitants of the United States.'[4] And on at length through a lawyer's paradise of protest and counter-protestation. For their part, the Newfoundland Government evoked the sacred doctrine of the Labouchere Letter.

'My responsible advisers', telegraphed the Governor in August, 'rely on assurance contained in despatch of the 26th March, 1857, that His Majesty's Government regard the consent of the community of Newfoundland as the essential preliminary to any modification of their territorial

[1] Mr Root to Sir M. Durand, letter of 12 October 1905, no. 1 in 'Correspondence respecting the Newfoundland Fisheries', U.S. no. 1 (1906), Cmd. 3262 C, vol. 137.

[2] No. 2 *ibid.*

[3] 4 Ed. VII, c. IV.

[4] Sir Edward Grey to Mr Whitelaw Reid, 2 February 1906, encl. to no. 3 in Cmd. 3262.

or maritime rights.'[1] As if copying straight from their French files, the Colonial Office replied that the British Government 'cannot but feel that your Ministers have failed to appreciate the serious difficulty in which their policy has placed both them and His Majesty's Government'.[2]

By now, both Washington and London were clutching at that time-honoured lifebelt, a further *modus vivendi*. While the American Ambassador in London saw grave difficulties in the way of abolishing 'Sunday fishing' and complained that it was sometimes physically impossible for his compatriots to break through the ice in compliance with the need to report at Newfoundland customs houses, the State Department appreciated London's good intentions as much as St John's resented them. Newfoundland Ministers were indeed hotly against the abrogation of their Bait Act as a price for patching up a quarrel. While 'keenly conscious of the responsibility that devolves on them as servants of the Crown to abstain from any action that would produce other than friendly and amiable relations between His Majesty's Government and the Government of the United States', they still expressed themselves as quite unable to understand why their policies should have excited so much American wrath. All that was at issue was the right of U.S. fishermen to buy bait locally or to engage Newfoundlanders to procure it for them. 'There is in this case no question of the lapse of Imperial authority to enforce Treaty obligations: no question as to territorial rights, nor any excitement or bad feeling manifested in connection with the conduct of the fishery...'[3]

This was certainly not the American view of the dispute nor of its atmospherics. The Newfoundland Government, as they saw it, had enacted hostile legislation which had driven their own ships' masters to the device of hiring Newfoundland fishermen abroad. When even this was prohibited by a further local law,[4] they looked to Britain to put Newfoundland in her place. Hence the fresh *modus vivendi* of 1906, to which Newfoundland Ministers refused to consent and which in effect sanctioned the employment of Newfoundland fishermen on American vessels fishing outside the three-mile limit.

Clearly matters could not long be left in so uneasy a state. Tempers in Newfoundland were high. In justifying his Government's attitude before the House of Assembly in May 1906 the Premier, Sir Robert Bond, had stated that, as soon as American vessels 'come within our territorial

[1] Governor Sir W. MacGregor to Earl of Elgin, telegram of 14 August 1906, no. 8 in Cmd. 3262.

[2] Earl of Elgin to Governor MacGregor, telegram of 3 September 1906, no. 18 in Cmd. 3262.

[3] Governor MacGregor to Earl of Elgin, dispatch of 7 September 1906, no. 28 in Cmd. 3262.

[4] 5 Ed. VII, c. 1.

jurisdiction, I hold that they are subject to our customs and other laws. In voicing this opinion I voice the opinion of the Government of this Colony.' And further, that 'The Foreign Fishing Vessels Act of last year (an amendment to which he was then moving) was passed in the interests of the people of the Colony...it is to be regretted that it was deliberately violated last year in order to render assistance to American fishermen in thwarting a policy that has been forced upon the Government of the Colony by the action of the fishing interests of Gloucester, Mass.'[1] At the Imperial Conference of the following year, Bond in fact proposed that the dispute should be submitted to the Hague Tribunal. That arbitration in some form was the best way out of the impasse had also occurred to the British Government, for in preparation for talks in the spring of 1907 between the United States and Canada on outstanding fishery issues, the Colonial Secretary had telegraphed to the Governor-General that: 'the present policy of Newfoundland has involved us in an awkward controversy as to the conditions on which the American rights of fishery under the Convention of 1818 are to be exercised. The attitude of the Colonial Government especially since the conclusion of the *modus vivendi* seems to leave us no alternative but to offer arbitration. Indeed, we shall probably very soon have to ask your Ministers to agree to this...'[2]

Such hints were certainly more warmly received in Ottawa than any suggestion that Britain might encourage the Colony to renew its previous efforts to enter into a separate Treaty with the United States.

Newfoundland–Canadian relations had in fact been under strain for a number of years. St John's saw little advantage in maintaining a common Empire front in respect of her fishery quarrels with the United States. Ever since Bond's abortive negotiations with the American Secretary of State, James G. Blaine, in 1890, Newfoundland Ministers had been pressing for a separate reciprocal trade treaty. This Canada had as consistently opposed on the grounds that such action would be out of keeping with 'the whole history of the fishery relations between the United States and British North America, in the conduct of which it had become traditional for Canada and Newfoundland to constitute a single bargaining unit'.[3] The Canadian Government had throughout maintained the strongest pressure on Britain to refuse Newfoundland the right to separate negotiations. In retaliation the latter had applied their controversial Bait Act of 1888, originally directed against France alone, to Canada. By then a tariff

[1] Sir R. Bond, speech in Newfoundland House of Assembly, 4 May 1906, app. no. 10 in Cmd. 3262.

[2] Colonial Secretary to Governor-General of Canada, telegram of 15 January 1907, no. 23 in N.A. no. 208.

[3] MacKay, p. 361.

war was raging and feelings on both sides of the Cabot Strait inflamed. A laborious conference at Halifax in 1892 failed to resolve the dispute; further United States–Newfoundland negotiations were blocked and it was not until Bond, by now Prime Minister, visited Ottawa in 1901, that the atmosphere once more improved. Discussion then led to agreement on the Canadian side that Newfoundland might once more reopen negotiations in Washington. But, as has already been seen, the resulting Bond–Hay Convention was blocked by the Senate in 1904, thanks largely to the New England fishing lobby, whose members saw their interests threatened by the proposed duty-free entry of Newfoundland fish.

Meanwhile, despite the ups and downs of piscatorial politics, Newfoundland since the century's start had been entering on a period of financial blessings. 'This Colony has for the last five years enjoyed unprecedented prosperity', wrote the Governor in January 1905. 'So recently as 1896–7, exports amounted to only $4,925,789, while last year they realized $10,381,897...In...1894 the export of dry cod was only 1,107,696 cwts: and in 1902–3 it was 1,429,274 cwts, which was an advance of 29 per cent on the former. In 1896–7 the average price a hundredweight was $2.48: in 1903–4 it was $4.37.' The Governor was commenting, 'despite the fragmentary nature of the statistics available' (a state of affairs which later economists were also to deplore), on the first comprehensive local report on the foreign trade and commerce of the Island. But, as he cautiously and rightly added: 'The fluctuations in the income of the Colony are so great as to demand that in ordinary prudence some provision should be made in years of plenty to meet bad seasons. Such precautions would be necessary in any circumstances in the face of such perturbations of income as are demonstrated in this report, but they are doubly necessary in a community that is dependent on other countries for its food, its clothing and its fuel.'[1]

With equal wisdom MacGregor went on to forecast that exports could be largely increased by the use of improved methods of curing fish and by cold storage, as well as by applying the aids of modern science to the search for new and the working of existing mineral deposits. To some slight degree these truths were already in evidence. While Britain, Gibraltar (for Spain), the West Indies and above all Portugal and Brazil remained Newfoundland's traditional markets for dried cod, the overall direction of trade was shifting gradually away from Britain towards the United States and Canada. The growing diversification of the economy was in part the cause.

Although the politics of fish still bred quarrels within the North American triangle, a rapid increase of iron ore and pyrites exports was now

[1] 'Report on the Foreign Trade and Commerce of Newfoundland', May 1905, Cmd. 2480 C, vol. 54, 1905.

developing to the North American market. In 1905 the Island's largest mines, at Bell Island in Conception Bay, had been opened by the Nova Scotia Steel Company of Canada. The deposits of high-grade iron ore, stretching far out under the sea, seemed unlimited and for a time the ore was to find a ready market. A decade later, the Harmsworth interests, which had already been active on the west coast prospecting the forests at the height of the 'French Shore' dispute, opened the Anglo-Newfoundland Development Company's first pulp and paper mill at Grand Falls in the centre of the Island. These major enterprises, forerunners of others to come between the two world wars, were materially to affect the economy of a country still desperately reliant on the products of the sea. Fresh avenues of employment were opened up, either permanently in the mines or mills, or as an alternative winter occupation, in the forests cutting and hauling wood. By 1906 exports of iron ore from Bell Island had risen to close on 5 million long tons, the bulk of it now going to Canada. This figure rose to 17 million tons before the first war ended. The output of paper at the Grand Falls Mill also rose rapidly from 120 tons daily in 1909 to 200 tons in 1912.

Thus, in so far as a basically primary producing country can ever afford the luxury of optimism, there were increasing grounds for local hope. Even on the fishery front, to which one must now briefly return, old quarrels were at last on the verge of solution. The Colonial Conference of 1907 was to pave the way to a final settlement of the American dispute.

Fair warning of what was in the wind was given to the House of Commons by the Colonial Under Secretary, Mr Churchill. Replying to a Question about the fate of the Newfoundland–United States *modus vivendi*, he stated on 20 February of that year that: 'It is proposed to discuss the fisheries question fully and in detail with the Prime Minister of Newfoundland when that gentleman is in London for the Colonial Conference.'[1] The British Government subsequently invited the Canadian delegation to take part in these discussions. Sir Wilfred Laurier's view of the dispute, as reported by his Governor-General, could be briefly put. It was that

His Majesty's Government should bring pressure to bear upon Sir Robert Bond to allow the Newfoundland fishermen to sell their bait (as many wished to) to the Americans. [But the American] contention that the Treaty of 1818 has exempted Americans from the operation of all laws passed since 1818 on the Treaty Shore should be treated as a preposterous suggestion which no Minister of the Crown should consider even for one moment. The idea of consenting to submit such a proposal to arbitration is regarded here as one that cannot possibly be seriously entertained by British statesmen. Sir Wilfred reminds me that

[1] No. 83 in N.A. no. 208.

> after the Rebellion the 'New Englanders' lost the right of fishing in our waters, which they had formerly enjoyed as British subjects. Our Government, not appreciating the value of these fisheries at the time, gave the New Englanders the same right to take fish in common with the subjects of the Crown as if they had remained Britishers: and now for the Americans to turn round and say that because we stupidly gave them the right to fish as though they were still British Subjects they had now rights superior to British subjects *est un peu trop fort*.[1]

It was a nice example both of Laurier's earthy common sense and of his ability to raise his mind above the previous levels of Canadian parochial thinking on this issue.

Meanwhile, as last vain efforts were being made to press the Bond–Hay Convention on a still reluctant Congress, the American Secretary of State laid out his cards in advance of the Colonial Conference. As regards Canada, he saw no hope of his Government agreeing to admit Canadian fish duty-free. Arbitration in that respect touching on the interpretation of the 1818 Treaty would be fruitless. As to Newfoundland 'some action was undoubtedly required...Regulations for the conduct of the fishery from American vessels should be framed by the Governments concerned, and best perhaps by the method of appointing a Joint Commission to consider and frame them.'[2]

Compared with the 'French Shore' dispute, which had raised major constitutional issues, put the peaceful relationship of two great powers at risk, and involved the actual occupation of sovereign territory by a foreign state, the reasons underlying the quarrels with America were trivial indeed. That Bond was pursuing them from principle—or indeed sheer cussedness—rather than for their material significance was self-evident. Nor, as the Governor emphasized, did his policies enjoy unhesitating support in Newfoundland. 'Fear of him (the Prime Minister) and the dread of being branded unpatriotic, restrain [many people] from expressing their opinion.'

MacGregor went on to state his anxieties at the way in which, within the Empire, minor Colonial issues of this kind could sometimes pose a threat to good relations between Britain and other major powers. In a scarcely remembered passage, he proposed a remedy which is worthy today of being reproduced in full:

> Surely, however, the gravest consideration arising from this question is the fact that a matter which is clearly not of vital moment to a Colony, which may even

[1] Governor-General of Canada to British Ambassador, Washington, letter of 12 March 1907, encl. to no. 150 in N.A. no. 208.

[2] British Ambassador, Washington, to Foreign Secretary, dispatch of 19 March 1907, encl. to no. 180 *ibid.*

be more personal than political, can be pushed by irresponsible persons, and be exploited in such a way as to threaten, or be a menace to, the good understanding existing between His Majesty's Government and the Government of another great Power.

Would the remedy not be to put a share of the responsibility in cases of this kind on those that have the power to create them, but are at present irresponsible in all that relates to the foreign relations of the Empire?

The case of Newfoundland, to which others can be added, proves that appeals to reason and to moderation in such matters may fall on deaf ears. Men of a certain stamp cannot see a local, or personal, or political advantage in the perspective of the common interest of the Empire; and, perhaps, only responsibility can provide a remedy against this. If Colonial Premiers had to answer to each other, as well as to His Majesty's Government, for action that may disturb the foreign relations of the Empire, they would not lightly enter on a policy that they could not defend in a General Council of State. At the present time there is no organ in the Empire of an executive nature that can enforce compliance with such an arrangement, as the *modus vivendi* of last season as applicable to this Colony; and for the action that renders that *modus vivendi* necessary the head of this ministry cannot be called to account. A certain latitude has been conceded to Colonies in shaping their commercial relations with foreign countries, and it is from this source that the present American question has really arisen in this Colony. Greater latitude will doubtless be conceded in future in the same direction; if it is unattended by responsibility, it must eventually produce very grave results. At present a Governor possesses in such affairs only the unknown quantity of moral power. And even that influence has been much reduced by conferring on Prime Ministers distinctions that overshadow those enjoyed by the majority of Governors.

My experience here has convinced me that an Imperial Council of some kind, of which Prime Ministers should be members, and to which they should be responsible for all action that bears on the foreign relations of the Empire, is an absolute necessity.

The question is, in my humble opinion, perhaps the most difficult that has presented itself in modern times. But it is as important as it is difficult, and I venture to say it will be found to be inevitable. It may also be true that it may be easier to deal with now if it is taken to have arisen over a case that is not of vital importance, while at the same time it presents clearly the principles involved in all cases of the kind.

It may be found possible to approach the subject at the present Colonial Conference.[1]

MacGregor's proposed remedy makes interesting reading not only in relation to the between-the-wars efforts of Australia to promote a centralized Dominions Secretariat for the coordination of Dominion foreign policy: but also in respect of the post-war 'Entrustments' to Southern Rhodesia and the Central African Federation. It could still well be studied

[1] Governor of Newfoundland to Colonial Secretary, letter of 2 April 1907, no. 186 in N.A. no. 208.

with profit by those now engaged in schemes for the 'free association' of the remaining small colonial territories with Britain.

That the British Government shared the Governor's apprehensions emerges from the verbatim record of a discussion—which must have been something less than amiable—between the Foreign Secretary and Bond, who had now reached London:

Sir E. Grey. You are trying to settle a big question on small points.
Sir R. Bond. The fishery was granted to *inhabitants* of United States only.
Grey. Then what regulations are applicable?
Bond. They cannot object to Regulations made unless they are specially aimed at them. His Majesty's Government should settle this point.
Grey. And carry them out by force?
Bond. Force would not be needed.
Grey. But we cannot be sure of this.
Bond. Carry the question to the Privy Council.
Grey. The United States will not accept that Court—you have no sense of responsibility because you know we have to bear the brunt.[1]

It was not a cheerful curtain-raiser to the Conference. Yet the latter proved far from unsuccessful, permitting the British Government as it did to propose through the American Ambassador to Washington in June that a further fishery *modus vivendi* should be agreed to pending full examination by both sides of the existing local fishing regulations. Meanwhile in deference to Bond's advocacy, Britain upheld nearly all his contentions as to the proper interpretation of the Convention of 1818. The American reply, though couched in the most friendly terms, left the immediate issues unresolved. 'With the utmost desire to find in your last letter', wrote the Ambassador, 'some practical basis for an agreement, we are unable to perceive it...The task of reconciling...the positions...seems hopeless.' But his Government offered one way out—'to propose a reference of the pending questions...to arbitration before the Hague Tribunal'.[2] It was not a course which commended itself to Newfoundland Ministers. Further acerbic correspondence passed to and fro across the North Atlantic, and before the year was out Britain, with a view to protecting larger interests, rode rough-shod over Island opposition, entering on a fresh *modus vivendi* with the United States and enforcing its local application through its naval officers by Order-in-Council. This action the Newfoundland Government denounced as 'intended to override both international and local laws, and

[1] Notes of an interview between Sir E. Grey, Sir R. Bond and others, 11 May 1907, no. 225 in N.A. no. 208.
[2] American Ambassador to Foreign Secretary, note of 12 July 1907, encl. to no. 77 in Cmd. 3765.

as calculated to prejudice the Colony's case before the Hague Tribunal'.[1] Once more a constitutional crisis was in the making. While Canada, the United States and Britain strove hard to agree upon the terms under which this increasingly unnecessary dispute should be put before the Tribunal, Bond, intransigent to the last, chose the following year's Speech from the Throne as a vehicle for criticizing the Imperial Government's policy. The Governor's position, now difficult in the extreme, was resolved only by the elections of November 1908. Then Bond was opposed by his former colleague, Mr E. A. (later Baron) Morris, who had meanwhile formed a new People's Party. The result, a tie, presented the luckless Governor with yet a further dilemma: but this was eventually resolved by fresh elections which resulted in Morris's return to power with a comfortable majority.

From this point on, the sorry dispute can be brought rapidly to its close. The Tribunal of Arbitration foregathered at The Hague in June 1910. Its eventual rulings were generally in favour of Newfoundland and of Canada. Thus, Britain's right to make fishery regulations in Newfoundland without the consent of the United States was found to be inherent in her sovereignty, provided such regulations were 'reasonable'. On the vital issue of the definition of 'bays', Britain also won the day, the Tribunal ruling by a majority that 'in the case of bays, the three marine miles are to be measured from a straight line drawn across the body of water at the place where it ceases to have the configuration and characteristics of a bay. At all other places the three marine miles are to be measured following the sinuosities of the coast'.[3] This disposed of the American contention that the 'three marine miles' formula should extend to the very bottom of all bays. On the American proposition that their fishing vessels were entitled to trade on the treaty coasts, the Tribunal, to quote Fraser, found that such vessels 'could go to the treaty coasts and fish in which case they could not trade, or they could go there and trade, in which case they could not fish'. The rights could not be exercised 'concurrently'.[3]

Generally speaking, the Tribunal's rulings were a victory for Newfoundland, as for Canada. A treaty giving binding effect to their recommendatory provisions was subsequently initialled by all parties to the dispute in Washington in 1912. Now, barring certain squabbles with the French which lingered on until the outbreak of war and one small issue of monetary claims and counter-claims, which was not finally resolved until 1925, a century of bickering, flaring sometimes to dangerous if sterile quarrelling,

[1] Minute of Newfoundland Executive Council, 11 September 1907, *Journal of House of Assembly*, 1908.
[2] Cmd. 5396 of 1910, p. 22.
[3] MacKay, p. 408.

was at last resolved. Honour on all sides had been satisfied and, whatever the economic hazards of the fishery, Newfoundlanders could now look forward to pursuing it unhampered by international complications. However irritating successive Newfoundland ministries had been—and however irritated successive Imperial Foreign Secretaries—obstinacy had paid off well.

It was a signal triumph for so small a community that two Goliaths in turn should have conceded defeat before this lesser David.

10

WAR AND PLENTY: PEACE AND THE GATHERING STORM

Newfoundland in the past decade has entered upon a new march that is destined to place her, within the next dozen years, in the front rank of the great small nations of the world. MR J. R. SMALLWOOD, 1931

By the eve of the First World War, the population of Newfoundland had risen to close on a quarter of a million. Her politicians had put her people firmly on the map. The Island enjoyed full internal autonomy and had won the right to be consulted on matters of concern to her in the international field. Newfoundland Prime Ministers attended the Imperial Conferences as of right, and despite the political strains which the enduring fishery disputes had caused, the loyalty of Newfoundlanders towards the Mother Country was no longer questionable. Proof and more of this was soon to be shown on the battlefields of France.

Meanwhile, the economic barometer was rising steadily. As early as 1908 a special visiting Commissioner from the Advisory Committee of the Board of Trade had been able to report that 'the total trade of the Colony has recently shown a steady upward movement and has more than doubled in the past eight years'.[1] While Newfoundland's exports found their way to many markets, Britain, Canada and the United States still had a virtual lien on her import trade. The Achilles heel, however, was the customs tariff. Newfoundlanders hardly knew the meaning of direct taxation. Revenue came overwhelmingly from import duties. When one considers that in the case of so humble an object as a wheelbarrow the *ad valorem* duty was as high as 75 per cent, and that in 1908 duties of between 40 and 50 per cent were charged on furniture, china, boots, shoes and ready made clothing, it becomes clear that the lower income groups were doubly punished, while the rich paid far less than they could afford to do. Not until 1934 was any serious effort made to revise the fiscal structure. Even then, so small was the population and so few were there in the direct income tax brackets, that the tariff still had to be looked to as the preponderant source of revenue.

The Board of Trade Commissioner expressed his anxieties not only on this score but on the march which North American businessmen were

[1] Report upon the Conditions and Prospects of British Trade in Newfoundland, Richard Grigg, Cmd. 4153, 1908.

stealing on their British rivals. 'I was informed in St John's', he wrote, 'that the commercial hotels there were supported almost entirely by American and Canadian travellers, and that they saw ten of these to one from the United Kingdom.' The United States Government of course had not been slow to sense the commercial opportunities. As early as 1905 a report published from the Department of Commerce and Labor foreshadowed the special Commissioner's later comments. 'The growth in the prosperity of Newfoundland during the last few years', it ran, 'which has resulted in placing the Colony in a very strong financial position with a balance of trade in her favour, has been due chiefly to the improved condition of the fishing industry, though the development of the pulp wood and other forest products and some increase in the output of the mines have had an appreciable effect.'[1] In world terms, the scale of activity—exports $10·4 million, imports $9·5 million—was small enough. What signified was the unprecedented optimism which lay behind these words. It seemed that it would no longer be good enough for British manufacturers 'to be indifferent to the Newfoundland market, regarding it as almost insignificant in comparison with their total trade'.[2]

These pre-war years were indeed a halcyon time for Newfoundland. Between 1901–7 the Treasury could report successive surpluses, and by the end of that time the Government had set aside a cash reserve of $450,000. 1906 in particular went down in the annals as the Colony's most prosperous and successful year. The British Commissioner's conclusions at the end of his stay could well have been written yesterday. More could be done by British traders, he urged, to increase their hold upon the Newfoundland market. Admittedly Canada and the United States were in a geographically favoured position. But

> British manufacturers should study Newfoundland conditions for themselves and not depend...upon merchants and agents. They should follow the example of their American competitors in entering as much as possible into direct communications with Newfoundland buyers, and turn their attention more than they have done in the past to the problem of distribution...It follows from this that the British manufacturer must either visit the market himself, or he must be prepared to select the best men obtainable, pay them well and thereby enable them to meet and fight their commercial competitors on their own lines... Newfoundland has adopted American standards...and if British manufacturers wish to sell in the Newfoundland market they must adopt for goods destined for that market the same standards also.

[1] Monthly Issue of Consular and Trade Reports, Dept. of Commerce and Labor, Washington, August 1905.

[2] Cmd. 4153.

And, by way of final warning: 'United States publications are very freely supplied, and Newfoundlanders have constantly exhibited before them the spectacle of the commercial and industrial greatness of the United States, whereas from the United Kingdom they receive practically nothing.'[1] *Plus ça change...*

War itself brought even greater wealth: not that this should be allowed to detract from the extreme and disproportionate sacrifices made by the small Colony to the allied cause. The figures speak for themselves. Of 5,482 men who went overseas, close on 1,500 were killed, 2,314 wounded and 234 decorated or mentioned in dispatches. The massacre at Beaumont Hamel remains, even today, a proud, sad memory to sacrifice. On 1 July 1916 753 Newfoundlanders went into action there. Next morning only 68 were left to answer to the roll-call.

But at home the material effects of war brought great comfort to the fishery. Oversea competition declined and the Island reaped the greatest catches of her history. As the demand for fish rose so did prices. Moreover, improved communications with the mainland enabled Newfoundlanders to cross the Cabot Straits in their thousands to seek lucrative employment in Canada and the United States. For once all sections of the community prospered and the general standard of living rose to levels never before experienced. Yet even before war ended, the writing was once more on the wall. Expenditure on public works, the continued extension of unprofitable branch railway lines and steamer services, the strains of contributing to the war effort itself, all sowed the seeds for future catastrophe, even though the dimensions of the crisis were to remain for some years hidden behind a smokescreen of false financial optimism. Loans amounting to $13 million—then a staggering figure for a community so small—had been raised to meet the Colony's war expenditure and shortly after peace returned the gross public debt had soared to $43 million.

There was much to encourage the illusion that the smoke screen of prosperity was a solid wall. 'Even hard headed businessmen prophesied a new era for the Newfoundland sailing vessels: throughout the Island, large fortunes were being made... the excitement of peace tempted men to think that prosperity would go on for ever.'[2] The Colony, moreover, had gained additional prestige and status from the war. Not only had her contribution been a gallant one, her Prime Ministers had been directly involved in the deliberations of the Imperial War Cabinet: her Governments had become used to being consulted, on an equal footing with the greater Dominions, on such international issues as the ratification of treaties

[1] Cmd. 4153.

[2] *Cambridge History of the British Empire*, vol. VI, *Canada*, ch. XXVIII, Newfoundland.

with foreign powers, commodity policies or the relationship of India to future Imperial Conferences. A measure of Newfoundland's growing involvement in the higher councils of the Empire (however infrequently she might contribute to them in practice) can be gauged from the press release issued on 19 August 1918 by the Prime Ministers then gathered in London. The Imperial War Cabinet, ran this statement, had been continuously in session for the past two-and-a-half months. These meetings had proved of such value that its members had

> thought it essential that certain modifications should be made in the existing channels of communication so as to make consultation between the various Governments of the Empire in regard to Imperial Policy as continuous and intimate as possible. It has therefore been decided that for the future the Prime Ministers of the Dominions, as members of the Imperial War Cabinet, shall have the right to communicate on matters of Cabinet importance direct with the Prime Minister of the United Kingdom, whenever they see fit to do so. It has also been decided that each Dominion shall have the right to nominate a visiting or a resident Minister in London to be a member of the Imperial War Cabinet at meetings other than those attended by the Prime Ministers.

The Newfoundland Government was proud to take advantage of this arrangement and the then Prime Minister, Mr (Later Sir William) Lloyd represented the Colony at both the London Conferences and the eventual Peace Conference in Paris.

That peace, as indicated, brought few seeming problems. The census of 1920 revealed a certain falling off of those gainfully employed in the fishery—25 per cent of the total population as compared with 28·5 per cent in 1901. But fishermen-farmers still made up the bulk of those working permanently for a living. And to the general prosperity to be gained from the sea, pulp and paper, forestry and mining added fresh dimensions. The accent in 1919, when first Sir Michael Cashin and second Mr (later Sir Richard) Squires succeeded as Prime Minister was on expansion. Later, in the wisdom of hindsight, the twelve ensuing years were to be scathingly described as: 'characterised by an outflow of public funds on a scale as ruinous as it was unprecedented, fostered by a continuous stream of willing lenders [*Pace* Nkrumah "ex Africa semper..." is not always true]. A new era of industrial expansion, easy money and profitable contact with the rich American continent was looked for and was deemed in part to have arrived. In the prevailing optimism, the resources of the Exchequer were believed to be limitless.'[1]

But even the knowledgeable failed to read the portents. Life had been so hard so long that two decades of prosperity suggested that the never

[1] Newfoundland Royal Commission, 1933, Report and Papers, Cmd. 4479, p. 43.

despaired of millennium had at last arrived. Writing as late as 1931, on the very eve of catastrophe the present Premier, the Honourable J. R. Smallwood, had this to say: 'After so long a period of primitive existence, Newfoundland has entered upon a new life, and a life very much akin to that of industrial America or industrial Canada...Never before did we have such healthy activity in education. Never did we have such comfort and efficiency in our railways. Never were there such fine ocean steamships connecting us with Britain, Canada and the United States. Never were there such good roads and such good hotels.'[1] Published with the sonorous title 'An account of the revolutionary developments which are transforming Britain's oldest colony from the "Cinderella of the Empire" into one of the great small nations of the world', Mr Smallwood's was a passionate if decidedly premature panegyric of the Island's assets. Certainly the roads, the railways, the hotels were enjoying a land-change. But at whose cost? And to what short-term benefit? And what of the fishery, still lingering outdatedly behind competitors who had returned to the arena with new fleets, new methods and new determination to capture what remained of ever shrinking world demand?

Yet for a time fresh ventures took the minds of politicians and electors alike off the financial pit that both were digging for themselves.

As an antidote to growing unemployment in the fishery and to the continuing fall in world demand, the development late in the post-war decade of lead and zinc deposits at Buchans in the centre of the island gave a new fillip to the economy, already all too artificially boosted by a large-scale programme of public works. But more important still was the opening, in 1923, of a second large pulp and paper mill at Cornerbrook on the west coast.

This bold project, often advanced and as often deferred, was finally undertaken by the Newfoundland Power and Paper Company at a cost originally estimated at some $20 million, the interest on and principal of which the British and Newfoundland Governments jointly guaranteed. However wildly out of true the construction costs might eventually prove (by 1925 when the mill opened they had risen to $45 million), this great enterprise at least offered steady employment to a larger number of workers than the Island had ever before seen assembled on one single project at one time.

But despite these developments, despite a gradual slowing of the downward slide of world trade, despite the stabilization of the currencies of the major trading nations and the sudden sensational prosperity of the United States, despite the superficial boom, the flowering of new businesses

[1] J. R. Smallwood, *The New Newfoundland*, pp. 7–8 (hereafter referred to as *N.N.*).

and the glamour of expanding railroad lines and new hotels, the Island's financial core was rotting slowly, invisibly away. Too many burdens had been accepted, too many optimistic plans embarked on: too little set aside for rainy days: too little attempt made to change old ways.

Self reliant and courageous though they were, Newfoundlanders still did little by their way of life to encourage great hopes for a constructive future. The settler mentality survived and flourished. Isolation rather than congregation was an ingrained habit, and denominational differences continued to run deep. Even by 1920 Newfoundland could boast only three settlements outside St John's with populations of more than 4,000. Scattered outports, strung around 6,000 miles of coastline, many of them still inaccessible by road or rail from the interior, would have placed an intolerable burden on a central administration far wealthier than Newfoundland could ever hope to support. The result was that medical and social services, communications and anything more than rudimentary education had to be supplied at excessive cost or not at all. And in the educational field the jealous vigour of the various faiths more often than not led to three or four understaffed and ill-equipped schools operating in competition with each other in one small community when a single school, providing ready access to all faiths for religious teaching, would have revolutionized and brought about great economies in educational systems and standards throughout the Island.

When retrenchment was most needed successive governments, still lured onwards towards destruction, marched boldly but blindly behind the banner of expansionism. Had they heeded them, statistics would surely have brought their column to a halt. For instance: 'In the years 1867–1921, while the population had increased by only 66%, revenue and expenditure had risen to fourteen times the amount of 1867, the average for three years ending with 1921 being $9,523,742 and $8,954,961 respectively. The debt was forty times as great. Trade was but six or seven times more valuable. The imports for 1921 were $28,909,727, the exports $22,441,267',[1] a heavy adverse balance of payments for so small a community to bear in addition to its public debt.

In fact the war alone had placed an almost impossible burden on a people with so little in reserve. The public debt, far from stopping at its 1920 all-time peak of $43 million, continued year by year to soar.

By no means all the financial failings could be laid at the door of politicians. Fecklessness there had been in plenty. Certainly improvidence had marched with bad judgement towards disaster. But it was also the Island's misfortune that fresh economic assets failed to come into play

[1] *Cambridge History, op. cit.* ch. XXXVIII.

before the fishery could be modernized and dependence on a single commodity, subject more than most to the cruel see-saw of sensitive price changes, eliminated or at least reduced.

Everything seemed now to be turning against the islanders, and save for cutting their coat according to their cloth they were virtually powerless to react. Right across the world tariff barriers were being raised. Spain and Italy, among Newfoundland's previous best markets, were cutting back their imports. France was once more encouraging her national fishing fleets. Refrigeration and canning were steadily reducing the demand for dried fish. Iceland and Norway were emerging as formidable, modernized competitors while the United States was gradually closing the door to working immigrants from Newfoundland.

It was fortunate as things were that the Cornerbrook mill, costly though its construction was proving, could yet prime the local pump. Between 1923–30 it generated over $40 million by way of wages, local purchases, taxes and the like. 'In sober truth', as Mr Smallwood later wrote, 'it has meant the difference between utter destitution and keeping our chins above water!'[1] Yet the 'sober truth' was that even miracles of this dimension could not fend off catastrophe. The whole economic programme—or rather a whole series of uncoordinated programmes undertaken at a time when economic nationalism was adversely affecting the primary producing countries—had gone awry. It was all very well to boast that, although railway modernization had cost the Exchequer over $15 million between 1920 and 1923 (in which year the whole system was taken over by government), 'new industries and the expansion of existing ones will surely wipe out the annual operating deficit'.[2] The harsh facts were that passenger and freight traffic were not expanding to reduce the deficit and that save in the pulp, paper and mining sectors, fresh capital from oversea was simply not available.

While exports of iron ore had been rising steadily from 16 million tons in 1918 to 21 million in 1925 and the production of paper was also creeping up, other and more vital figures told another story. By now the current budgets were running on average a deficit of $2 million per annum. Loans were being raised continuously, but save in one instance no provision for a sinking fund was made. By 1923 the public debt had topped the $55 million mark. Three years later it stood at $72 million. 'We need not perhaps enter into details of the expenditure of this period', the Royal Commissioners later and primly commented, 'apart from noting that it was marked by waste and extravagance on a reckless scale.'[3]

[1] Smallwood, *N.N.* p. 49. [2] *Ibid.* p. 90.
[3] Cmd. 4479, p. 48.

Nor was the political situation much happier. The boom–slump–boom conditions of the immediate post-war years had destroyed the sense of unity and patriotism which the war-time Coalition Government had fostered. Newfoundland's greatest public figure, Sir Robert Bond, had long since retired from the political scene, embittered by the split of the Liberal party and unable to face the aggressive tactics of a new crusading force, the Fishermen's Protective Union. The rival Liberal leader, Sir Edward Morris had taken his seat in the House of Lords, and in 1919 the Island and Empire had witnessed the unprecedented spectacle of the Minister of Finance, seconded by his own Prime Minister, Sir William Lloyd, moving a vote of no confidence in their own administration. In this novel fashion, the Coalition Government fell. A new force in local politics, Mr (later Sir Richard) Squires, now joined forces with the Fishermen's Union and, under the party label 'Liberal Reform' and the slogan 'Industrial Development of Newfoundland', proceeded to sweep the country. But in the Tory opposition leader, the late Sir Michael Cashin, the Liberal reformists found a foe as implacable as he was bitter. Once more political behaviour and ethics came dangerously close to emulating the bad old nineteenth-century days. Squires, adulated and reviled in turn, carried his expansionist banner forward to 1923 when, for reasons best left to be unravelled at a later date, the Liberal Government collapsed. Cashin, Squires, and the Fishermen's leader, Coaker, temporarily retired from politics and the Tories under a newcomer, Mr Walter S. Monroe, returned to power. They were to stay in office for four dismal years. Today their brief tenure of the helm is perhaps better remembered for their share in seeing to a close the long-standing Labrador boundary dispute than for any notable achievement in other fields. For, as the ensuing chapter shows, Newfoundland, at a time when she was least able to afford it, was about to acquire a 'Colony'.

11

THE LABRADOR DISPUTE

Si quis sinus additus ultra,
Si qua foret fellus, fuluum quae milteret aurum,
Hostis erat PETRONIUS ARBITER

I trust that...an early and satisfactory settlement of this long outstanding question may thus be reached.
GOVERNOR OF NEWFOUNDLAND to Lord Grey, 2 October 1907
(P.C. 1694M)

On 1 March 1927 the people of Newfoundland retired to their beds richer by some 110,000 square miles of territory than they had arisen that morning. Thus ended, almost thirty years after the Governments of Canada and Newfoundland had first agreed to submit their claims to the Imperial Privy Council, the long-standing dispute over the exact location of the boundary separating Quebec from Newfoundland Labrador.

Prestige and patriotism required that the decision be hailed locally as a signal triumph and as a vindication of Newfoundland's ever-romantic expectations of the riches of her soil. But, viewed against the impending financial storm, this bonus from the Judicial Committee, which more than doubled Newfoundland's domains, was to prove in the short-term a hindrance, not an asset. It could only serve still further to strain the Island's meagre administrative resources. Moreover, with the exception of the coastal and salmon fisheries, which were already in decline and the known existence of large forests of pulp wood round the landward shores of Lake Melville—in themselves the immediate cause of the boundary dispute—the Labrador had little to offer Newfoundland in terms of wealth. Few in 1927 foresaw the latter-day significance of the Judicial Committee's decision in terms of mineral, railway, hydro-electric and air developments.

Ever since the Treaty of Paris of 1763 successive Governors and later Governments of Newfoundland had exercised marginal control over the Labrador coastline stretching south and easterly from Cape Chidley at the entrance to Hudson Strait to Blanc Sablon on the Strait of Belle Isle. Small fishing settlements gradually established themselves along the shoreline south of Hamilton Inlet. Northwards from there, with the agreement from time to time of the Imperial Government, the Moravian Missionaries established posts, notably at Nain and Hopedale, where they traded with and administered to the spiritual and material needs of the Esquimaux. Apart from this handful of men perched on the edge of a continent, the interior was left to roaming tribes of Indians, to the lone Quebec and Newfoundland trapper and, as the nineteenth century drew to a close, to occasional teams of geologists, surveyors and foresters.

It was in all respects a forbidding land: the coastline heavily indented, treacherous and often fog- or ice-bound: the interior a tormented, lake-studded mountainous mass whose average temperature never rose above −2°C: where in the long winter the ground froze six feet deep and in the short summer months great mosquitoes and swampy tundra repelled all but the most determined. Its winter perils were once graphically—though purely imaginatively—evoked by H. G. Wells.[1] To all save the hardiest enthusiasts it was indeed well named 'the Land that God gave Cain'.

The Labrador cod fishery, which from the start had been the main cause of British and Newfoundland interest in the peninsula, was no longer in the 1920s such as to hold out great hopes. The industry was by tradition in the hands of 'liveyeres' and 'planters'. The former, as their (probably) West of England corruption of 'live here' implies, were residents of the coast; the latter fishermen from Newfoundland who in local parlance 'sailed down to the Labrador' each summer. Most of the 'liveyeres' were no doubt correctly described as 'descendants of those pioneer fur animal hunters and seal catchers who married Eskimo or Indian women'.[2] But some of them would certainly have been Newfoundlanders by birth and Labradoreans by adoption. Whatever their origins, their life had always been a hard one. In 1927 the Labrador could boast only one coastal settlement, Battle Harbour at the south-easterly tip of the peninsula, which in any way approximated to a town. For the rest, the 'liveyeres' existed in scattered outports fishing for salmon in the early summer, bartering their catch to visiting traders for the basic necessities of life; then taking to their boats for the cod fishing and finally moving inland in mid-winter when the trapping season opened. Save for rare visits from coastal steamers during the few open months, and from west country schooners occasionally loading salt cod for Mediterranean ports, contacts with the outside world were few and far between.

In economic terms the 'liveyeres' made little impact. The bulk of the Labrador fishery was prosecuted by the 'planters' who again, in local parlance, fell into two categories—the 'stationers', i.e. those who came down through the ice from Newfoundland ports in early summer, taking up temporary residence at and fishing from a shore base; and the 'floaters'; that is men working powered vessels and fishing from them between July and September, splitting and wetsalting their catch on board. However

[1] H. G. Wells, *The War in the Air* (London, Bell, 1908).

[2] V. Tanner, *Acta Geographica, Helsinki*, VIII (1944), 1–909.

the fishery was conducted, it was 'a specialised and commercially risky venture, when compared with the bank and shore fisheries, which are the two longer and stronger sides of the Newfoundland fishing triangle'.[1] It was indeed as much custom as economic good sense which continued to drive the schooner fleets yearly up along the barren Labrador coast. Only in recent years have economic facts, combined with other and more fruitful means of livelihood, led to the decline and virtual eclipse of the Labrador fishery. Two sets of figures mark the extent of the change. In the summer of 1881 the migratory population of 'floaters' and 'stationers' was estimated[2] at 30,000 and their weight of dried cod produced at 42,000 metric tons. In 1945 the comparable figures were 4,000 men and 12,500 tons.

But at the time the Labrador dispute came before the Privy Council, the cod fishery was still far and away the most important economic asset of the territory. Because of the climate, terrain and distances involved, timber extraction on any scale was as yet little more than a pipe dream. For the same reasons, exploitation of the known resources of water power seemed impossible of achievement. And to have talked then in terms of minerals would have been to anticipate the future by twenty years or more. All that the Labrador could offer between the two world wars, in addition to its perennial cod, were modest returns from the salmon and herring fisheries and from the small seal and whaling industries. It was therefore more in expectation of future miracles than on account of tangible riches, more out of national pride than in hopes of immediate gain, that Newfoundland and Canada agreed to submit their differences to the Judicial Committee.

The boundary issue was, as Fraser points out,[3] first raised 'in a semi-academic manner' by a Newfoundland judge in 1888. Mr Justice Pinsent then pointed to a discrepancy between the extent of Newfoundland's jurisdiction in Labrador as defined by the Letters Patent of 28 March 1876 and as shown by a map published under the authority of the Canadian Government. The judge urged that a practical and essential problem arose in respect of the administration of justice in the territory. He appealed to the then Governor to seek some exact definition from the British Government. Efforts were made at the abortive conferences at Halifax, Nova Scotia, on confederation in 1888 and 1892 to resolve the matter. But even

[1] G. W. St J. Chadwick, 'The economic resources of Labrador', *Polar Record*, v (1948), 155–62.

[2] Joseph Hatton and M. Harvey, *Newfoundland: The Oldest British Colony* (London, Chapman, 1883).

[3] MacKay, p. 463.

an agreement reached at the latter meeting that the Newfoundland and Canadian Governments should each appoint geographers to study and to report on available documents on the boundary came to nothing. The issue 'was at that time of little practical importance'.[1]

The immediate origin of the eventual reference to the Privy Council can be directly traced to a letter[2] of 18 December 1902 addressed by the Lieutenant-Governor of Quebec to the Canadian Secretary of State in Ottawa. With this was enclosed an *aide-mémoire*, with supporting documents, from the Provincial Minister of Lands, Mines and Fisheries. The Quebec Government complained that the Newfoundland Government had earlier in the same year granted to the Grand River Pulp and Lumber Company a fifty-year licence to cut timber on both the north and south sides of the Hamilton River. The Government of Newfoundland had apparently taken this action in the mistaken belief that it enjoyed jurisdiction in the Labrador peninsula 'north of the 52nd parallel of latitude east of the 64th degree of longitude'. Quebec disputed this claim and asked that 'the necessary steps be taken to prevent any encroachment by the government of New-Foundland [*sic*] on the territory of the Province of Quebec'.

A Committee of the Canadian Privy Council studied the Quebec complaint and on 10 March 1903 recommended to the Governor-General that he should move the Colonial Secretary to arrange for the cancellation of the Newfoundland licences. In their submission[3] the Privy Counsellors first referred, in defence of the Quebec complaint, to that fateful word 'coast' which twenty-three years later was to echo and re-echo for fourteen consecutive sitting days in the august ears of the members of the Judicial Committee in London. 'Even upon an interpretation of the legislation most favourable to the Colony of Newfoundland', ran the Canadian submission to the Governor-General,[4] 'nothing can be included within the Newfoundland Labrador but coasts and islands..."coast" cannot possibly be so interpreted as to include the territory through which the Hamilton River flows, hundreds of miles from the ocean.' The Governor-General in forwarding the correspondence to the Colonial Office observed merely that it was the request of his Ministers that the offending licences be

[1] *Ibid.* p. 465.

[2] In the Privy Council, In the matter of the boundary between the Dominion of Canada and the Colony of Newfoundland in the Labrador Peninsula, Report of the Lords of the Judicial Committee of the Privy Council, vol. 1 of Joint Appendix, sec. 2, no. 4, pp. 130–1.

[3] In the Privy Council, In the matter of the boundary between . . . Canada and . . . Newfoundland, vol. 1 of Joint Appendix, sec. 2, no. 3, p. 129.

[4] *Ibid.* vol. 1 of Joint Appendix, sec. 2, no. 3, p. 129.

cancelled.[1] The President of the Pulp and Lumber Company, on learning that he had unwittingly sparked off so weighty a legal argument, was more outspoken. 'We', he wrote from his Nova Scotia office to the Quebec authorities, 'are not stealing anything.'[2] Clearly not. He was indeed to be robbed of his own expectations, for the next moves were to take the matter far beyond the competence of local law officers and to keep unfortunate licensees in suspense for many years to come. First under cover of a dispatch[3] from the Governor of Newfoundland to the Colonial Secretary came a minute from the Newfoundland Council briskly rejecting, by reference to the Imperial Acts of 1809[4] and 1825[5] and to an Order in Council of 1880, all claims advanced by Canada and concluding that the Labrador peninsula was within the jurisdiction of the Government of Newfoundland. Next Lord Minto, having referred the Newfoundland counterclaim to his own Ministers and through them to the provincial government of Quebec, transmitted to London the request of the Canadian Privy Council that the question of the position of the boundary between the Dominion and the Newfoundland Labrador 'may be submitted for decision to the Judicial Committee of the Privy Council under the provisions of Section 4 of the Imperial Statute 3 and 4 William IV, c. 41'.[6] To this the Colonial Secretary replied in the month following[7] that in the view of His Majesty's Government the Canadian request was a proper one and that it was his hope that the Governments of Canada and Newfoundland would be able to agree on the evidence and case to be submitted to the Judicial Committee.

The search for agreed terrain on which to disagree was, however, of painful slowness. Over three years passed before the Governor of Newfoundland was again substantively in touch with the British Government. Even then it was only to report that his Ministers concurred in the proposal to refer the dispute to the Judicial Committee 'and will be prepared to submit their case forthwith'. 'I trust', he added with unconscious irony, '...that an early and satisfactory settlement of this long outstanding question may thus be reached.'[8]

[1] *Ibid.* Lord Minto to Mr Joseph Chamberlain, 18 March 1903, p. 128.
[2] *Ibid.* 1369L (*b*), no. 6, p. 132.
[3] *Ibid.* Sir Cavendish Boyle to Mr Joseph Chamberlain, no. 53, 24 July 1903, nos. 10 and 11, pp. 115–37.
[4] 49 Geo. III, c. 27.
[5] 6 Geo. IV, c. 89.
[6] In the Privy Council, In the matter of the boundary between . . . Canada and . . . Newfoundland, Lord Minto to A. Lyttleton, no. 118, 20 April 1904, no. 14 and 15, pp. 139–41.
[7] *Ibid.* A. Lyttleton to Lord Minto, Canada no. 143, 20 May 1904, no. 16, p. 141.
[8] *Ibid.* W. MacGregor to Lord Grey, P.C. 1694M, 2 October 1907, no. 17, p. 142.

His optimism was ill-rewarded. The First World War interrupted the massive legal and documentary preparations on either side. It was not until 1922 that a memorandum of agreement[1] was finally approved by both Governments, setting forth the terms of reference of their joint submission to the Judicial Committee. Put in interrogative terms, these read:

What is the location and definition of the boundary as between Canada and Newfoundland in the Labrador peninsula under the statutes, orders-in-Council and proclamations?

Even with this triumph of accord to their mutual credit, the two contestants were still not to come to grips for four further years. But if in this case the layman is rash enough to conclude that the law is a ponderous dray-horse and that what was first queried in 1903 could well have been settled by 1913, let alone 1923, then the very weight and intricacy of this dispute, even leaving aside its imperial importance, must confound him. When at long last, on the morning of 21 October 1926, the Judicial Committee assembled in the Council Chamber on the corner of Downing Street and Whitehall, the members of the board had before them a mass of material such as can rarely have been assembled for a Committee hearing. The two Government cases and counter-cases; the historical surveys, whether common ground or in dispute, the Statutes, Orders in Council, Instructions and Proclamations; the affidavits, supporting notes; the documents and correspondence relevant to the issue, occupied no less than nine large printed volumes running to close on 5,000 pages. The verbatim evidence taken over fourteen days was to add a further 1,600 sheets. Little wonder that their Lordships, at the close of this written and verbal marathon, should require four further months before finally tendering their advice to the King in Council.

The Board was composed of the Lord Chancellor, Viscount Cave, supported by Viscounts Haldane, Finlay and Sumner and by Sir Thomas Warrington. Leading Counsel for the Colony of Newfoundland was Sir John (later Lord) Simon, assisted by Sir P. McGrath, Mr M. Furlong and the Hon. W. J. Higgins, K.C. The leader for the Dominion of Canada was the Rt. Hon. H. P. (later Lord) Macmillan of the Scottish Bar, supported by a strong Canadian team.

Before attempting to summarize the arguments advanced on both sides or to isolate the main legal and practical issues in dispute, it will be useful to refer to certain basic matters governing the history of the Labrador and to the Statutes and other instruments affecting the territory which, even

[1] *Ibid.* Terms of reference to Judicial Committee, 11 November 1920 as amended 20 November 1922, vol. 1 of Joint Appendix, pt. 1, sec. 1, pp. 125 ff.

before the hearing opened, were conceded by either party to be common ground.

It was not for instance disputed that the Hudson's Bay Company had in 1670 obtained from Charles II a Royal Charter giving it sole rights of trade and commerce of 'all those seas, straits, bays, rivers, lakes, creeks and sounds in whatsoever latitude they be that lie within the entrance of Hudson's Straits'.[1] No question arose therefore of a Newfoundland territorial claim to the areas previously held by the Company as confirmed by Article x of the Treaty of Utrecht, 1713—a Treaty which had at the same time declared Newfoundland itself to belong in exclusive sovereignty to Great Britain.

Nor were the following facts, of legal import, disputed. First that by the Treaty of Paris, 1763, France had ceded to Britain without restriction Canada with all its dependencies, including the whole peninsula of Labrador saving those areas restored to the Hudson's Bay Company in 1713. Secondly, that by a Royal Proclamation of 7 October 1763 made in consequence of the Treaty of Paris, 'the coast of Labrador and the adjacent islands—from the River of St John's to Hudson's Streights, together with the islands of Anticosti and the Madelaine and all other smaller islands lying upon the said coast...' were put 'under the care and inspection of our Governor of Newfoundland'. Thirdly, that by the Quebec Act of 1774[2] all the territories above mentioned which had since the Treaty of Paris 'been made part of the Government of Newfoundland were now during His Majesty's pleasure annexed to and made part and parcel of the Province of Quebec'. Fourthly, that by an Imperial Act of 1809[3] these same territories (less on this occasion the island of Madelaine or Magdalen) were again reannexed to the Government of Newfoundland. Or fifthly and finally: that by a further Imperial Act of 1825[4] 'so much of the said coast of Labrador as lies to the westward of a line drawn due North and South from the bay or harbour of Anse Sablon inclusive as far as the fifty second degree of North Latitude with the island of Anticosti and all other islands adjacent to such part as last aforesaid of the Coast of Labrador' were now 'reannexed to and made part of the said province of Lower Canada'.

The effect of this bewildering succession of legal instruments will be more readily understood from a glance at the accompanying map (p. 263).

[1] In the Privy Council, In the matter of the boundary between . . . Canada and . . . Newfoundland, The case on behalf of the Colony of Newfoundland, vol. 1 of Joint Appendix, p. 6.

[2] 14 Geo. III, c. 83.

[3] 49 Geo. III, c. 27.

[4] 6 Geo. IV, c. 59.

Such was the strictly statutory background to the dispute. The battle itself was pre-eminently one of interpretation of words and intent; of the significance to be attached to the key word 'coast': to the question of effective occupation; to the issue of settlement as against the long-standing Imperial policy of using Newfoundland—and Labrador—as mere training grounds for seamen and as a seasonal fishing ground. 'Words', as leading Counsel for the Dominion of Canada was to say in arguing his case 'have their own significance. The fortune of a word is in the ear that hears it.'[1] His observation was a telling one.

Of necessity, the Canadian case and counter-case were narrowly deployed, narrowly argued and based on legal and political premises which, however relevant to the eighteenth and early nineteenth centuries, tended to ignore practical local developments since that date. The Canadian argument which, in view of the Committee's ultimate ruling, may conveniently be summarized first, was developed from Mr Macmillan's statement that the Judicial Committee was faced with the task of placing the true interpretation on the words 'all the coasts of Labrador', as used in the Royal Proclamation of 1763. It was, he said, 'a tribute to the ambiguity of the English language that an apparently simple phrase such as that should have afforded material for so prolonged and so elaborate a debate'.[2] Mr Macmillan first disputed the Newfoundland contention that in this particular case 'coast' could be read as meaning all the territory between the coasts and the ascertainable height of land or watershed behind it. Next he suggested that when the Labrador coast had first been placed under the jurisdiction of the Governor of Newfoundland, the sole aim of the Imperial power had been that it should be used as a margin of the sea for fishing purposes. He compared the exact language used in defining the territorial concessions granted to the Hudson's Bay Company under their Charter of 1670 with that of the Royal Proclamation of 1673 and subsequent Instructions to successive Governors of Newfoundland. If, he argued, it had been the intention of His Majesty's Ministers to confer on their Governor in Newfoundland as huge an area as the Newfoundland Government now claimed, then surely they would have used language more precise than the shorthand description 'all the coasts of Labrador'. To suggest more than the cession of a coastline exclusively for fishing purposes would be to read into the language of legislators one hundred and fifty years ago intentions which they had probably never entertained. The true intent of the Royal Proclamation of 1763 had been to entrust the Governor of Newfound-

[1] In the Privy Council, In the matter of the boundary between . . . Canada and . . . Newfoundland, 13th day, 12 November 1926.
[2] *Ibid.* 13th day, Mr Macmillan, p. 906.

land, who was at the same time a servant of the Board of Admiralty, with the care and inspection of the fishery prosecuted along or from the coasts of Labrador.

Mr Macmillan then drew attention to the Commission[1] passed under the Great Seal in April 1763 appointing Thomas Graves as 'Governor and Commander-in-Chief in and over the island of Newfoundland, the Coast of Labrador etc.'. The Newfoundland claim, he said, had made considerable play with the fact that the word 'territories' occurred several times in that document. But this, surely, was the appropriate word to use of any area of jurisdiction. It by no means inferred that such jurisdiction carried to any depth inland. Indeed, the greater burden of the Commission was that the Governor was to do nothing 'contrary or repugnant to the Act' (of 1699) for 'encouraging the Trade to Newfoundland'. And the 'trade to Newfoundland' meant the cod fishery and nothing else. It implied too that settlement, whether of Newfoundland or the Labrador, was to be resisted in the Imperial naval and mercantile interest. Counsel for Canada then went on to quote one particular example, among many others cited in the course of the hearing, pertaining to the meaning of the word 'coast'. It related to the French Shore question. In 1853 negotiations opened between the French and British Governments had led to the Convention of 1857 governing 'the rights of fishing on the coast of Newfoundland and on the neighbouring coasts'. After much argument as to the territorial rights going with the right to use the coastline for fishing purposes, it had been laid down in Article x of this Convention that—so far as the west coast of Newfoundland was concerned—'The strand reserved for French exclusive rights for fishing purposes shall extend to one third of an English mile inland from high-water mark, from Rock Point to Bonne Bay, inclusive...and from Bonne Bay to Cape St John, to half an English mile inland from high-water mark.' The Convention also stated at Article III in respect of concurrent fishing rights on the Labrador Coast—and this was of significance in relation to Lake Melville—that 'the said French concurrent right of fishing shall terminate at the embouchures or outlets of rivers and creeks'.[2]

A Canadian argument was then deployed in regard to the Indian reservations said to have been created in the Labrador by the Proclamation of 1763 to the exclusion of any justifiable territorial claims from Newfoundland. The number of these Indians, Montagnais, Nascopies and others,

[1] Patent Roll, 3 Geo. III, p. v, no. 15.

[2] In the Privy Council, In the matter of the boundary between . . . Canada and . . . Newfoundland, Convention between Great Britain and France, London, 14 January 1883, vol. v of Joint Appendix, no. 930, p. 2188.

was estimated at roughly two to four thousand at this time. They lived in both the Hudson's Bay Company territories later annexed to Quebec and in that part of the Labrador peninsula which was now the subject of dispute. The Proclamation, Mr Macmillan reminded the Committee, had been concerned not only with the disposal of Lower Canada and Newfoundland following the Treaty of Paris but also with East and West Florida and Grenada. It had declared it

> to be our Royal will and pleasure... to reserve under our sovereignty, protection and dominion, for the use of the said Indians, all the land and territories not included within the limits of our said three new governments, or within the limits of the territory granted to the Hudson's Bay Company—as also all the land and territories lying to the westward of the sources of the rivers which fall into the sea from the west and northwest as aforesaid: and we do hereby strictly forbid, on pain of our displeasure, all our loving subjects from making any purchases or settlements whatever, or taking possession of any of the lands above reserved, without our especial leave and licence for that purpose first obtained.[1]

Mr Macmillan went on to argue that there were two persons, at the time of the Proclamation, recognized as concerned in the Labrador peninsula—the newly appointed Government of Quebec and the Governor of Newfoundland. But to the latter there had been entrusted only the care and inspection of a coastal strip. The Governor of Quebec on the other hand had received under his own Commission detailed Instructions as to his duties towards the Indian tribes, and these same tribes, living in the hinterland of Labrador now claimed by Newfoundland, had in 1763 applied to that Governor for protection. Thus 'instead of finding the Governor of Newfoundland equipped to grant licences to trade and all these things regulating the Indians, the Governor of Quebec has all those powers and the Governor of Newfoundland has not any of them'.[2]

Seen, therefore, from the Canadian viewpoint the chessmen on the board at the time of the Royal Proclamation of 1763 and later were, the Hudson's Bay territory: the Quebec territory, which later absorbed it, the Indian reservations and the Governor of Newfoundland with his coastal territory. There was thus no undistributed hinterland such as the Newfoundland side were claiming. Even though the Indian reservations might not have been subject to any precise or definite government, they none the less remained in the hands of the Crown under the direct personal responsibility of His Majesty.

[1] *Ibid.* Royal Proclamation of 7 October 1763, vol. v of Joint Appendix.

[2] In the Privy Council, In the matter of the boundary between ... Canada and ... Newfoundland, oral evidence, 14th day, Mr Macmillan, p. 983.

I humbly submit [Mr Macmillan said in closing the Canadian case] that the watershed line down to the backbone of Labrador which my friend [Sir John Simon] maintains was the implied boundary of the coast of Labrador, and the line along the coast above the St Lawrence, which my friend also claims as his boundary, have not been established. I have shown that there was an Indian territory there which was reserved to the Crown. That again fits in with my humble submission at the outset, that these matters were not in the minds at all of the persons whose governing consideration was the use of the sea for an open and free fishery. The submission which I make that the grant was limited to the preservation and fostering of an open and free fishery by giving a limited territorial jurisdiction along the coast between the points on the coast, is not only the most natural, but the most appropriate interpretation of this grant.[1]

If, Mr Macmillan concluded, he had successfully established that no more than a littoral jurisdiction in the Labrador had been afforded to the Governor of Newfoundland and his successors, then there remained to be determined whether, in the light of other precedents, this jurisdiction should run 200 yards, half a mile, a mile or say five miles inland from the sinuosities of the coastline. The Canadian Government had instructed him to propose one mile as fairly meeting the interests of the timber industry. But 'the matter is in your Lordships' hands...As far as my clients are concerned, whatever figure your Lordships thought was a maximum so as to ensure the embracing of as much territory as could on any reasonable view be appurtenant to the jurisdiction, would in no sense be resented by my clients at all.'[2]

We may now conveniently turn back to a consideration of the Newfoundland counter-case. Compared with the narrowly legalistic and relatively defensive Canadian presentation, Sir John Simon's was a masterly, sweeping tour de force. Like some well-tuned engine he drove on for days, sometimes ingeniously deflecting the course of his argument in the face of an obstacle thrown up by the Board, but more frequently demolishing with silken firmness the irrelevant observations with which Viscount Haldane in particular seemed to delight in interrupting his case. Indeed, viewed at this distance in time certain of these exchanges have an Alice in Wonderland quality. On the 'height of land' argument, for instance, the following occurred:

Viscount Haldane. There is no evidence to show that there was the height of land which they thought there was.

Sir John Simon. I may perhaps be wrong, in these scientific matters one is easily misled, but I should have thought that dealing with a country which was

[1] In the Privy Council, In the matter of the boundary between . . . Canada and . . . Newfoundland, oral evidence, 14th day, Mr MacMillan, p. 990.

[2] *Ibid.* p. 991.

known not to be as flat as a table...it followed inevitably there was a height of land.

Viscount Haldane. It does not tell you there is a height of land in the document.

Sir John Simon. It does not.

The Lord Chancellor. The words are 'on the river which lie within'. That carries you up.

Sir John Simon. One is clear that water would run downhill even in Labrador. Therefore if you give people the land upon the rivers...

Lord Sumner. Sometimes the rivers are frozen in that district.

Sir John Simon. I agree, and sometimes for the greater part of the year, but even then water will not run uphill.[1]

However, their Lordships doubtless felt that some light relief was by now essential. They were then well into the twelfth day of the hearing.

Sir John Simon's must have been one of the longest addresses in the Judicial Committee's history. It was a case, he said in opening, which 'my friends and I have been at pains to try to prepare...in the most convenient form, because the volumes before your Lordships, one red bound volume, and I think seven[2] green volumes, have a very formidable aspect'.[3]

Like Mr Macmillan, Sir John Simon insisted from the outset that the Judicial Committee was not being called on to settle such boundary between Quebec and Newfoundland in the Labrador peninsula as might seem to them reasonable, but to determine what that boundary actually was. And that decision had to be settled on some principle. The principle which Canada had sought to apply was that the coasts and territories referred to in the many relevant documents meant no more than 'a selvedge of one mile from the water's edge without even penetrating the land in places where there are inlets—as there are on this coast'.[4] Hamilton Inlet, for instance, was a very large opening.

Sir John then deployed the main Newfoundland argument. It was that 'the location and definition of the boundary to which Newfoundland is entitled in Labrador is a boundary which is to be ascertained by reference to the height of land. It has Cape Chidley at one end, and has a terminus which has differed from time to time at the other end'.[5] The definitions of 'height of land' and 'coast' were vital to the outcome of the case. There were many authorities and much documentation which could be quoted in defence of either party. Newfoundland would seek to show that

[1] *Ibid.* 12th day, pp. 805–6.

[2] There were in fact eight.

[3] In the Privy Council, In the matter of the boundary between . . . Canada and . . . Newfoundland, oral evidence, 1st day, Sir John Simon, p. 2.

[4] *Ibid.* pp. 4–5.

[5] *Ibid.* p. 16.

it had never been the practical intention of the Imperial power to restrict the authority of successive Governments in Newfoundland to a mere coastal band of the Labrador. Such an aim had certainly not been in the minds of those who had granted their Charter to the Hudson's Bay Company. Moreover, when one came to study contemporary maps of, for example, the Colony of Virginia, it could be seen that, although described as 'les costes de Virginie', the area embraced all the territory lying between the coasts and the height of land behind them. The Newfoundland Government did not seek to claim that, prior to the discovery at the close of the nineteenth century of large tracts of timber suitable for pulpwood, the interior of the Labrador had been of any significance to them. Earlier than that date both Quebequers and Newfoundlanders would have been hard put to it to place any value on this inhospitable and virtually unknown land. Now, however, it had to be administered by someone, not only along the coastline, but in depth.

Sir John Simon then sought to show that, as early as the Treaty of Utrecht, attempts had been made by Commissarys appointed by the French and British kings to determine the limits of the lands allotted to either country under the Treaty in the area of Hudson Bay. Even the inconclusive lines then drawn on inaccurate maps went some way to support the deductions he was drawing as to the correlation between 'coasts' and watershed. In the same way the Treaty of Paris, when referring to the French cession to Britain of Canada with all its dependencies including the island of Cape Breton and 'all the other islands and coasts', did not and could not imply that a mathematical line or a strip a mile wide was being ceded. What had been at issue was a great land mass bounded on the sea by the seashore. Thus, whatever the language of the Treaty, whatever the terms of the Commissions to successive Governors of Newfoundland from Graves onwards, however much the coastal limits of Newfoundland Labrador might have been altered by statute between 1763 and 1825, precedent alone demanded that coast and watershed go hand in hand.[1] If proof positive of this intent on the part of earlier legal draftsmen was required, it could be found in the Act of 1825, which removed from Newfoundland and gave to Quebec a southerly portion of Labrador described as 'The Coast of Labrador'. Yet that definition was such as to annex to the province, not a mere coastal strip, but a piece of land 40 miles deep at its eastern and 120 miles deep at its south-western sides. The same Act was of further significance to the Newfoundland claim in that it referred to parts of the territory to be reannexed to Quebec as reaching 'as far as the fifty-

[1] For the development of this argument much credit was due to the work of Mr Furlong and Mr F. J. Morris of Newfoundland.

second degree of north latitude'—at which level it had been contemporaneously recorded that the St John River had its source.

As the relevant documents showed, Newfoundland was totally excluded from the Labrador peninsula in favour of Quebec between the passage of the Statutes of 1774 and 1809. But here too dispossession favoured the Newfoundland case since in the recital to the Act of 1774 it was stated that 'Whereas by arrangements made by the said Royal Proclamation [of October 1763] a very large extent of country...was left, without any provision being made for the administration of civil government therein...'. It seemed irresistible, so ran the Newfoundland argument, that anything less than a substantial continuous area of territory—and not merely selvedge—was then being statutorily transferred. 'My whole case', Sir John Simon re-emphasized, 'is that what Newfoundland got was not a strip a mile wide, but it got a territory and this territory is now being taken away from it. I want to put the point to the Board and I can put it without any map...'[1] In other words, whatever the Government of Newfoundland acquired on the mainland in 1763, that same area, neither more nor less, passed by the Statute of 1774 and was again returned to Newfoundland by the Act of 1809. The sole question was—How much was this area?

Here the maps of a distinguished Canadian geographer, Mr A. P. Low, printed following his expeditions to the Labrador peninsula between 1892 and 1896 could be called in evidence. Mr Low had marked in from Cape Chidley southwards the approximate watershed dividing coastal from continental Labrador. The size of the area shown as lying to the east of the height of land was not lost on the Judicial Committee when read with the Imperial Order in Council of 1880. This, in consequence of successive British North America Acts, had laid down that 'from and after the first day of September, 1880, all British territories and Possessions in North America not already included within the Dominion of Canada...shall (with the exception of the Colony of Newfoundland and its dependencies) become and be annexed to and form part of the said Dominion of Canada...'[2] As Lord Sumner commented after studying Low's maps: 'You have to say that the area you want, whatever it is, is Newfoundland according to the Order in Council of 1880; so it rests on you to march inland and establish your line if you can.'[3]

The Newfoundland case, thus far presented, had sought to demolish the Canadian argument that no more than the definition of a mere coastal

[1] In the Privy Council, In the matter of the boundary between . . . Canada and . . . Newfoundland, oral evidence, 1st day, Sir John Simon, p. 53.
[2] *Ibid.* Order in Council of 31 July 1880, vol. 1 of Joint Appendix, no. 41, p. 241.
[3] *Ibid.* oral evidence, 2nd day, p. 84.

selvedge was at stake. But there were other issues to be faced. Not least of these were the political, strategic and mercantile interests and intentions of the Imperial power in regard to Newfoundland and the Labrador from 1763 onwards. Was the Labrador a mere fishing station? If so, how far inland, if at all, could the Governor's writ be said to run?

On the issue of jurisdiction, for instance, the Commission granted in 1825 to Sir Thomas Cochrane as Governor of Newfoundland had declared it to be 'our will and pleasure that there shall henceforward be a Council without our said Island and Territories'; and further that the Governor should have power to 'erect and appoint or set apart convenient Court Houses for the holding the [*sic*] Supreme Court and Circuit Courts within the said Island and territories'.[1] Admittedly, in an area so sparsely inhabited as the Labrador then was, the duties of Circuit Courts could not have been onerous. But contemporary records show that justice had at least reached to the inmost end of Hamilton Inlet which itself was close on 120 miles from the sea. In fact a Circuit Court heard cases there in August 1827. It could therefore hardly have been the intention of the drafters of the Governor's Commission that 'the Supreme Court was going to sit on the sands of the seashore'.[2]

Weighty historical arguments had also been adduced on the Canadian side to show that throughout the period in which the Labrador was being kicked like a lawyer's football between Quebec and Newfoundland, it had been the deliberate policy of successive British Governments to keep the Island and its dependencies free from settlement. That story has already been briefly traced in the first chapter of this book. The antecedents of the anti-settlement policy had also been graphically described in the 'Representation of the Lords Commissioners for Trade and Plantations to His Majesty relating to the Newfoundland Trade and Fishing dated 19th December 1718'.[3] While this document looked back to events long before the Treaties of Utrecht and Paris, its whole burden was to show how injurious permanent settlement or attempts at it had always been to the English mercantile and fishing interests, and how at various times measures had been taken to prevent or limit it. Thus, the so-called 'Western Charter' granted by Charles I in February 1633; the Letters Patent of January 1660, confirming the Charter and adding further restrictions on settlement; and the new Charter of January 1678 followed more particularly by the Act of

[1] In the Privy Council, In the matter of the boundary between ... Canada and ... Newfoundland, Commission passed under the Great Seal appointing Sir Thomas Cochrane to be Governor, etc., over Newfoundland, 20 August 1825, vol. II of Joint Appendix, no. 179, p. 718.

[2] *Ibid.* oral evidence, 2nd day, Sir John Simon, p. 94.

[3] *Ibid.* vol. IV of Joint Appendix, no. 756, p. 1815.

1699 'to encourage the Trade to Newfoundland'. While all these measures contained severe sanctions on settlers intending or actual, the Lords Commissioners were forced to the conclusion that they had failed. The only solution for the survival of the fishery which they could then offer to the King was 'to remove the inhabitants or Planters to Nova Scotia or to some other of Your Majesty's Plantations in America'.[1] Equally to the point was the reference to Newfoundland in a survey of the Charter and Constitution of each of the American colonies which was submitted to the First Lord of the Treasury in May 1752 by James Abercromby. 'Newfoundland', he reported, 'though ranked amongst the Best and first in point of property belonging to this Kingdom, from the discovery thereof by Cabot...; yet the object of that Government relates to a kind of Police amongst Fisher Men and to them only.' Such references to the mercantile and naval policies of the Mother Country are familiar enough. The issue in this case was whether those policies, as applied in the sixteenth to eighteenth centuries, could be said still to be relevant at the time Newfoundland Labrador's coastal limits had been finally defined by the Imperial Statute of 1825.

On this point Sir John Simon was not slow to point out that only thirty years elapsed between that Act and the introduction of responsible government in Newfoundland. This forward step could hardly be interpreted as a continuation of the policy of discouraging settlement. Indeed, by 1870 and possibly several years before that date, numbers of Labrador 'liveyeres' were permanently settled not only along the coast but a long way up the various rivers.

This mass of counter-argument led Sir John Simon, when he completed his address on 28 October 1926 to hand in and interpret to the Committee ten propositions. These were:

First: that the basic document to be construed was Governor Grave's Commission of 1763 with its references to 'all the coasts and territories of Labrador'.

Second: that the Act of 1825 removing a southern area of the Labrador peninsula from Newfoundland: defining its extent and annexing it to Canada proved that the whole area in dispute was no mere coast line.

Third: that what was re-transferred in 1825 implied that what remained under Newfoundland jurisdiction also ran inland at least to the 52nd parallel.

Fourth: that the best available contemporary maps indicated that the headwaters of the River St John would be found in approximately latitude 52 or slightly further north.

Fifth: While the primary object in including a part of Labrador in Newfound-

[1] In the Privy Council, In the matter of the boundary between . . . Canada and . . . Newfoundland, vol. IV of Joint Appendix, no. 765.

land had been to extend and maintain the open and free fishery, it by no means followed that the area annexed was limited to a mere fringe.

Sixth: The immediately preceding proposition could the more readily be sustained in regard to an area which at the material time, and indeed long afterwards, was considered to be worthless.

Seventh: The word 'coast' had been in constant use since at least the 16th century to indicate a territory with a defined sea frontage which stretched to the height of land.

Eighth: The above interpretation could be confirmed by the three following considerations:

(*a*) It secures that the additional area entrusted to Newfoundland does not trench upon the area already belonging to the Hudson's Bay Company, for the height of land running South from Cape Chidley will be at one and the same time the Western Boundary of the one and the Eastern Boundary of the other;

(*b*) it explains why the area retransferred to Quebec in 1825, though bounded on the North by the 52nd parallel, was known to be part of the 'coast' previously annexed to Newfoundland;

(*c*) it provides a scientific and practical test which enables the actual course of the boundary to be delimited with precision by the application of a prescribed formula to the physical facts, as and when those facts become precisely ascertained.[1]

Ninth: The views advanced from the Newfoundland side had been continuously supported by the official maps and public declarations of the Dominion of Canada right down to the time when the backland of Newfoundland Labrador was first known to be worth having.

Tenth: No other interpretations could lead to the proper location and definition of a boundary.

And so, concluded Sir John: 'I most respectfully submit on behalf of the ancient Colony of Newfoundland that the considerations which it has been my duty to endeavour to lay before the Committee should lead to the conclusion that the boundary is a boundary to be fixed by reference to the height of land.'[2]

The decision of the Judicial Committee was delivered by the Lord Chancellor on 1 March 1927.[3] It was unhesitatingly in favour of the Newfoundland claim. It was, moreover, in view of the wealth of documentation and pleading which had preceded it, a masterpiece of compression. In an issue 'worthy of the judicature of a Roman Senate', to quote the language of an earlier judge, Lord Hardwicke, the duty of the Board had been, as their

[1] In the Privy Council, In the matter of the boundary between . . . Canada and . . . Newfoundland, oral evidence, 4th day, Sir John Simon, pp. 295–6.

[2] *Ibid.* p. 296.

[3] In the Privy Council, In the matter of the boundary between . . . Canada and . . . Newfoundland, report of the Lords of the Judicial Committee of the Privy Council, vol. XII.

report re-emphasized 'not to consider where the boundary in question might wisely and conveniently be drawn but only to determine where, under the documents of title which have been brought to their notice, the boundary is actually to be found'.[1]

After traversing the history of North America from the capture of Quebec onwards and referring to the Commission and Instructions of 1763 to Governor Graves, the Committee's report drew attention to the fact that in neither of these documents was any distinction made between the island of Newfoundland on the one hand, and the coast of Labrador on the other. Both were included in identical terms in the territories placed under the care of the Governor. The powers applicable to the one were equally applicable to the other. Nor was the oft-quoted Royal Proclamation of 7 October 1763, in so far as it dealt with Newfoundland, the Labrador and the creation of Indian reservations, more than declaratory of an annexation already effected under the Commission to Graves. The Proclamation was not in fact the origin of the title of Newfoundland to its territory in Labrador. Nor did it take anything from the rights conferred on the Governor by his Commission.

The basic matters in dispute, continued the report, were that the Dominion of Canada contended that the relevant documents should be construed as meaning that Newfoundland's territorial rights in the Labrador should extend no further inland than one mile from high-water mark. The Colony of Newfoundland's contention on the other hand was that, between the fifty-second degree of North latitude and Cape Chidley, the boundary should follow the course of the watershed of the rivers flowing into the Atlantic. In presenting their arguments, both parties had agreed that the word 'coast' was one of undefined meaning. Yet, in the Committee's view, much evidence could be adduced (cf. Gold Coast, Coromandel Coast) to show that the word had frequently been used as signifying a whole country. It had also been common ground that the practical effect of the statutes, etc., in question had been to give the Government of Newfoundland 'not mere rights of inspection and regulation exercisable upon a line of shore, but territory which became as much part of the Colony as the island of Newfoundland itself, and which was capable of being defined by metes and bounds'.[2] Whatever the Canadian argument about the language of the Proclamation of 1763, the plain inference to be drawn from the other documents cited was that what had

[1] *Ibid.* p. 2.

[2] In the Privy Council, In the matter of the boundary between . . . Canada and . . . Newfoundland, report of the Lords of the Judicial Committee of the Privy Council, vol. XII, p. 11.

then been added to Newfoundland was 'a tract of land, having a boundary which can be located and defined'.[1] No alternatives had at any time been advanced other than that that boundary should be defined by reference either to the sinuosities of the coastline or to the height of land.

Moreover, references in the Commissions to Graves and his successors between 1763 and 1774 to 'territories', 'planters or inhabitants' and to the holding of quarter sessions supported the contention that 'coast' could properly be construed as including a considerable area of land. In addition, use of the watershed or height of land was certainly familiar at the material time in British North America and was shown in many contemporary maps. It had also been accepted as a doctrine of international law—and here the report cited Hall,[2] Westlake[3] and Lawrence[4] in support—that the occupation of a sea coast carried with it a right to the whole territory drained by the rivers which empty their waters into its line. But above all, the Statute of 1825 pleaded in Newfoundland's favour. The very definition of the southern area of the Labrador then re-annexed to Lower Canada showed conclusively that the territory must have a sizeable hinterland. It was, therefore, as difficult to sustain the Canadian thesis of a mere coastal strip in face of this legislation as it was to suggest in practice that the coastal boundary should now be drawn one mile inland on the grounds that this would provide a territory accessible and useful to the fishery. What would then happen on the long stretches of coast bounded by high cliffs and thus inaccessible from the sea? Or to the many deep inlets? Was it to be supposed that a realistic boundary could be drawn by treating the great Hamilton Inlet as part of the sea coast? And had it really been the intention of the statesmen of 1763 that the whole interior should be put 'entirely at the mercy as regards customs duties and otherwise of the Government of Newfoundland'?[5]

Admittedly the Canadian Government had advanced strong reasons to show that the fisheries had supplied the principal, if not the only motive for the annexation of the Labrador coast to Newfoundland. Like the island, it was to be a base for fishing and a nursery of English seamen. But what George III and his advisers had in effect sought in 1763 went far wider.

[1] *Ibid.*

[2] William Edward Hall, *A Treatise on International Law* (5th ed. Oxford, Clarendon Press, 1904), p. 104.

[3] John Westlake, *International Law*, part I (Peace, 2nd ed. Cambridge, University Press, 1910), p. 113.

[4] T. J. Lawrence, *The Principles of International Law* (3rd ed. Boston, Heath, 1905), p. 151.

[5] *Ibid.*

They had envisaged not only a fishery but a government on the coast with power to administer justice; to encourage trade and to erect forts for purposes of defence. Even on the fisheries question, the Canadian argument failed since not only cod, seal and sea-cow were involved. The salmon fisheries too had been mentioned in Graves's Instructions and the salmon fishery could only be fully protected by the grant of jurisdiction over rivers and inland lakes as well as over the seashore. On this issue the Committee's report concluded that 'the reference to the fisheries tends rather to extend than to limit the grant'.[1]

There was still further matter to the advantage of the Newfoundland case—the grants between 1765–1871 of 60,000 acres of land, sometimes running thirty miles inland from the Labrador coast, to the Moravian missionaries: and further grants from the King in Council in 1774 to John Agnew and others to prospect for minerals up to sixty miles inland from low-water mark. Effective jurisdiction and customs duties exercised or levied by successive Governments of Newfoundland since 1825 had, moreover, never been challenged from Canada. Nor *per contra* could the Board find any evidence of the exercise of Canadian jursidiction in the territory in dispute. Furthermore, the Committee found it significant that no Canadian authority had ever challenged—indeed a Committee of the Canadian Privy Council had approved its very language—the terms of a dispatch, dated 12 November 1874 from the Governor-General of Canada to the British Ambassador in Washington.[2] Written in reply to an inquiry made of the latter by the U.S. Secretary of State 'whether any part of Labrador is separated from the jurisdiction of either the Dominion of Canada or that of Newfoundland', Lord Dufferin had written:

The Honourable the Secretary of State to whom this despatch, with enclosures, has been referred, reports that the boundary-line between the Dominion of Canada and Labrador is a line drawn due north and south from the Bay or Harbour of Anse au Blanc Sablon, near the Straits of Belle Isle, as far as the 52nd degree of north latitude; that Labrador extends eastwards and northward from that point of Hudson's Straits.

That the division-line in the interior separating Labrador from the Dominion of Canada has only been defined as far north as the 52nd degree of north latitude, but it has been assumed that the boundary-line in the interior would have taken the direction laid down on the accompanying map, which follows the height of land.

[1] In the Privy Council, In the matter of the boundary between . . . Canada and . . . Newfoundland, report of the Lords of the Judicial Committee of the Privy Council, vol. XII, p. 16.

[2] *Ibid.* p. 21

That Labrador, with the islands adjacent thereto, is annexed to Newfoundland, and under the Government of that Island.

Attached to the Report of the Secretary of State are extracts from the Imperial Statute bearing on the question, and a map showing the exact boundary on the coast and the assumed boundary in the interior.[1]

To complete Canadian discomfiture, the Committee's report rubbed in the fact that this and other maps indicating the supposed inland boundary of the Labrador were Canadian in origin. Not until 1900 was the boundary now claimed by Canada to be found in any map. Given this weight of argument, it was scarcely surprising that the Judicial Committee should conclude 'that the claim of the Colony of Newfoundland is in substance made out'.[2] The Committee now finally declared the boundary between Canada and Newfoundland in the Labrador peninsula to be

a line drawn due north from the eastern boundary of the bay or harbour of Anse au Sablon as far as the fifty-second degree of north latitude, and from thence westward along that parallel until it reaches the Romaine river, and then northward along the left or east bank of that river and its head waters to their source and from thence due north to the crest of the watershed or height of land there, and from thence westward and northward along the crest of the watershed of the rivers flowing into the Atlantic Ocean until it reaches Cape Chidley; and they will humbly advise His Majesty accordingly.[3]

It might well be asked why so much attention should be paid to a dispute which has long since passed into the academic pigeon holes. But this would be to ascribe to the case less legal, constitutional and practical significance than it deserves. In legal terms alone the hearing was unique in the Privy Council's annals. Not only was it of singular length. It was also the first occasion on which two States within the Commonwealth had agreed to invoke Section 4 of the Judicial Committee Act of 1833 to decide a matter in controversy between them. There has been no comparable case since then: and the only previous dispute involving boundaries within Her Majesty's dominions—the Ontario–Manitoba dispute of 1884—had been one domestic to Canada alone.

Although the case was decided in strict law it was also unique in that it cast the Judicial Committee virtually in the role of a Board of Arbitration between two self-governing countries within the Commonwealth. This too is a fact not without significance, given latter-day suggestions from within

[1] In the Privy Council, In the matter of the boundary between . . . Canada and . . . Newfoundland, report of the Lords of the Judicial Committee of the Privy Council, vol. XII, p. 21.

[2] *Ibid.* p. 22.

[3] *Ibid.* p. 23.

the modern Commonwealth itself that the steadily declining oversea functions of the Judicial Committee might be revived by giving it, or some analogous body, some supreme arbitrating authority on behalf of the Commonwealth association. When the Labrador case was heard in 1926 the then Dominion Governments all freely accepted the Judicial Committee as an ultimate court of appeal both in relation to municipal law and in respect of constitutional issues. But today, as the independent Commonwealth expands and the concept of a common allegiance to the Crown and with it that of the Sovereign as the Fountain of Justice has diminished, increasingly few Commonwealth member countries still retain the right of appeal to the Privy Council.[1] At some future date, when the nationalist sensitivities of the newer member states have lessened, the 1926 case might well be looked back to as a precedent on which to build some new relationship between the Judicial Committee and the Commonwealth.

But above all the settlement of the Labrador boundary was to prove of significance far beyond the rosiest dreams of the disputants at the time. While Newfoundlanders had always clung with the optimism of despair to the illusion that the ground beneath their feet was packed with hidden wealth, it was probably the Canadian Government which had the shrewder idea of the potential mineral, timber and water resources of the Labrador. Neither Government, however, could foresee the astonishing developments which the pressures of a second world war were to bring about—the construction of the great airbase at Goose Bay: the discovery of huge deposits of high-grade iron ore in central Labrador and the construction of a railway from the Gulf of the St Lawrence into the heart of this forbidding territory. The recital of these developments must be left for a later chapter. Here it is enough to say that the ruling given in that quiet room in Downing Street nearly forty years ago is still revolutionizing the economy of Newfoundland. What began as a wrangle over limited timber concessions finally endowed a small, one-commodity community with diversified sources of wealth and livelihood beyond even its wildest hopes.

[1] They are Australia, New Zealand, Ceylon, Malaysia (by special provision involving the Head of State of that country), Sierra Leone, Uganda (on matters solely relating to the constitution), Jamaica, Trinidad, Malawi, Malta and The Gambia.

12

SINS OF OMISSION: ROYAL COMMISSION

> The difficulties with which the country is faced, while accentuated by the effects of the world depression are in reality the result of persistent extravagance and neglect of proper financial principles on the part of successive Governments prior to 1931. Royal Commission Report, 1933

1929—Public debt $87·7 million: Revenue $11·5 million, of which over 75 per cent came from customs and excise duties: the value of exported codfish $12 million compared to wartime peak figures of some $25 million per annum. And still the bonanza continued. By now Squires had returned to public life as leader of a Liberal 'Cabal of all the Talents'. 'Appealing to the country on his record of achievements in industrial development, Sir Richard was welcomed back by the people with amazing enthusiasm. The country opened its arms to him: and such was the people's faith in his promise of still more industrial development and expansion should he be returned to power, they gave him an overwhelming victory at the polls.'[1]

Alas! for faith: alas! for expansion. Had there been money in the till, reserves to fall back on, all might yet have been well. As it was, the lessons of the 1890s had been brushed aside. Assets had been mortgaged, the future pledged, the siren voices of hire purchase bagmen all too often listened to entranced, and the Island embarked on a course from which no remedy could now rescue it save retrenchment of the strictest kind. Even by 1930 the landslide might have been averted. One year on it was too late.

There has since been much controversy about the true reasons for Newfoundland's financial plight. Some Canadian apologists have vigorously rebutted the charge that the blame lay squarely with local politicians. Their argument has been that, when the economic blizzard of the 1930s struck the world, no primary producing country as small and badly placed as Newfoundland could conceivably have survived unaided. Nor, in default of her own currency, could she resort to devaluation. And there were overriding exchange difficulties in her way; since, while she exported mainly to Europe and the sterling area, much of her imports had to be bought against the dollar. Moreover, in those pre-war days there was still something faintly immoral about currency manipulation.

But in Britain the general opinion was that the Colony had grossly mismanaged its own affairs and must therefore shoulder the main burden

[1] Smallwood, *N.N.* p. 192.

of guilt for all that subsequently befell it. Certainly both Governments and merchants had proved selfish and shortsighted. Not even in the halcyon days had any real effort been made to eliminate the vicious Truck system, which still held the fisherman in thrall to his supplier. Scant energy had gone into applying scientific and rational methods to the conduct of the fishery. In the headlong pursuit of an industrial chimera, Newfoundland's basic industry had been neglected. The politicians concentrated on vote-catching at the expense of a gullible and still largely undereducated population: a gulf and a sense of enmity divided rich from poor. Greed, graft and corruption stalked the land. By the time the storm broke, not only the financial structure but the moral fibre of the country had been sapped.

Even the Ottawa Agreements of 1932, which might in time have benefited exports of fish and iron ore to Britain, were to prove of no avail. Collapse was already imminent. The financial year 1931/2 showed a deficit on current account of over $4 million and the public debt was by now perilously close to the $100 million mark. It represented in fact almost $400 per head of a population composed chiefly of fishermen on the very borderlines of subsistence. Interest payments on the debt had reached the staggering proportion of 65 per cent of average revenue over the preceding years. Not surprisingly, with the onset of world depression, the seemingly inexhaustible supply of loans from overseas dried up almost overnight. In the fateful period between 1931 and 1932 the value of fishery exports slumped from ten to six million dollars and of exports overall from $33·5 million to $26·6 million.

Dry docks, railway extensions, tourist highways, telegraph and steamship services—all in themselves desirable—had been financed from loans. War pensions and an increasing commitment in respect of unemployment relief hung, additional heavy albatrosses, round the now struggling Government's neck. To add to the general gloom, the inshore fishery failed and many fishermen were driven to seek the pitiful help in kind—$1·80 worth of tea, flour, pork and molasses per month—which was all the state could offer. The last loan to be negotiated—for $5 million in 1930—was followed by damning silence when next year efforts were made to raise a further $8 million. Faced with an—in local terms—enormous deficit in the coming financial year, the Government appealed urgently to London for advice. It was the first public admission of defeat. In response, the British Government dispatched a senior member of the Board of Inland Revenue and a Treasury official to St John's. Thanks to their help and persuasive powers temporary relief was gained through a loan of $2 million from the Canadian banks and an internally raised 'Prosperity' Loan of $2½ million. The desperate nature of affairs could, however, be judged from the conditions attaching to these loans. The banks stipulated that all revenue raised from customs duties should in future be paid into a special account with the Bank of Montreal. The Imperial Oil Company, which subscribed the bulk of the 'Prosperity' Loan received in return a monopoly on the import, manufacture and distribution of all petroleum products. Even though, paradoxically, some $26 million were still on deposit in the banks, hardly an individual Newfoundlander could be found to subscribe.

Some effort was now made to set the financial house in order. In 1932, under the Newfoundland Treasury Control Act, a measure of financial control was belatedly introduced under which new expenditure could only be incurred by written consent of the Department of Finance: and administrative economies were made. But as expenditure was pruned so, of necessity, customs revenue declined and the bill for able-bodied relief increased. By the autumn of 1933 default on the next interest payments on the public debt was averted only through joint emergency action by the Canadian and British Governments. Such stopgap measures could not long continue. Newfoundland was dropping out of the bottom of the world. It was time now not for first aid, but for surgery. It fell to the new and, as it proved, last Prime Minister of an independent Island, Mr F. C. Alderdice, to make one supreme appeal to his countrymen to rescue Newfoundland from the twin spectres of default and bankruptcy. Speaking to the new budget in June 1933 he urged that: 'The only possibility of a real and lasting revival of prosperity in this country depends upon the realization by every member of the population that the qualities of self-help and self-reliance are not only a very precious possession, but are indispensable qualities for ensuring the future welfare and independence both of the individual and of the Dominion.'[1]

But even before that date, the Newfoundland Government had realized that they could go no further without external help. At their request a Royal Commission had, in February, been appointed to investigate the whole situation.

'Whereas', ran the sonorous first preamble to the Royal Warrant, 'on the advice of our Ministers in our United Kingdom of Great Britain and Northern Ireland, in our Dominion of Canada and in our Island of Newfoundland We have deemed it expedient that a Commission should issue forthwith to examine into the future of Newfoundland and in particular to report on the financial situation and prospects therein.'[2]

The terms of the Warrant were themselves significant. Although by now

[1] Hon. F. C. Alderdice's Budget Speech, *Newfoundland House of Assembly Proceedings*, 29 June 1933.

[2] Royal Warrant, 17 February 1933, Cmd. 4479.

it was a question for Newfoundland of 'needs must', this was not an investigation thrust upon an independent country against its will. The terms of the Balfour Declaration and the spirit of the Statute of Westminster were safeguarded to the hilt. Only following a request from the sovereign Parliament of Newfoundland was the Royal Commission invited and empowered to take evidence in the Island. Significantly its high-powered three-man team consisted of representatives from Canada and Newfoundland as well as from Britain. Whatever they might later have to say about the highly critical tone of the Report, Newfoundlanders could not subsequently complain that the Royal Commission had been foisted by an Imperial power upon an unwilling people.

The Commissioners were quickly off the mark, assembling in St John's on 13 March and holding their first public sitting three days later. The Chairman, Lord Amulree, was supported by Mr C. E. M. Magrath and by Sir William Stavert, K.B.E., a prominent Island lawyer. Their Secretary was Mr P. A. Clutterbuck[1] of the Dominions Office. The eventual report, published in October of the same year, owed much to the latter's grasp of the complex problems with which Lord Amulree and his colleagues were faced. For a government publication it was (and indeed still is) an eminently readable document. As the Parliamentary Under Secretary for Dominion Affairs, Mr Malcolm MacDonald, was to say later in Parliament: 'I went one day on a three hour train journey and I took with me this forbidding looking Book and also a very attractive novel...But at the end of three hours, I found myself still immersed in this Report.'[2]

The Report made a penetrating analysis of Newfoundland's political and economic ills. It covered in detail the conditions prevailing in the various industries; dissected their failings, and proposed reforms. It pulled no punches in its criticisms of the behaviour of Government, religious bodies, merchants and industrialists and framed a series of far-reaching constitutional recommendations which, while causing serious misgivings at the time, now prove to have been amply vindicated by events. The one principal accusation running through the Report, which in retrospect lays the Royal Commission open to some criticism, was its unremitting attack on local politicians and merchants for their responsibility in allowing their country to drift into so parlous a situation. Time and again the Report was to underline the reckless and extravagant use of public funds as one of the principal reasons leading to Newfoundland's near bankruptcy.

[1] Later to become after a distinguished career as British High Commissioner to Canada and India and Ambassador to the Irish Republic, Permanent Under Secretary of State, Commonwealth Relations Office, as Sir Alexander Clutterbuck, G.C.M.G., M.C.

[2] Parliamentary Debates, Commons, vol. 284, cols. 215 ff., 12 December 1933.

As to the physical and moral condition of the people the Report if anything understated the case. The effects of the starvation diet of those bitter years, which saw an alarming increase in such illnesses as rickets and tuberculosis, are still to be traced in the faces of those who were young men at the time. But feckless though successive Governments had been, it is only fair to repeat that the root cause of Newfoundland's collapse was not political or even financial, but economic. As an export community she had been among the first to suffer from the world-wide recession. There was no fat on which she could live: no alternative resources on which she could call. Her fisheries admittedly seemed inexhaustible but: 'Natural resources at any given time are worth only what they can be sold for in raw or processed form in the market. In the case of the fishery, Newfoundland producers were not dissimilar from producers of Canadian wheat—they could produce much more than the market could at the time absorb.'[1]

The members of the Royal Commission travelled widely through the Island, holding some 100 formal sittings, receiving many memoranda and hearing upwards of 250 witnesses. They also took evidence in Canada. Their report, published in October 1933, contained a descriptive and historical introduction: a survey of current financial, economic and social conditions: a detailed analysis of all aspects of the fishery: a forecast of the prospects lying ahead in other industries; an examination of alternative solutions to the island's problems which raised, only to discard them, the questions of the sale of Newfoundland Labrador to Canada and the old bogey of confederation: and a definitive plan for political, constitutional and financial reconstruction.

The arguments for and against disposing of Newfoundland Labrador recall in some degree those mooted at the time of the sale of Alaska to the United States. It was agreed that the Labrador possessed water power facilities of a high order, including one waterfall on the Hamilton River estimated to be twice as high as the Niagara Falls. One day these natural resources might well be exploited. But in terms of sale, local witnesses estimated the value of the Labrador at figures as far apart as fifty and five hundred million dollars. Views on the future of the territory varied to a like degree. Some were for outright sale to Canada in return for her acceptance of Newfoundland's public debt. Others suggested that the administration of the territory should be turned over to Britain or that it be sold or leased to a trading company operating under charter. Yet other witnesses argued that it would be improper to transfer the sovereign rights which had been won in 1927 and that it was the duty of Newfoundlanders to preserve the Labrador for future generations. It was to this latter view

[1] Cmd. 4479.

that the Royal Commission itself inclined, emphasizing that 'the general opinion is that the territory is capable of great possibilities. Hitherto those possibilities have only been guessed at. As soon as funds permit, an aerial survey should be undertaken to ascertain...the nature of the territory and its approximate value.'[1]

Given all that has since happened in the development of this huge and unknown land, present and future generations of Newfoundlanders must bless the members of the Royal Commission for their prescience. Their refusal to give way to the short-term temptation of palliating the Island's financial ills by recommending the lease or sale of the Labrador was indeed a case of casting bread hopefully upon the waters.

On the issue of union with Canada the Commission agreed that this at first sight offered an attractive solution to the Island's difficulties. There had in the past few years been a revival of pro-confederation feeling in Canadian political circles. But it was in the last resort a matter of the terms which Newfoundland herself could negotiate. In this respect the Commission's analysis of the difficulties and advantages of achieving confederation threw a searching forward light on the negotiations of 1947–9, through which union was eventually achieved.

As the Report made clear a large part, if not the whole, of Newfoundland's public debt would have to be assumed by the Federal Government of Canada. The latter would also perforce take over certain public services of a federal character. But—and here was the rub—Newfoundland would become subject to the Canadian tariff, the revenue from local customs duties being paid into the Canadian exchequer. Canadian goods would therefore enter the Island duty-free.

> This would [ran the Report] doubtless have the beneficial effect of reducing the present cost of living; but the likelihood that branches of the Canadian department stores would be introduced into the Island would create consternation among the storekeepers in St John's. There is a very general apprehension in St John's that, in such circumstances, it would be impossible for local storekeepers and business houses to compete successfully with Canadian firms operating on a basis of mass production, and that in a short time they would find themselves swept away. Similarly, it is feared that the farmers would be unable to dispose of their produce in competition with Canadian hay and vegetables while the local factories would also be overwhelmed by the products of the Canadian manufacturing centres.[2]

But in the last resort, it was not on the sole insistence of the St John's merchant class, powerful and self-interested though it was, that the thought of confederation was brushed aside. It was rather for lack of any marked

[1] Cmd. 4479. [2] *Ibid.* p. 188.

enthusiasm on the mainland, combined with a general sentiment in the Island that 'the people of Newfoundland would much prefer to be master in their own home, however poor, than to play the part of Cinderella in the Canadian mansion'.[1] Or, as certain African politicians have more recently phrased it: 'Better to be free though poor, rather than not be free at all.'

While, therefore, the Royal Commission concluded that confederation was not at that time a practical issue, they went out of their way to emphasize that contacts between Newfoundland and Canada were constantly increasing. There was a shared currency; Canadian imports were by now half of total imports; educational links were being continuously strengthened; the powerful Methodist movement in Newfoundland had recently become part of the United Church of Canada; Canadian mining and life insurance companies were expanding their activities, and the development of a regular transatlantic air service would bring the two countries into still closer relationship.

But although these and other factors were to work unobtrusively over the next quarter of a century in shaping Newfoundland's ultimate destiny, it was clear that in the short-term Canada could not be looked to to save her neighbour. Such aid as could be given must come from Britain alone.

In framing its main recommendations, the Royal Commission was—in the atmosphere of the hour quite properly—guided by the principle that the country 'should be given a rest from politics for a period of years'.[2] Even the ideas of extending the life of the then government exceptionally so that it might run on unhampered until 1940: or of forming a National Government of Reconstruction were turned aside. 'We cannot', as the Report acidly commented, 'escape the conclusion that even if a National Government could be established on a basis which led to a suspension of political rivalry, the underlying influences which do so much to clog the wheels of administration, and to divert attention from the true interests of the country, would continue to form an insuperable handicap to the rehabilitation of the country.'[3]

References such as these: phrases such as 'the legacy of a generation of misgovernment' or 'an atmosphere tainted by political and party influences' were later to earn the Royal Commission and the Dominions Office in London much ill-will. But even if, by the wisdom of hindsight, the Report did somewhat exaggerate the misdeeds of politicians and their parties, the hard fact remains that a succession of misfortunes; a subsistence diet and the very struggle for survival had reduced the average Newfoundlander to a state of apathetic a-politism. As he in his heart well knew, the

[1] Cmd. 4479, p. 189. [2] *Ibid.* p. 195. [3] *Ibid.* p. 195.

politicians had long since tried and failed. He and his family were on the edge of starvation. He was in no mood to contest any solution, however revolutionary or draconian, provided it put bread in the mouths of his wife and children.

It was against this background that the Report, with suitable apologies to the British taxpayer, recommended that 'an immediate appeal should be made to the sympathy and good offices of the government of the United Kingdom'.[1]

Such good offices would have to take two forms: financial since it was now wholly beyond the resources of the people to support the current level of indebtedness; and political, because of the crying need for honest, clean and efficient government. Only through such a two-pronged approach could Newfoundland hope to win free from the 'malign influences which, developing from a prolonged period of misgovernment, have demoralised the people and warped their outlook'.[2]

The Royal Commission then launched its novel, and as it seemed to many at the time undemocratic, broadside—a recommendation for the suspension of the existing Legislature and Executive Council, Letters Patent and Royal Instructions, and the introduction in their stead of Government by Commission. Such a Commission, to consist of three members from Newfoundland and three from the United Kingdom, would be presided over by a Governor-in-Commission, in whom full legislative and executive power would be vested, but who would remain responsible to the British Government for his actions. Laws would be enacted by the Governor on the advice of his Commissioners, the power of disallowance being reserved to the Sovereign, who in turn would be advised by his United Kingdom Ministers, in practice the Secretary of State for Dominion Affairs. Appointments to the public service would also be the responsibility of the Governor-in-Commission, and the Commissioners, each of whom would take charge of a group of Government departments, would be collectively responsible for the proper working of the administrative machine. In any matter in which the Commissioners were divided in their opinions, a decision would be reached by voting, the Governor himself enjoying a casting vote. The suspension of the existing form of government would remain effective 'until such time as the Island may become self-supporting again'[3]—a phrase of which much was to be heard in later years.

In a country less physically and morally defeated such recommendations might well have led to disorders, if not bloodshed. It is a measure of the island's anguish that a people who had struggled for so long to gain and to

[1] *Ibid.* p. 192. [2] *Ibid.* p. 193. [3] *Ibid.* p. 201.

maintain their separate identity, could now be judged as having no more than an academic regard for the constitutional niceties, which seemed of small importance compared with the necessity of rescuing the country from its parlous state.

From the financial viewpoint, Lord Amulree and his colleagues urged that, as a *quid pro quo* for Newfoundland voluntarily surrendering her Dominion status and placing herself in the hands of a Commission, His Majesty's Government should for a time assume general responsibility for the finances of the Island. This responsibility should include the provision of an annual grant-in-aid and such measures as might seem necessary to reduce the burden of the public debt.

The Royal Commission summed up its general conclusions as follows:

> The objectives of the new Government will be twofold, (*a*) immediate, (*b*) such as can only be attained over a period of years. The immediate objective must be to rescue the country from the peril of collapse which now threatens to overwhelm it, to instil new heart and confidence in the people...the next objective must be the formulation of a long range plan, based on an exhaustive study of local conditions and calculated...so to strengthen the economic structure of the Island as to prevent the recurrence, at least in such extreme form, of those periodical visitations of pauperism and distress to which it has hitherto been subject.[1]

The Commission thus proved at once radical and conservative in its thinking—radical in recommending the suspension of responsible government; conservative in advocating no more than an immediate financial rescue operation. There was to be no capital grant for development; no five-year plan. It is tempting to speculate what their conclusions would have been a decade later when the Colonial Development and Welfare Acts were in full flood and budget financing and stringent Treasury control were no longer the twin pillars of Whitehall policy. But, looking to the future, the most important recommendation of all was that 'as soon as the Island's difficulties are overcome and the country is again self-supporting, responsible government, on request from the people of Newfoundland, would be restored'.[2] Morally, this sentiment was impeccable; politically the Report could hardly dare fail to contain it; practically, it was to give rise to much heart-searching ten years hence.

With the publication of the Commission's report on 4 October 1933 the scene of activity switched to London. British Ministers, impressed with the urgency of Newfoundland's plight, acted with speed. On 19 November Mr J. H. Thomas, then Secretary of State for the Dominions, telegraphed the Imperial Government's views to the Newfoundland Prime Minister.

[1] Cmd. 4479, p. 221. [2] *Ibid.* p. 224.

His Majesty's Government were, he said, ready, subject to the approval of Parliament, to accept the main recommendations of the Royal Commission. If the Newfoundland Government and Legislature were likewise disposed, the British Government would invite Parliament to pass the necessary legislation. Such legislation 'would be twofold in character i.e. both constitutional and financial. The first part would relate to the new constitutional arrangements to be made...and the second part would give concrete shape to the financial recommendations of the Commission, whereby general responsibility for the finances of the Island would be assumed by the United Kingdom...'[1]

With sad hearts but equal speed the Newfoundland Legislature debated and, by a large majority approved, an Address to His Majesty praying that new Letters Patent be issued for the period during which it had been suggested that His Majesty's Government should take over responsibility for the Island's affairs. It was now the turn of Parliament at Westminster to act.

[1] Royal Commission Report, papers relating to the Report, pp. 4–8, Cmd. 4479.

13

INTERLUDE AT WESTMINSTER

All the best countries default nowadays.

MR C. R. ATTLEE, 12 December 1933

On 7 December 1933, against a background of unemployment at home, financial stringency and scant sympathy for shorn Empire sheep, the House of Commons, where a small but vocal Labour minority faced the massive Government ranks, began its marathon debates on Newfoundland. It was a country of which most Members knew little. But even though many might have little financial warmth of heart, the House as a whole was well alive to the constitutional significance of what it was now being asked to underwrite.

The scene was set by the Chancellor of the Exchequer, who moved a Resolution to give effect to the financial aspects of the proposed settlement, including the provision of grants and loans and guarantees of the principal of and interest on Stock issued by the Government of Newfoundland. Mr Neville Chamberlain emphasized at the outset that the House was faced with 'a step which is unprecedented—the suspension for a time of the present status of the Dominion...'[1] Any Honourable Member, he added, would agree that some of the Royal Commission's Report, which was extremely plain spoken, made very painful reading. But apart from Britain's moral debt to an Empire partner, there were strong economic reasons why Newfoundland's financial credit should be preserved and confidence restored. His Majesty's Government proposed therefore to arrange for the issue to holders of Newfoundland Stock of Stock of equal face value with their present holdings, backed by the British Government and bearing interest at 3 per cent. In addition and in order to avoid yet further increases in the public debt, any advances from the British Exchequer to make good deficiencies in the Newfoundland budget would, between then and 1936, be in the nature of free gifts. These gifts would supplement a grant of £550,000 which the Government had already made to tide the Island over her immediate difficulties.

Looking to the future, the Chancellor said while the measures he had described would not make Newfoundland self-supporting in the short-term, there was no reason why she should not reach that stage in time. 'Her misfortunes are due to misgovernment and also to the fall in prices. Now,

[1] Parliamentary Debates 1933/4, vol. 283, cols. 1845 ff.

with efficient administration and with a prospect of better times generally in world trade altogether, I think that her future is not at all unhopeful. We must remember that Newfoundland is a country of great potential resources.'

The Governor-in-Commission [said Mr Chamberlain in conclusion] will no doubt be faced with very formidable difficulties but to anybody with an imaginative and adventurous mind there are great opportunities of a singularly absorbing and fascinating character in the task which will be before him. He has to create a new State, to rehabilitate the ruined finances of the country, to develop her resources, to rebuild the political system of the country on a new basis and to bring back to the people of Newfoundland some measure of material prosperity and contentment with their lot.

While at this distance in time the remaining stages of the debate scarcely merit close attention, it is worth pausing at the principal speech from the Labour benches, delivered by Mr Lunn. Its line and contents cast an interesting reflective light on the distance Government and Opposition have since moved in developing a common approach to the broad issues of Commonwealth and Colonial policy. Mr Lunn vehemently opposed the Financial Resolution, urging that at a time of unemployment at home the British taxpayer should not 'be called upon to make good bankruptcy brought about by wrong-doing'. He referred to the Chancellor's proposals as a 'shocking ramp', and to the Newfoundland Government as a 'bandit government'. It was proposals of this kind in these circumstances which made him 'hesitate in giving support to this Dominion or to any other Dominion'. Let Newfoundland, he concluded, 'provide the means for its own restoration. It has the necessary resources.' When the Question was put, however, the House by the overwhelming majority of 227 to 38 approved that the Resolution be reported on the morrow—a procedural formality.

The Commons next addressed themselves to the constitutional issues. On 12 December Mr J. H. Thomas opened the debate on the second reading of the Newfoundland Bill.[1] This proved to be a short, general measure providing for the suspension of the existing Letters Patent, dated 1876 and 1905, and making provision for the administration of the Island during the interim period. Any further Letters Patent reversing the new procedure would have to be laid before Parliament for the statutory period of twenty-one days. To the Bill were scheduled the Address from the Legislative Council and House of Assembly of Newfoundland praying His Majesty to suspend the existing Letters Patent: and a summary of the principal recommendations contained in the Royal Commission's report.

[1] Enacted as 24 Geo. V, 21 December 1933.

The debate[1] was lengthy, often acrimonious, sometimes moving. Its main importance today is as a commentary on the ethic of suspending constitutional government in a country which had, for close on a century, exercised full control over its internal affairs and which since the passage of the Statute of Westminster could, had it so wished, have assumed full control of its extraterritorial relations. From the outset the Dominions Secretary was at pains to emphasize that it was at the express request of the Newfoundland people that this drastic step was now being taken. Constitutionally the setback would not be so great as in other of the self-governing Dominions since Newfoundland, although referred to in the Statute of Westminster, had never requested that its provisions should be applied in her respect. The sole aim of the British Government was to help the islanders until they could put their house in order.

But the Labour Opposition saw things in a different light. Mr Attlee at once moved an amendment designed to block the passage of the Bill through second reading. His argument was that, far from providing for the abolition of the 'inefficient and vicious system of competitive capitalism, truck and exploitation by the economic system organised in the interests of the merchant community', the Bill imposed an unjustifiable burden on the British taxpayer 'by the provision of grants and guarantees in the interests of banks, of moneylenders and stockholders'.

Mr Attlee based his case against the Government on 'the exploitation of Newfoundland which has been going on from year to year'. Ministers voiced any amount of righteous indignation against the corrupt politicians but had nothing whatever to say against the whole degrading economic system. The Government spoke of sympathy and honour. As to the former, his party would like to see more of it directed towards South Wales. Talking of honour, 'all the best countries default nowadays'. The Government were setting a dangerous precedent. Soon the British taxpayer might become the guarantor of the finances of the rest of the British Empire, including even the equal partners in the Commonwealth of Nations. It was a cruel thing, concluded Mr Attlee, that Newfoundland should be nursed back to health for a little time and then returned to competitive capitalism. A scheme should be worked out of 'Newfoundland for the Newfoundlanders'. But what that scheme should consist of the Labour Party's spokesman failed to show.

From the Conservative backbenches, Sir E. Gregg voiced his sorrow that at the very moment Parliament was considering the grant of self-government to India they should be withdrawing it from Newfoundland. He regretted the absence of any measure of constitutional representation for

[1] House of Commons, Parliamentary Debates, vol. 284 (12 December 1933), cols. 215 ff.

Newfoundland public opinion in this new experiment, which itself ran counter to Britain's long experience in oversea government. Sir E. Gregg also sought enlightenment on the precise status of the six Commissioners who were now to run the country. Would they be regarded as civil servants or as Ministers and politicians? If all form of local representation was to be ruled out then Newfoundlanders should, in the twilight period on which the Island was now embarking, be permitted to send representatives to Parliament at Westminster, which was about to assume control of the Island's affairs. After all, it was only just that the taxable Newfoundlander should continue to enjoy some form of representation.

This concern that democratic principles should at least be preserved, and that some new forum for the expression of public opinion should be devised, ran like an anxious thread through the debate. Colonel Wedgewood, elaborating on Sir E. Gregg's suggestion of Newfoundland representation at Westminster, proposed that the House should arrange 'for a really new departure, the beginning of an Imperial Parliament with representation here of those Dominions which through difficult financial circumstances have decided to come back to the Mother Country'. But other Members argued that Newfoundland representatives elected to Westminster might well embroil the situation locally as and when they found themselves in opposition to the policies which the new Commissioners were trying to carry out. Only one Member spoke with persuasion and vision about what he regarded as a further opportunity for confederation which had now been missed. 'I hope', said Mr Ander, 'that...we shall use all our good offices in the most friendly and diplomatic way...to bring the two countries [Newfoundland and Canada] together, so that when finally we have set Newfoundland on her feet again, she will find her future destiny not as an independent unit. She has shown herself too small an area for that.'

The Under Secretary for Dominion Affairs, Mr Malcolm MacDonald, wound up the debate that evening. As he saw it, there was one point at least on which both sides of the House agreed—the wretchedly poor state of the Island and its people. Whereas the Government sought, as part of their programme of relief, to underwrite the pledges to which successive Newfoundland governments had committed themselves, the Opposition had quite frankly urged default. But default would hurt not only the bondholders; it would shatter the credit of the Island; still further reduce the prospects of trade and add to the already sizeable number of Newfoundlanders living on the dole. Mr MacDonald accepted the force of one of the arguments advanced: namely, that, once the situation was less desperate, political agitators might start to undermine the work of the Commissioners and to arouse local opinion against them. This made the Government all the more determined to choose the three British nominees not only for their administrative ability, but also for their experience in handling political problems. 'They are not going to be civil servants bound down by all the rules of the Civil Service.' They would have to travel widely among the people, make speeches and explain the new administration's policies. They would also, in concert with the British Government, have to press ahead with development and reconstruction plans. The fishery would have to be modernized; the evils of the Truck system gradually eradicated and municipal government, which so far existed only in the capital, extended as a basis for political training. The Government's policy, concluded the Under Secretary, 'is a policy which bristles with difficulties', but the great imperial reputation of Britain would not suffer through her determination to come to the aid of the oldest British colony.

The Second Reading debate on which the House eventually divided 250–42 had not shown the Commons in their best light. With all allowances made for the plight and bitterness of the small Labour Opposition against a background of widespread domestic unrest and unemployment this was neither a dignified nor a particularly generous episode. The House had spent more time berating the 'corrupt politicians' of Newfoundland and in defending or attacking the rights of bondholders than they had in considering the plight of the ordinary Newfoundlander. Even from the Government benches financial help had been somewhat grudgingly conceded, while the Opposition had frankly used the occasion for an onslaught on capitalism. The Committee stage, taken on 14 December, found Members in more sympathetic vein and increasingly conscious of the need both to emphasize the temporary nature of the suspension of responsible government and to find some outlet for the expression of public opinion in Newfoundland.

Sir Stafford Cripps opened with an amendment designed to suspend rather than revoke the existing Letters Patent and to limit the period of suspension to three years. In his view, the inclusion of the word 'revoke' in the Bill implied a conclusive step which would put the existing constitution of Newfoundland out of action for all time. There was no system of local government in the Island and, unless alternative means of expression were provided, the people's political consciousness would be dulled. They must, therefore, be given some incentive, such as a firm limit to the suspension of Parliamentary government, if they were not to sink into hopelessness. This argument Mr Aneuran Bevan reinforced with the remark that, as things stood, the constitution could only be restored 'upon the initiative of the bailiffs'. This was not fair to Newfoundlanders, who should be allowed to determine when they wanted to resume charge of their own affairs.

There was sympathy on both sides of the House for these views and before the amendment was defeated the Dominions Secretary promised to see whether the all too categorical word 'revoke' could be excised. But he felt unable to accept any definite time limit on the Bill. To include this would be a temptation to the local politicians to say to the people, 'Do not do what these people [i.e. the Commissioners] want because in two or three or four years the whole thing will be altered again and you will be all right.'

A second Opposition amendment, moved by Mr Maxton, would have allowed the Bill to proceed only following a plebiscite in Newfoundland. The very people, his argument ran, who would be affected by the removal of their constitutional rights—the ordinary people of Newfoundland—were the only ones not to have been consulted. To this Mr Thomas's reply was that Newfoundland was still a Dominion. The Humble Address on which Parliament was now acting was constitutionally within the discretion of the Newfoundland Government and Legislature. As the Imperial Conference of 1926 had established, it was within the discretion of a Dominion to decide what should be the form of a request to the Imperial Parliament to legislate on its behalf. It was no part of the latter's duty to say: 'You have to express your consent or your request in this or that particular form.'

Having suffered defeat on this amendment, Mr Maxton next proposed that the new arrangements should come into force only after the other Dominion Governments had signified their approval. While accepting that no machinery existed under the Statute of Westminster which would make such approval a prerequisite to action, Mr Maxton urged that 'the conception of consultation with the Dominions on all matters affecting the Dominions is implicit in the whole Statute of Westminster, which is the setting up of a new conception of equality between the various parts of the British Empire'. Mr Thomas replied that, ingenious though the amendment was, it had no relevance to the Bill. Other Dominion Governments would not wish to express an opinion on such legislation. Moreover, Newfoundland had ruled herself voluntarily out of the ambit of the Statute of Westminster. The measure now being debated was a domestic issue between Newfoundland and Britain. The amendment was, therefore, wholly unacceptable to the Government.

The debate now focused more narrowly on the issue of representation. The next Opposition amendment proposed that any taxpayer in Newfoundland should be allowed to petition the House of Commons regarding any proposals for imposing taxation upon the people of Newfoundland. Mr Thomas based his rejection of this proposition on the grounds first that it would be impracticable, and second that it would destroy from the outset the trust which the British Government would be placing in the new Commissioners. Their task would be difficult enough as it was. Moreover, the House could not hope to rival the Commissioners' local knowledge of fiscal needs and prospects.

After numerous further divisions the Bill was finally reported without amendment by a majority of 142 to 28. Three days later the Dominions Secretary moved that it be read a third time.[1] By then there was little fresh that he or the House could add to the exhaustive and exhausting debates which had gone before. The Secretary of State emphasized, however, that the new experiment on which Newfoundland was now embarking would largely stand or fall on the character and performance of the six Commissioners whom it would fall to his lot to select. He also announced that to meet the widely expressed anxieties about the use of the word 'revoke' the Government would introduce an amendment designed to make clear that what the Government intended amounted to no more than temporary suspension of the Newfoundland Constitution. At the same time he held out no hope that the Bill could be so altered as to set a time limit to the new arrangements.

The Upper House took the Bill on the following day, 19 December. Here it will be enough to single out one speech, that of the Chairman of the Royal Commission, Lord Amulree. After reciting the reasons, historic and economic, which had led his colleagues and himself to their conclusions, he emphasized that they had not lightly recommended that responsible government be suspended. The effect of the Report, he added, had already been to restore financial confidence locally. What was needed now was

> a well thought out policy on all the trading facilities of the island, rebuilding Newfoundland anew, and lifting the island to a new plane of economic life. The vast majority of the people [he concluded] wish a rest from Party politics and Party strife. The proposals in the Bill give that rest. The measure is only temporary. The people have suffered much and have endured long. They now see a ray of hope, and seem to feel that their deliverance is near.

Next day, with the Lords in Committee, the Government spokesman carried out the promise already given by the Dominions Secretary, moving that the word 'revoke' be struck out of Clause 1 in favour of the words 'suspension of the operation of the existing Letters Patent'.[2] This and

[1] House of Commons, Parliamentary Debates, vol. 284 (18 December 1933), cols. 931 ff.
[2] House of Lords, Parliamentary Debates, vol. 90 (14 December 1933), cols. 566 ff.

other minor consequential amendments were approved without a division: and the Bill was at once read a third time and returned to the Commons. There the Lords' amendments were approved without demur.[1] On 21 December the Bill received the Royal Assent.

It remained now only to bring the new Letters Patent and the Royal Instructions to the Governor into effect, and this was done on 30 January 1934, the date on which the six Commissioners took up their appointments. Considering the many complex and unprecedented steps that had had to be taken, both Government and Parliament had moved with remarkable speed. Little more than three months in fact elapsed between the publication of the Royal Commission's Report and the establishment in Newfoundland of Government by Commission.

Thus ended the first sad phase of a unique experiment. Never before had a sovereign partner in the Commonwealth been reduced to straits such as Newfoundland was now experiencing. Never had a Dominion voluntarily surrendered its independent status. The whole situation was without precedent. But whatever strictures might be levelled against the British Government, then or later, no one could complain that the people of Newfoundland had been bullied into submission. The Royal Commission Report, in which they had had an equal voice with Canada and Britain, was unanimous. The Commission itself was appointed only on request from the Newfoundland Assembly. Its painful and far-reaching recommendations were put into effect with the full and free consent of that Assembly. The foresight shown by the framers of those recommendations may be judged from the story that now unfolds.

[1] House of Commons, Parliamentary Debates, vol. 284 (20 December 1933), col. 1447.

14

SUSPENDED STATUS

All the furniture of a Parliament more than a hundred years old had been stripped and put away in a loft—nobody seemed to know where. The place was occupied by civil servants.

A. P. HERBERT, *Independent Member*, p. 260

What was this constitutional oddity which had now been so hastily, if reluctantly, launched into the Imperial pool? Had Newfoundland ever been, in the commonly understood sense of that term, a Dominion? If so, must she now once more be regarded as a Colony? And if not that, how was one to describe her?

Lawyers and historians alike have spent much time propounding arguments for and against the thesis that the effect of the Newfoundland Act, 1933, was to cause the Island to revert to the status of a Crown Colony. Suspension of the constitution of a dependent territory was and is no novelty. It has happened time and again in Imperial history, particularly in the West Indian colonies. Newfoundland herself had experienced a similar setback in the first period of representative government. But by the end of the First World War, the Island had reached a far more advanced constitutional stage. She had dabbled, if only locally, in foreign affairs. She had been represented at the Paris Peace Conference. Her Prime Ministers had attended post-war Imperial Conferences and had been directly associated with the drafting of the Report of the Inter-Imperial Relations Committee from which flowed the Balfour Declaration of 1926.[1] That report had emphasized that, while not holding the same title, the Governor of Newfoundland was in the same position as the Governor-General of a Dominion. Under the Statute of Westminster, moreover, Newfoundland had been described as a Dominion—an autonomous community equal in status to Britain, Canada or Australia. Where doubt had previously arisen as to Newfoundland's status in practice was in the field of external relations. She was not a member of the League of Nations and in the course of the inquiries into the right of Dominion Parliaments to legislate extra-territorially, which flowed from the Imperial Conference of 1926, had made it clear that she did not seek the same privileges as other Dominion Governments. Yet the very presence of Newfoundland Prime Ministers at the Imperial Conferences and the citation of Newfoundland

[1] Imperial Conference 1926, summary of Proceedings, Cmd. 2768.

in the Statute of Westminster must be taken as confirming the Island's right to the title 'Dominion'. It is therefore proper to conclude that with the passage of the Newfoundland Act, 1933, the Island became, in constitutional parlance, a 'Dominion with suspended status'. If and when she should revert to her previous constitutional position, the terms of the Statute of Westminster would, if she so desired, enable her to take full control of all her affairs, both internal and external.

These, however, were academic considerations. The Act of 1933 was now being rapidly translated into practice by means of the new Letters Patent and Instructions to the Governor of 1934.[1]

The Letters Patent laid down, in the usual archaic language, that the Commission of Government should consist of six persons, 'of whom three shall be persons ordinarily resident in our said Island and three shall be persons ordinarily resident without our said Island'. They empowered the Governor on the advice of the Commission to make laws for the peace, welfare and good government of Newfoundland, all such laws and other matters being enacted or decided by unanimity or by a majority of votes given. The disallowance of any law within one year of its enactment by the Governor was reserved to the Sovereign. The Royal Instructions, which issued simultaneously, more specifically enjoined the Governor not to assent without the authority of a Principal Secretary of State to a limited category of Bills, including those relating to divorce, currency, differential duties, or measures which might conflict with United Kingdom treaty obligations or prejudice the Royal Prerogative in establishment, trade or shipping matters. Nor finally was the Governor to absent himself from the Island 'upon any pretence whatsoever...without first having obtained leave from Us for so doing under our Sign Manual and Signet'.

The stage was thus set for the Commissioners to take up their duties. This they did on 16 February 1934 when the Letters Patent were gazetted locally. The three Newfoundland appointees were Mr F. C. Alderdice, the outgoing Premier (Church of England); one of his Ministerial colleagues, Mr J. C. Puddester (United Church), and a barrister, Mr W. R. Howley, K.C. (Roman Catholic). On the British side, the choice fell on Sir John Hope-Simpson, a retired official of the Indian Civil Service, Mr E. N. Trentham, a Treasury official already on loan to the Newfoundland Government as their financial adviser; and Mr T. Lodge, who had been both civil servant and businessman. The British Commissioners took the portfolios of Finance, Natural Resources, and Public Utilities; the three

[1] Letters Patent passed under the Great Seal of the United Kingdom, constituting the Office and Commander-in-Chief of the Island of Newfoundland and its dependencies, 30 January 1934.

Newfoundlanders those of Education and Home Affairs, Justice (later to include Defence), and Health and Welfare.

The new experiment was launched under difficulties which are easier to discern at this distance than was the case at the time. But it had these points in its immediate favour. Confidence was already flowing back and, leaving aside a small section of the population which remained virulently opposed to the suspension of responsible government, the bulk of the people were clearly thankful for a breathing space from politics and grateful that their affairs were for a time at least to be ordered by an impartial Committee with no obvious axe to grind.

As to the handicaps facing the Commission, some at least were more theoretical than real. The fact that it was to operate *in vacuo*, and without apparent guidance from public opinion, had already caused anxiety to Parliament at home. The fact that the Governor-in-Commission not only combined within himself both executive and legislative functions but was answerable for both to His Majesty's Government and to the House of Commons suggested that the new administration would always be operating with one hand tied behind its back. But to these doubts the real answer was that exceptional circumstances demand exceptional remedies. More to the point were certain of the charges which one of the British Commissioners levelled at the new system following his retirement from three years' control of the Department of Public Utilities. Mr Lodge's main criticisms can be summarized as follows. First, the Royal Commission had been misled in concluding that Newfoundland's ills had stemmed from corrupt and spendthrift administration rather than from external economic causes beyond her own control. From this misconception sprang all subsequent errors of judgement on the part of the British Government. Secondly, the constitution now imposed on Newfoundland 'suffered from the vice of inflexibility' in that no amendment which experience might show to be desirable could be introduced without recourse to Parliament at Westminster. And matters would have to be very pressing before the Whips would agree to find time for this. Thirdly, the Dominions Office, under whose care Newfoundland remained, was not equipped 'for dealing effectively with a discontinuity', nor trained to handle administrative problems thrown up by what was now to all intents and purposes a dependent territory. And, finally, the control which Parliament at Westminster exerted on the Commission's financial acts was bound to have an inhibiting effect on the long-term policies of the Commission itself.[1]

One could debate at length the validity or otherwise of these charges. If, for instance, the British Government had bowed to Mr Attlee's dictum

[1] T. Lodge. *Dictatorship in Newfoundland* (Cassells, 1939).

that all the best governments defaulted nowadays, Newfoundland might conceivably have struggled out of its difficulties without recourse to so radical a constitutional sacrifice. But once the decision had been taken to place the Government in Commission and to guarantee both the public debt and a balanced budget, it followed that Parliament, as controller of public monies, must have the final say in the activities of the Commissioners. To have arrived at any other solution would have involved remodelling the British Constitution itself as well as the policy and procedures of the British Treasury in respect of the many other dependent territories receiving grants-in-aid. Nor was it fair to describe the Dominions Office as ill-equipped to deal with the affairs of this new-style island. In the first place, there were at the time many civil servants in that Office with direct experience either of Newfoundland itself or of the problems of dependent territories. Secondly, it would have been a retrogressive step, and one unacceptable to both Parliament in Britain and public opinion in Newfoundland, to place the affairs of the Island in the hands of the Secretary of State for the Colonies.

Lodge's contention that the Royal Commission had directed overmuch of their fire at the politicians of the twenties and had paid insufficient attention to the Island's incapacity to influence the terms of external trade struck closer to the bone. But while this judgement may temporarily have clouded the minds of those in London with whom the Commissioners had now to deal, it was in the immediate context of Newfoundland's misfortunes already an academic argument. For it failed to address itself to the more vital question how a people suffering from widespread unemployment and physical distress, which showed itself in an alarming incidence of tuberculosis, rickets and other effects of malnutrition, were to be raised from the despair and penury into which they had sunk.

If there are two more practical charges which may be laid at the Royal Commission's door, and thus at that of the British Government of the day, they are first that the new administration in Newfoundland found itself from the outset virtually committed to a policy which insisted that the fishery was the unchallenged mainstay of the island's economy; and secondly (although this ignores the political and financial climate in Britain at that time) that the opportunity was missed to embark forthwith on a bold, long-term development plan, or at least to provide that such a plan should be drafted by some competent body of outside experts. The effect was to create a general mental atmosphere in which traditionalism rather than fresh initiative was to prevail and where the Commissioners felt obliged—no matter how minor the subject at issue—to work with one weather eye cocked always in the direction of the British Treasury. The scope for any radical departure of policy was thus severely limited and it became the primary task of the Commission of Government to modify, to streamline or to clear up the existing system rather than to branch out into fresh experiments. The conjured ghost of the British taxpayer was one which must constantly have lingered at their collective elbow.

It is, therefore, hardly surprising that between 1934 and the outbreak of the Second World War the performance of the Commission of Government was one rather of sober and solid administration than of spectacular advance. The tariff structure was thoroughly overhauled; realistic efforts were made to modernize the fishery and through the establishment of a Fisheries Board (one of the major feathers in the Commission of Government's cap) to improve marketing arrangements. Land settlement was also encouraged with varying results. On the social side the most marked advance was in the field of public health, where many enduring improvements were carried through. But the frailty of the economy was still apparent from the immediate effects of the Spanish and Italo-Abyssinian wars, and of the coffee slump in Brazil, on three of Newfoundland's traditional markets. Nor did the mild recession in Britain over the same period do anything to improve the hopes of the local mining and pulp and paper industries in that direction. These events alone were enough to re-emphasize that no Government, whatever its composition, however high its standards of morality, could hope to find an immediate panacea to Newfoundland's basic unease: overdependence on an out-of-date, uneconomic industry, resulting in inability to stand alone and uncushioned against the vagaries of world trading booms and slumps.

Two facts at least stand out from the early years of Government by Commission. First, that there was not, as some Jonahs had forecast, a sharp and continuing cleavage between the Newfoundland and British members. In fact, on the infrequent occasions where the Government was unable to arrive at unanimous decisions, the weightage of votes had nothing to do with nationality. Newfoundlander would often be ranged against Newfoundlander; Englishmen would find themselves in the same camp with Newfoundlanders against another Englishman. Votes in fact were cast, when they had to be cast, from individual conviction, not from any sense of patriotism or nationality. Even Lodge, who was otherwise highly critical of the whole system, supported the decision to create a mixed Commission rather than one composed of Newfoundlanders or Englishmen alone. From personal experience he could confirm that the detached approach of the latter was constantly illumined by the detailed local knowledge of their Newfoundland colleagues.

The second fact to stand out was that the essentials of democracy were not killed with the establishment of the new régime. Admittedly, as some Newfoundlanders later suggested, the position of the Commission of Government would have been greatly strengthened had the terms of the Newfoundland Act of 1933 first been approved—as they undoubtedly would have been at the time—by national plebiscite. But the local press was still free both to criticize, which it did unhesitatingly, and to publish for public comment the drafts of Bills which the Commission had prepared. Moreover, the individual Commissioners travelled continuously, kept in close touch with trade and church interests and opened their doors wide to individual Newfoundlanders, with whom it had always been the tradition to bring personal or local grievances, however petty, to the direct notice of their Ministers. Thus, while by the very nature of its being the new instrument was bound to be imperfect, its failings turned out to be considerably less grievous than many of its critics had foreseen.

Whether, if war had not intervened, some later steps would have been taken to modify the Letters Patent, is hardly a fruitful field for speculation. Apart from his view that the British Government kept all too inhibiting a control of the Newfoundland pursestrings, Lodge's opinion (supported some years later by a visiting Parliamentary Mission from Britain) was that the Governor should be divorced from the executive responsibility which went with his chairmanship of the Commission, and that his place as Chairman should be taken by an administrator of high calibre. But this and the many other variants on the régime which were proposed from both sides of the Atlantic could not conceal the fact that, when war broke out, Newfoundland was in little different shape economically than she had been when the Commission of Government took office. Improved social services had brought with them higher recurrent liabilities; the deficit on the Budget was still being met from the British Exchequer; all efforts to eradicate certain medieval processes from the fishery were frustrated by the continuing contraction of overseas markets. In harsh terms 50,000 men, or one-sixth of the population, were still on relief in 1939. And this despite all efforts on the Commission's part, not merely to modernize all branches of the fishing industry but also to survey potential mineral resources. In short, while the Commission could offer honest and impartial administration, reform of the civil service and improved health and welfare services—no mean achievements in themselves—they could not control the terms of world trade. They could not hope even in a generation to remove another basic handicap to the Island's progress—a population spread uneconomically in hundreds of scattered communities along six thousand miles of coastline. Faced as they were with a nation of rugged individualists, it was beyond their capacity, even had the means been available to them, to carry through a drastic programme of resettlement. Lacking a popular mandate, subject day in and day out to Treasury control from Whitehall, they could only 'depend on persuasion as a means of securing approval for change of policy'.[1]

Had there been no second war, Newfoundland might have lingered on in her suspended status, her fortunes little altered. But the fall of France in the summer of 1940 brought about changes even more abrupt than those which followed on the start of the First World War. Overnight, Newfoundland's position, exposed and undefended, at the western end of the North Atlantic convoy route and at the gateway to the St Lawrence, struck home to military planners in London, Ottawa and Washington alike.

As earlier chapters have shown Newfoundland, from the sixteenth century onwards, had been regarded as a nursery for seamen. Fighting between individual ships, privateering raids, and later engagements between rival European fleets took place in and around her waters. Sporadic efforts had been made to fortify St John's and other strategic points along the coastline. But even in the early years of the twentieth century no Imperial strategic importance attached to the island. Halifax rather than St John's was the preferred British naval base, and so long as Britain 'held a general sea superiority, the defence of Newfoundland was primarily a matter of trade protection, without any wider strategic implications. Even during the Great War of 1914–18 no harbour of Newfoundland was used as a main convoy base.'[2]

The advent of the long-range bomber, the isolation in which Britain found herself, and the consequent increase in the German submarine menace in North American waters rapidly and radically altered Newfoundland's role in allied strategy. By September 1940 the British and U.S. Governments had entered into negotiations which were to lead in the following year to the conclusion of the Leased Bases Agreement. Writing on 2 September to Cordell Hull the British Ambassador in Washington stated that

> Her Majesty's Government will secure the grant to the Government of the United States *freely and without consideration* of the lease for immediate establishment and use of Naval and Air bases and facilities for entrance thereto and the operation and protection thereof on the Avalon Peninsula and on the Southern Coast of Newfoundland and on the East coast...All of the bases will be leased to the United States for a period of ninety-nine years, free from all rent...[3]

[1] MacKay, p. 217. [2] MacKay, p. 261.

[3] Agreement between the Governments of the United Kingdom and the United States of America relating to the bases leased to the United States of America (and exchange of notes) together with protocol between the Governments of the United Kingdom, Canada and the United States of America concerning the defence of Newfoundland, London, 27 March 1941, Cmd. 6259.

The Agreement, which also covered the leased bases in the Caribbean, set forth in detail the rights and powers of the United States in the various leased areas, with particular reference to their use in the event of the United States Government becoming involved in hostilities. It also covered issues of jurisdiction, customs, taxation, assignment and compensation. What significantly it could not include was any reference to the wishes or co-operation of the people of Newfoundland in signing away to a foreign power for close on a century sizeable areas of their own territory.

There is no doubt that the Newfoundland members of the Commission learnt with misgivings of the British Government's intentions. They were in a peculiarly difficult situation in that, as Ministers of a Government at war with Germany, they clearly saw it as their duty to do all in their power to assist the war effort, whereas as patriotic citizens they were deprived of any representative body through which they could consult or guide public opinion. In the last resort they could and did fall back on the argument that the British Government were responsible for the external affairs and defence of Newfoundland. On that basis all they could do was work with the British negotiators to secure the best possible terms for Newfoundland in the purely domestic sense. In the event any qualms which the people of Newfoundland felt about the Leased Bases Agreement were suppressed in the general backs-to-the-wall spirit of those days and, more materially, in the knowledge that the construction of the bases would bring with it undreamt of chances of employment and prosperity.

Two further points should be noted in respect of the Agreement. On the date of signature, 27 March 1941, Mr Churchill put on record with the American Ambassador in London that 'upon the resumption by Newfoundland of the constitutional status held by it prior to the 16th February, 1934, the words "the Government of the United Kingdom", wherever they occur in relation to a provision applicable to Newfoundland in the said Agreement, shall be taken to mean, so far as Newfoundland is concerned the Government of Newfoundland, and the Agreement shall then be construed accordingly'.[1] To this declaration the United States Government promptly acceded, as they did to a Protocol of the same date, signed also by the Governments of Canada and the United Kingdom.[2] This document proclaimed the interest of Canada in the defence of Newfoundland and her right to be consulted in respect of operations involving the use of leased bases in the island. Thus were simultaneously revived or strengthened hopes of an eventual return to responsible government; and Newfoundland's links with her Canadian neighbour.

Meanwhile the Canadian Government were also playing a major role

[1] *Ibid.* p. 39. [2] *Ibid.* p. 43.

in the defence of Newfoundland. As soon as war broke out the R.C.A.F. began patrolling the Island's waters and the seaplane base at Botwood on the east coast was placed at their disposal. By June 1940 Canadian troops, with the Newfoundland Government's approval, had assumed garrison duties at the main airbase at Gander and were guarding other key points. As the allied position worsened Newfoundland forces were placed under Canadian command: the airbases were taken over and extended by the R.C.A.F. and the Canadian Government constructed an additional fighter base at Torbay, near the capital. Next year Canada, acting for the British Admiralty, also constructed a naval repair base at St John's. By now, Britain, Canada and the United States were collaborating closely in the defence of Newfoundland.

But undoubtedly Canada's greatest wartime contribution to the economy and protection of the Island was the construction of the great airbase at Goose Bay. This was to revolutionize the future of the Labrador once peace returned.

By 1941, the Allies were beginning to search urgently for a short Atlantic air ferry route to Britain. Aerial surveys carried out in the late summer of that year led to the choice of Goose Bay, 'a sandy plateau overlooking the extreme western end of Lake Melville',[1] some 120 miles inland from the coast in Newfoundland Labrador. Secret negotiations opened forthwith between the British, Canadian and Newfoundland Governments regarding the rights to be accorded there to Canada. But in view of the wartime urgency, construction of the airbase began later in the same season. It was pushed forward and completed with remarkable speed. It was not until the autumn of 1944 that a formal Agreement, under which Canada in turn obtained a 99-year lease backdated to 1941, was signed, the Newfoundland Government on that occasion being a principal party to the Agreement. The terms initialled on both sides provided *inter alia* that 'for the duration of the war and for such time thereafter as the Governments agree to be necessary or advisable in the interests of common defence' the control of the air base should be under the direction of the Royal Canadian Air Force and (an important point for the future) the use of the base 'for civil and commercial operations after the war...will form the subject of discussion between the Governments of Canada, the United Kingdom and Newfoundland'. The Commission of Government also secured that the Government of Canada would as far as practicable employ Newfoundland labour at the Air Base.[2]

[1] J. Chadwick, 'The economic resources of Labrador', *Polar Record*, v (1948), 155–62.

[2] Memorandum of Agreement between Canada and Newfoundland relating to the establishment of an air base at Goose Bay, Labrador, signed at St John's, Newfoundland, 10 October 1944, Treaty Series 30 of 1944 (Ottawa, King's Printer, 1947). For full text see appendix III.

Thus, within eighteen months from the outbreak of war six large military bases were either under construction or in the planning stage—a land base at Pleasantville (Fort Pepperell) outside St John's; a naval-cum-airbase at Argentia on the southern shore; further airfields at Stephenville (Harmon) on the west coast; at Torbay (St John's) and Goose Bay in Labrador; and the naval base at the capital. Unemployment, which had already declined following Newfoundland enlistment in the rapidly formed Forestry Unit and in the British and Canadian Forces, now dwindled to vanishing point as more and more men were taken on by American and Canadian contractors. At the height of the building boom close on 20,000 Newfoundlanders found employment at the bases at rates of pay hitherto undreamt of.

The effect on the economy was to prove remarkable. Whereas at the end of the first year of Government by Commission revenue had amounted to $9·6 million and expenditure to $11·6 million, leaving a deficit of $2 million to be found by Britain, the comparative figures for the year ending 1942 were $23·5 million and $16·1 million, providing a surplus of over $7 million, a figure itself running close to the total annual revenues of the early 1930s. Put briefly, the cumulative deficit for the six years ending 30 June 1940 was $18 million. The cumulative surplus resulting from the war years was $32·5 million.

This marked change in the Island's fortunes should not be allowed to obscure the concurrent rapid rise in the price of imported goods, on which Newfoundland was so heavily dependent and which in turn almost doubled the cost of living between 1940 and 1945: nor the fact that the increase in national income did little more than bring the average Newfoundlander from subsistence level to receipt of an adequate living wage. But despite these items on the debit side, the point was not lost sight of in London that when war ceased the British Government might well face urgent demands from Newfoundland for some further change in her constitutional fortunes. 'Until such time as the Island is again self-supporting', the Act of 1933 had proclaimed. Clearly that position was rapidly being achieved. Whether it would last once peace returned or whether, as in the 1920s, the Island would once more fall victim to external stresses, was problematical. At all events, the Deputy Prime Minister and Secretary of State for the Dominions, Mr Attlee, decided in September 1942 to pay a personal, exploratory, visit to Newfoundland. It was a wise gesture. At the same time it was to open the way to the final solution of Newfoundland's constitutional status.

15

MEN OF GOODWILL

> If the three British Commissioners were men as able as Mr Churchill, Mr Roosevelt and Mr Stalin, they would still be foreigners...The fact remains that Government by Commission is an alien and anomalous regime, repugnant to the instincts and traditions of a freedom-loving British people... A. P. HERBERT, *Independent Member*, pp. 259–60

As Deputy Prime Minister, Mr Attlee must have found Newfoundland a minor problem compared with the issues of global strategy and the blue prints for Britain's future which were even now beginning to emerge. In addition, as Dominions Secretary, he carried direct responsibility for British political relationships with Canada, Australia, New Zealand and South Africa. As the war effort of the Dominion partners grew so their determination to have their rightful say in the conduct of operations increased. Inadequately supplied with staff, the Dominions Office fought its way from one crisis to the next. Yet hidden in its midst there still survived a handful of officers concerned with Newfoundland affairs. They could rarely expect to be dealing with front page news. But it was typical of Mr Attlee's sympathy with the political underdog and of his keen interest in training the unenfranchised in the arts of politics that their problems and recommendations invariably received his full attention.

Indeed it was less the growing strategic importance of the Island which led the Secretary of State to decide on a personal visit than the question how best and how soon Newfoundlanders could be led back to a truly democratic way of life and what form their new institutions should take.

Brief though they were, Mr Attlee's discussions with the Governor and the Commissioners served to focus attention on both sides of the Atlantic on the problems that peace would bring. It seemed to be tacitly accepted that, as an independent unit, Newfoundland could never hope to be truly viable. Equally it was agreed that some scheme must soon be worked out through which public opinion could once more be tested. It was now over ten years since an election had last been held. In that decade the Commission of Government had done much good if unspectacular work. But however excellent its performance, it was doubtful whether dictatorship, benign though it might be, would remain acceptable for long.

The question was what alternatives could be offered? The idea of confederation still seemed anathema. Many older people would shrink from the restoration of responsible government in its previous form. Some half-way house involving a measure of representative government was one possibility, provided this could be geared to continuing British and perhaps also Canadian aid. In Canada also minds were turning to the idea of some kind of rental services, falling short of outright confederation, under which the Federal Government might make themselves responsible for operating the Newfoundland railway and such other public utilities as the postal and telecommunications services.

While many projects were in the air, and Newfoundlanders themselves were beginning to savour a new taste for political debate, Mr Attlee's visit was clearly the spark which set off the subsequent chain of events culminating in the majority decision of the people to seek terms of union with Canada. One early outcome of the Dominions Secretary's discussions in St John's was the passage of a resolution by the Newfoundland Board of Trade (in British parlance Chamber of Commerce) dated 8 March 1943 calling for the urgent establishment of 'some form of representative government'. A special Committee subsequently appointed by the Board, to examine how best such a change could be brought about, reported back in April. In its view the great majority of Newfoundlanders now desired political representation. There were widely differing views as to the form such representation should take: but many people would be dissatisfied with anything which fell short of the full restoration of responsible government. Since opinion was divided, the Committee urged that the British Government should appoint a Royal Commission, with a majority of Newfoundlanders, which would be empowered to take evidence 'not only on questions relating to the Constitution but also with respect to the financial, economic and social problems of the country'.[1]

These recommendations were adopted by a full meeting of the Board which moved that the Royal Commission be appointed forthwith. There followed a minor outburst of petitioning. The West Newfoundland Association also called for a Royal Commission, deeming the present Government to be 'out of sympathy with the people'. On the other hand, the presidents of seven labour unions, in a joint resolution countering that passed by the Board of Trade, opposed the appointment of a Royal Commission. In their view, if and when a change should prove desirable, the former constitution should be restored 'on a petition to His Majesty to that effect being signed by the electors of Newfoundland'. Meanwhile the present form of Government should continue.

These three petitions were of some significance in that they foreshadowed the sharp cleavage of opinion which was to emerge when the time came for Newfoundland's future to be put to the popular vote. Mercantile

[1] Lord Ammon, *Newfoundland: the Forgotten Island* (Victor Gollancz, 1944), p. 8.

interests, as represented by the Board of Trade, favoured the early return to some form of representative government. The west coast, out of sympathy with thinking in the capital, its attitude coloured by its proximity to Canada, its growing prosperity and its dependence on its trade links with Britain, favoured a release from what it considered to be the overcautious policies of the Commission, but without going so far as to call for a return to the *status quo ante*. Finally the Trade Unions, severally weak, but in unison a force to be reckoned with, revealed the continuing suspicions of the working man for the old political system. Beneath the surface, the antipathy between merchant and fisherman; carpetbagging politician and now cynical elector still survived.

But at the climax of a world war the British Government saw little advantage to be gained from the appointment of so formal a body as a Royal Commission. They accepted none the less that some visible step forward must now be taken. Accordingly, on 5 May 1943, Mr Attlee made the following statement in the House of Commons:

As the House is aware, I visited Newfoundland myself last September, accompanied by my hon. Friend, the member for Pontypool [Mr Arthur Jenkins]. Under war conditions Newfoundland has become a centre of great activity; it is an important naval and air base and is making a most valuable contribution to the war effort in men and resources. This has resulted in a great improvement in economic conditions; but it has also given rise to economic and social problems which may be a difficult legacy when employment for war purposes comes to an end. Therefore, while concentrating on the winning of the war, we must think and plan ahead so far as this can be done. It would be premature at present to attempt to reach conclusions but I feel, from my own experience, that it would be valuable if fuller knowledge of Newfoundland's war effort, and of the problems likely to face the Island after the war, could be made available to Parliament. I am therefore arranging for a small Mission, composed of three Members of this House to visit the Island during the early summer. I am happy to say that my hon. Friend, the member for North Camberwell, has consented to lead this mission; his colleagues will be the hon. and gallant member for Thornbury and the senior burgess for Oxford University.

This mission will not be a formal body charged with a specific enquiry, constitutional or otherwise. Conditions at the end of the war cannot be foreseen, and the present war preoccupations of Newfoundlanders and the absence of many of the younger generation with the Armed Forces make a formal enquiry into the Island's future constitution inappropriate at the present time. The mission will be of an informal goodwill character. It will have no defined terms of reference and will not present a written report, but I should hope that my hon. Friends on their return would give members of the House orally an account of their impressions. The mission's objects will be to acquaint itself with all that the Island is doing in the war, to give to Newfoundlanders a first-hand picture of our own war effort, and to go about amongst the people in the outports as well as in the towns so as to see something of their way of life. In view of the United Kingdom Government's special responsibility for the welfare of Newfoundland, I feel sure that the House will regard such a mission as most valuable, and I am confident that it will be cordially welcomed by the Government and the people of Newfoundland.[1]

The Members of Parliament selected for this task were the late Mr C. G (later Lord) Ammon (Labour); the late Sir Derrick Gunston (Conservative) and Mr A. P. (later Sir Alan) Herbert (Independent).[2] They were accompanied by a Secretary[3] from the Dominions Office. The mission arrived in St John's on 21 June 1943 and from then until the end of August toured extensively within and around the Island and down the Labrador Coast.

Their journeyings took them somewhat upward of 3,000 miles sometimes by rail, sometimes by air: infrequently by road and for the most part in a series of small boats which tested not only the members' goodwill but their fortitude to the full. By the end of their tour the Mission could justly boast that they had seen more of the Island than most Newfoundlanders would visit in a lifetime. And, as Sir Alan Herbert subsequently commented in his graphic description of the journey:

Mr Attlee did very sensibly...in sending out a small patrol of back-benchers... instead of a portentous Royal Commission...such a necessarily heavy body could not go everywhere, see everything and everybody, as we few and unpretentious persons could and did. It could not sit on the fish wharves and argue with fishermen and merchants, magistrates and Rangers and Ministers of religion: and get so near as I think we did to the minds of a shy and rather reticent people.[4]

It would be fair to say that the more they saw of Newfoundlanders the more the Mission came to like and respect them: but equally the more they talked with these 'gay, good-humoured and generous: tolerant, temperate, tough, God-fearing, sabbath-keeping and law abiding' (the description is Sir Alan Herbert's) people, the more bewildered they became. The Senior Burgess for Oxford University had his own views and expressed them pungently. He was struck by the 'Englishness' of Newfoundlanders; warmed by the patriotism which had made and kept them independent minded; shocked by the state in which he found the Parliament buildings; worried at the absence of local government machinery and convinced that Newfoundlanders no more 'belonged' to the American continent than he himself did. His colleagues had differing views.

[1] House of Commons, Parliamentary Debates, vol. 389 (5 May 1944), cols. 177–8.
[2] Gunston was a compulsive fisherman: Ammon an unbending disciplinarian. Bruised between Scylla and Charybdis, the Secretary was once heard to murmur that he 'could not serve both Rod and Ammon'. [3] The author.
[4] A. P. Herbert, *Independent Member* (London, 1950), p. 262.

Each of the three merchants of goodwill [as Sir Alan was later to describe it] wrote his own independent report. When I saw Derrick Gunston again I found that, in odd corners and moments he had nearly finished tapping out his version of Newfoundland. And John Chadwick, at the more stately speed of the Civil Service, was drafting a most able report for our leader. This, I think, was a good arrangement. I do not believe very much in the modern technique of artificial unanimity...And the remarkable, valuable thing was that, scribbling away in separate corners we agreed about many things. I had, I think, a little more faith than the others in the desire, and capacity, of Newfoundland to return to self-government soon...Certainly not one of us recommended that Newfoundland should cease to be a Dominion and be absorbed by any other country: and we all agreed about the Ten Years' (Development) Plan.[1]

The fact that the Goodwill Mission was unable to present an unanimous report was proof enough of the conflicting evidence with which it was presented and of the partisan approach into which any earnest examiner into Newfoundland affairs was likely to be inveigled. All that the three members could do on returning home was to deposit their troika of reports on the desk of the Dominions Secretary and await reactions. They must have been somewhat vexed to find that, before he had time to act on them, Mr Attlee had been succeeded at the Dominions Office by Lord Cranborne. The first move on the British Government's part came in the course of a general debate on Imperial affairs which took place in the House of Commons on 2 December 1943. The Parliamentary Under-Secretary for Dominion Affairs, Mr Emrys Evans, then announced that, while not wishing to anticipate a fuller discussion on the upshot of the Parliamentary Mission's findings, he proposed to comment on the constitutional position of Newfoundland, which the Government had recently reviewed. He rejected suggestions that the Island was 'being kept in subjection under a system imposed by a tyrannical home Government against the will of the people'. He referred to the prosperous conditions which Newfoundland was enjoying, at the same time reminding the House that, however self-supporting the Island might now appear to be, there was as yet no sign of any unanimous request from the people that responsible government should be restored forthwith. Opinion was still much divided as to what form of self-government, or what form of government, would best suit Newfoundlanders in future.

The Under Secretary then made the following important declaration of policy:

After reviewing the position, the Government decided that their policy should be based on the following main points:–

The arrangements made in 1933 included a pledge by His Majesty's Govern-

[1] Herbert, *op. cit.* pp. 286–7.

ment that as soon as the Island's difficulties had been overcome and the country was again self-supporting, responsible government, on request from the people of Newfoundland, would be restored. Our whole policy is governed by this undertaking.

Owing, however, to the existing abnormal conditions caused by the war which make it impossible for the Newfoundland people as a whole to come to a considered conclusion as to the Island's future prospects, there should be no change in the present form of Government while the war lasts.

As soon as practicable after the end of the war that is, the war in Europe, machinery must be provided for enabling the Newfoundland people to examine the future of the Island and to express their considered views as to the form of Government they desire, having regard to the financial and economic conditions prevailing at the time. In the meantime the Secretary of State will be taking soundings in order to ascertain what kind of machinery would be acceptable to the Newfoundland people.

If the general wish of the people should be for a return to full responsible government we for our part shall be very ready, if the Island is then self-supporting, to facilitate such a change.

If, however, the general wish should be either for the continuance of the present form of Government or for some change of system which would fall short of full responsible government, we shall be prepared to examine such proposals sympathetically and consider within what limits the continued acceptance of responsibility by the United Kingdom could be recommended to Parliament.

In the meantime a vigorous attempt should be made to push on with the development of local government, on which the members of the Mission have made some interesting recommendations, as well as with general reconstruction plans. Every effort should be made to encourage the development of local government institutions, which would afford a base for an effective central Government.

In accordance with this statement of policy, my Noble Friend [Lord Cranborne] will take steps to ascertain what machinery would be most acceptable to Newfoundland public opinion, and to discuss means to enable it to be put into effect at an appropriate moment. Possible methods might include, for example, the setting-up of some National Convention, but this is for further consideration in the light of views expressed in Newfoundland. I would like to add that there is no desire on the part of the Government to impose any particular solution. The Government will be guided by the freely expressed views of the people. It is for Newfoundland to make the choice, and the Government, with the assent of Parliament, will be very ready to give effect to their wishes. Although it is not my intention to say very much about the financial, economic and social conditions of the Island, they, of course, have an important bearing upon the constitutional issue.[1]

The Government statement was as significant for what it omitted as for what it included. No reference was made to the prospects, however faint,

[1] House of Commons, Parliamentary Debates, vol. 395 (2 December 1943), cols. 596–600.

of confederation. Indeed, this still seemed almost unthinkable to those who knew the local climate of opinion. On the other hand, the suggestion that a National Convention might be established to ascertain the wishes of Newfoundlanders as to their future was borrowed directly from Sir Alan Herbert's report to the Government. Although he was to complain later that it was never published—'a shocking blow to a professional writer'—he also made clear in his reminiscences that the Government statement meant that Mr Attlee had 'accepted the machinery I had myself proposed, the National Convention, followed by a plebiscite'.[1] Indeed, the Government's request to the members of the Parliamentary Mission that their reports should remain confidential was honoured more in the breach than in the undertaking. A résumé of Lord Ammon's report was published in the following year by the Fabian Society.[2] Truncated and badly edited though it was, it at least made clear the basic views of the leader of the Mission. These were that Newfoundland was not then ripe for full responsible government: that while confederation with Canada could not in 1943 be considered as a serious solution 'the possibilities should be borne continuously in mind'[3] and that the best immediate prospect was the continuation of Commission Government in a modified form. Lord Ammon did not exclude a return to responsible government. As a politician he could hardly dismiss such a solution out of hand. But he gave it as his view that it would doom Newfoundlanders to a second bankruptcy. His central proposal therefore was that the Newfoundland members of the Commission of Government should henceforth be elected by universal suffrage, their British colleagues continuing to be appointed, as previously, by H.M.G. and that the Commission should collectively appoint its own independent Chairman who might be drawn from any country of the Commonwealth. His recommendations (as published in précis) continued:

> It might be that two years from the annulment of the local Defence Regulations a referendum should be held, the people being told that H.M. Government would be prepared to continue its help to Newfoundland on a large scale; and that the machinery of Commission would be broadened, and then being asked to vote for or against this policy. Should they reject it, thus showing their desire for an immediate return to responsible government...these proposals fall. If they voted for the continuation of Commission Government in a modified form for a number of years, then I would urge that the development plan be put into operation without delay.[4]

The implied threat of 'no subservience—no cash' running throughout these recommendations as published does less than justice to their author's

[1] Herbert, *op. cit.* p. 286.
[2] Ammon.
[3] *Ibid.* p. 9.
[4] *Ibid.* p. 12.

real intentions. For a fairer picture of what was in the minds of the three members of the Mission, it is necessary to turn back to the full-scale debate on Newfoundland which took place in the House of Commons on 16 December 1943.[1]

Mr Ammon (as he still then was) opened by moving the following motion:

That this House welcomes the statement [of 2 December] made on behalf of H.M.G. of the acceptance in principle of the right of Newfoundland to self-government and urges H.M.G. to give effect to such approach by taking the necessary preliminary action as soon as possible.

Mr Ammon referred to the Mission's extensive travelling, sometimes in very difficult conditions: to meetings on wharfsides, in sheds, churchyards, school halls and stores and to the overall impression he and his colleagues had gained that while no one wanted a return to the political atmosphere of pre-Commission days, equally 'nobody seemed to know quite what he wanted'. Some seemed to favour a continuance of the *status quo*: others confederation with Canada, and a few accession to the United States. But there was 'an overwhelming number' against any link with Canada. The answer seemed to lie either with the restoration of responsible government or in a middle course, beginning perhaps with the election of the Newfoundland Commissioners, the appointment of a separate Chairman in place of the Governor, and some immediate relaxation of day to day Treasury control.

The Conservative Member, Sir Derrick Gunston, echoed Mr Ammon's perplexity about the real wishes of the Newfoundland people, adding his view that 'nobody wanted responsible Government now'. 'Trade unions and co-operative societies', he said, 'were more apprehensive about a return to responsible government than the merchants of St John's. They said they wanted responsible government *X* years after the war, but the further we journeyed from St John's the greater the size of the *X* grew.' He concluded by proposing a thoroughgoing ten-year development programme, and the extension of the social services, at an overall cost of some £20 million.

Mr Maxton having then moved an amendment, calling on the Government to restore representative government in Newfoundland forthwith, the Deputy Prime Minister, Mr Attlee, intervened. He reminded the House of the distaste he himself had expressed in 1933 prior to the establishment of the present régime. However, as he had found on his own recent visit to the Island, there was no unanimous desire to return to the particular form

[1] House of Commons, Parliamentary Debates, vol. 395, cols. 1743–1804.

of government which Newfoundlanders had previously enjoyed. What in his view was deplorable was the continuing lack of any kind of local government outside St John's. 'Adults right up to the age of 30 have never cast a vote.' It was now essential, as the Government had already said, that 'we should try to get from the Newfoundland people by consultation, their view of the kind of machinery they would like to set up—to determine their future constitution rather than to act on purely a priori lines and put them back where they were ten years ago, and where it certainly does not appear they necessarily want to go now'.[1]

Mr Maxton's amendment having been defeated, it was left to Mr Herbert, the third member of the Parliamentary Mission, to propose the course of action by which the British Government were very largely to be guided. Mr Herbert began in typical vein, confessing both that it was a new experience for him to write 30,000 words, not merely without pay but without publication, and that Newfoundland had seemed to him 'about the most testing and complicated puzzle in the whole Imperial scene'. Some, as he put it, 'of the religious, political and indeed industrial problems of Ireland and of India, the size of Ireland, the title of a Dominion, the population of Bradford, the history and habits of Dominion Government and the social services of a neglected Crown Colony'.[2]

To the questions whether Newfoundland was likely to be in the strict economic sense self-supporting when peace returned and whether she was to be denied self-government until she was, the double answer, in Mr Herbert's view was 'no'. However, there would be no thanks from the Island if the British Government merely restored the *status quo ante* with no reference to the economic future. Therefore, the Government should seriously consider the following programme. They should announce that, three years after the end of the war, full responsible government would be restored to Newfoundland 'unless by a plebiscite one year before that they had chosen some other form of government'. In the interim period a Council of Citizens should be formed from Newfoundlanders in all walks of life. This body, over which should preside a British constitutional expert, would help to prepare the people for a return to political activity and would frame the questions to be put at the suggested plebiscite. Mr Herbert did not rule out that these might include the absorption of Newfoundland into the United Kingdom, somewhat on Northern Ireland lines, and the re-emergence of the local Parliament as a unicameral legislature. The main aim should be to provide Newfoundlanders with a body, whether nominated or elected, which could act as a sounding board for public opinion and pave the way for a return to democratic institutions.

[1] *Ibid.* col. 1772.

[2] *Ibid.* col. 1780.

Replying for the Government Mr Emrys Evans rejected the proposals that the Newfoundland Commissioners should henceforth be elected and the Commission presided over by an authority other than the Governor. This would give rise to a constitutional division of loyalties and could not be accepted so long as the Governor remained responsible to the Dominions Secretary and, through him, to Parliament. On financial aid, the Minister was cautious to the point of negation. He was equally so in regard to any link between Newfoundland and Parliament at Westminster. As to the constitutional proposals advanced by Mr Herbert he would say no more than that 'H.M.G. have an open mind on the whole of this question and are prepared to await the conclusions of the people of Newfoundland with regard to the machinery to be set up before coming to a final decision'.[1] But even if the Government's mind was open, the fact that Mr Herbert's proposals had sunk home in Whitehall was evident from Mr Emrys Evans's reference to the 'machinery to be set up'.

The Government's statement of 2 December and the subsequent debate awakened keen if somewhat jaundiced interest in Newfoundland, the *Daily News*[2] commenting sourly that the desire for change locally would have been much less apparent if the Commission of Government had made a greater success of its conduct of affairs. The *Star*[3] a few days later added that if Newfoundland could not exist without assistance from England, or confederation with Canada, 'by all means let us ask for assistance from England'. But by and large newspaper and popular opinion could be summed up in the phrase—everything remained exactly as it had been before. While the ball had now moved back into the Newfoundland court, no one had any real idea in which direction it should be kicked, or any burning desire to be the first to kick it. It was in this atmosphere of simmering puzzlement that peace returned to a now prosperous Island and that the penultimate phase of Newfoundland's constitutional odessey cautiously unfolded.

As a Canadian economist wrote shortly before these events took place:

> Whatever the political decision as to the future and whatever financial and administrative arrangements may be made, without the miracle of some undreamt of discoveries Newfoundland will still remain a relatively sparsely populated country, very much dependent on outside markets, and outside sources of supply, and fighting hard to keep abreast of the other countries of the Western world. Her greatest asset is a growing number of capable young men with a well-balanced faith in their own ability and their country's future.[4]

It was fair comment.

[1] *Ibid.* col. 1801.
[2] 7 December 1943.
[3] 11 December 1943.
[4] MacKay, p. 242.

16

NATIONAL CONVENTION

Mr Stanley. Has the hon. Gentleman's attention been called to a statement which appeared in this morning's Press by one of the members of the delegation complaining of the treatment that they received here? Could the hon. Gentleman assure the House that while recognizing, as we all do, the practical limits of any financial assistance we give, the Government will do everything they can within those limits to assist Newfoundland along the road that they want to choose for themselves?

Mr Bottomley. The answer to the latter part of the question is, yes. With regard to the other part of the question, there were six delegates and when there are six representatives from different sources it is hardly to be expected that you will get an unanimous view.

Hansard, House of Commons, 13 May 1947

Throughout 1944 and 1945 discussions continued between the British and Newfoundland Governments both on the steps to be taken to discover the future wishes of the islanders and on the possible content of a long-range economic reconstruction programme. Speaking in the House of Lords on 3 May 1944 Viscount Cranborne, Mr Attlee's successor as Dominions Secretary, re-emphasized that once the war in Europe had ended Newfoundlanders must be trusted to choose their future for themselves. Meanwhile the machinery to provide for this must be got ready. He for his part was inclined to favour Mr Herbert's suggestion for a National Convention. But it would be useless, he added, 'for us to prejudge the consideration of the matter by the Convention by ourselves advocating this or that policy'.[1]

Three members of the Commission of Government visited London in August of the same year to continue the dialogue. Shortly thereafter a senior Newfoundland district magistrate was released from ordinary duties to prepare a comprehensive scheme for elections to a Convention, the size and purpose of which were as yet undetermined. Meanwhile the war in Europe had dragged on into another winter, Britain's own balance of payments difficulties were becoming monthly more apparent, and a great many young Newfoundlanders were still serving overseas. In these circumstances the British Government concluded that all plans, whether for the launching of a generous development programme or for a grand debate on the Island's constitutional future must remain in cold storage. These unpalatable decisions were announced by the Dominions Secretary

[1] Parliamentary Debates, Lords, vol. 191, 5th ser.

in the House of Lords on 30 January 1945.[1] As he then made clear, a full understanding of how Newfoundland stood economically and financially, when war ended, would be an essential prerequisite to the taking of decisions on the constitutional issue.

It was not in fact until 11 December 1945, with the war in Europe ended and a Labour Government in power in Britain, that definitive policy statements on Newfoundland were at last made. Speaking in the Commons,[2] the Prime Minister endorsed the Coalition Government's earlier statement of 2 December 1943. He went on: 'H.M.G. have decided to set up in Newfoundland next year, as early as climatic conditions permit, an elected National Convention of Newfoundlanders. Election to this Convention will be broadly on the basis of the former Parliamentary constituencies. All adults will be entitled to vote...The Convention will be presided over by a Judge of the Supreme Court of Newfoundland.' The terms of reference of the Convention, Mr Attlee announced, would be

> to consider and discuss among themselves, as elected representatives of the Newfoundland people, the changes that have taken place in the financial and economic situation of the Island since 1934 and bearing in mind the extent to which the high revenues of recent years have been due to war-time conditions, to examine the position of the country and to make recommendations to H.M.G. as to possible forms of future government to be put before the people at a national referendum.

To help the Convention, the British Government proposed to make available the services of an expert adviser[3] to give guidance in constitutional forms and procedure. Mr Attlee also promised that a factual and objective statement of the Island's financial and economic situation would be made available to members of the Convention. Reconstruction plans would meanwhile be carried forward on the basis of an approved two to three year development plan, but, as Mr Attlee warned the House, 'the special difficulties of (Britain's) financial position over the next few years may well preclude us from undertaking fresh commitments'.

Now that all uncertainty had been cleared away, the Commission of Government pressed forward with local legislation providing for elections to the Convention, while the British Government in February 1946 dispatched two officials[4] to Newfoundland to prepare the promised economic

[1] *Ibid.* vol. 194, 5th ser.

[2] Parliamentary Debates, Commons, vol. 417, 5th ser.

[3] Professor K. C. Wheare, later Master of Exeter College and Vice-Chancellor of Oxford University.

[4] Mr Edgar Jones of the Treasury and the author.

and financial survey of the Island. It may be useful at this stage to summarize the main points emerging from this survey, which was later to be presented to Parliament[1] and to the National Convention. It was in itself a self-contained commentary on the Commission of Government's stewardship and on the state of the Island as it had emerged from the end of the Second World War.

The principal difficulty facing the compilers of the report was, as Governor MacGregor had complained in 1906, the absence of comprehensive statistics. They could, however, point out in broad terms that the accumulated national debt stood on 31 March 1946 at $82 million. As against this there were available exchequer balances and interest free loans to Britain totalling nearly $29 million. Annual revenue had risen sharply from $8·7 million in 1934 to $33·4 million in 1946. Reconstruction expenditure over the twelve years in which the Commission of Government had held office amounted to close on $30 million. Overall revenue still depended to a dangerous degree on customs and excise receipts, but it was a marked indication of the prosperity which war had brought that receipts from income tax and excess profits tax had risen from a mere $1·5 million in 1940 to $9·5 million in 1946. Deposits with the banks had also trebled between 1935 and 1945. A more disturbing feature of this new found prosperity was that the cost of maintaining the Public Services, excluding salaries, had nearly quadrupled over the same ten-year period. Exports meanwhile had shown a healthy and continuing increase; but to balance that gain imports had risen even more sharply. During the war years, the United States had replaced Britain as Newfoundland's best export market. Perhaps most significant of all, in the context of the changing pattern of trade, was the place now allotted to the export of fresh and frozen as opposed to salt cod. While in 1934 the former had earned a mere $4,000, it produced in 1945 a return of nearly $4 million or one-third of the value of the traditional fishery. As to employment, the number of men on relief at the end of 1945 was less than 8,000, compared with a peak unemployment figure of 75,000 on the eve of war.

Statistics on employment by industries were not available in any accurate form and, excluding the war-time building boom on the military bases, the compilers of the report could still only rely on the rule of thumb 1935 calculation that about 45 per cent of the working male population was employed in various branches of the fishery; 15 per cent on logging, agriculture and mining; 25 per cent in manufacturing services, industries and trade; and about half the balance in professional, personal and governmental services.

[1] As Cmd. 6849, 'Report on the Financial and Economic Position of Newfoundland'.

Such were the factual data to be laid before the National Convention. But as the Report itself could not fail to emphasize, the considerable improvement in Newfoundland's lot had been largely due to outside influences. Work on the military bases had achieved what peace-time trade and public expenditure had failed to bring about. 'Such an expansion was artificial and should not hide the fact that the long-term prosperity of the Island ultimately depends on a flourishing trade.' And at that moment in time no one could foresee how wide open Newfoundland's traditional fish markets would remain. The White Paper's comment on this basic industry was that 'its future prosperity would depend mainly on the retention of a proper balance between the various types of fish produced: on the maintenance of high marketing standards; the constant study of existing and potential markets and of world demand for fishery products and on careful attention to production costs'.[1]

In statistical terms the Report also paid due credit to the stewardship of the Commissioners. Admittedly the war had in some directions immensely eased their burden; but while concentrating on such essentials as education and health services, they had resisted the temptation to plunge heavily for development works which it might later prove difficult for a successor government to maintain. Thus while the number of hospital beds rose in ten years from 1,000 to over 2,400, and free and compulsory education to a maximum age of 14 had been introduced in 1942, the National Debt had at the same time been reduced and the reserves considerably strengthened. Strong encouragement in the form both of advice and grants had been given to embryo Town Councils: membership of the various trade unions had more than doubled and now stood at over 42,000; and imaginative steps had been taken to ease the housing problem, particularly in the capital. But although the Report's immediate message was (to coin a phrase) 'You've never had it so good', the lesson it sought (rather too polysyllabically) to drive home was 'It may be too good to last'.

With the financial and economic survey still in draft, the Commission of Government announced in February 1946 their detailed plans for the setting up of the National Convention. The Island was to be divided into 37 electoral districts. Certain of these would, on a population basis, return more than one candidate, and a special new district, comprising the whole of the Labrador, was to be created. For candidates themselves there would be residential or armed services, but no property qualifications. Nor would a candidate be required to put down a deposit. In the following month a draft Bill for the establishment of the Convention and the conduct of its proceedings was published locally for comment.

[1] Cmd. 6845.

These signs of activity stimulated interest among Newfoundlanders in their own future. The press was increasingly occupied in urging good candidates to stand and in analysing the advantages or drawbacks for Newfoundland of every conceivable form of future government. By June the Governor was able to report that candidates had been nominated in every district—as many as seven for one seat in several localities—and that already there had been seven unopposed returns. The elections themselves were now fixed for 21 June, except for the three most northerly areas where polling was to be deferred until 11 July because of weather conditions. By 23 July the full returns were available. It emerged that 8 members had been returned unopposed and 35 by majority vote; of the latter, 8 represented St John's.

It is instructive to note the occupations of the 43 men who were now to recommend what kind of government their country should have. They were, and this was no small advantage, a markedly mixed bag—13 merchants, 3 ex-servicemen, 3 trade unionists, 6 professional men, 2 co-operative workers, 2 journalists, a smattering of retired public servants, a farmer, a teacher, clerks, accountants, insurance agents and one candidate describing himself simply as 'gentleman'. Denominationally, the Church of England headed the list with 16 members. The Roman Catholic and United Churches provided 13 and 11 candidates respectively. As expected, the more highly populated and industrialized areas tended to return members from the merchant or professional classes, while the outports favoured trade unionists, civil servants, or teachers. From the composition of the Convention it was clear, even before discussion began, that the views of its members would be likely to divide almost equally between those committed to the restoration of responsible government, those who sought a further moratorium on all political activity, those who were sympathetic to the idea of confederation with Canada, and those who, while in principle favouring a return to self-government, wished first to examine all the available facts and evidence. The Convention was summoned by Proclamation to meet on 11 September 1946. It was to remain in session until March of the following year. In the early stages, the deliberations were marred by the death of its Chairman, Judge Fox. He was eventually succeeded, at the wish of the Convention itself, by one of its own members, Mr F. G. Bradley, K.C., a former Solicitor-General.

At the outset, the Convention worked chiefly through sub-committees set up to consider and report on various aspects of the economy. Before the Christmas recess, however, some plenary sessions were held at which the mercantile faction began a sustained attack designed to discredit the Commission form of Government. This, on the resumption of plenary sessions late in January 1947, broadened into a succession of debates, all basically unfriendly to the existing form of government. Resolutions were now passed in rapid succession; a first, dated 4 February, urging the Convention to find out how 'economic or fiscal relationships between the U.S.A. and Newfoundland, particularly bearing in mind the present occupation of certain Newfoundland territory by the said U.S.A.' could be improved. The same resolution went on to declare that the British Government must be asked what financial relationship would obtain between them and Newfoundland (1) if the Commission form of Government continued: (2) under a revised form of Commission Government with elected representatives; (3) under responsible government as before; (4) under any other suitable form of government. Finally the resolution inquired what would be a fair and equitable basis for Federal Union between the Island and Canada.

The Convention then dispatched a sub-committee of its members to discuss this omnibus self-exhortation with the Governor and certain of the Commissioners. As regards financial relations with the United States, the body was advised that such matters did not fall within the Convention's terms of reference. In any event, the impending international conference on tariff and trade questions, which was to lead to the establishment of the G.A.T.T., did not suggest that this was a propitious moment for Newfoundland to seek to enter into separate bilateral tariff negotiations. On relations with Britain and Canada, the Governor promised that the views of the Convention would be forwarded to both these Governments, either or both of which might agree to receive a delegation from the Convention. Having heard the Governor's statement, the Convention lost no time in passing, early in March, two further resolutions. The first, unanimously adopted, requested the British Government to receive a delegation consisting of their Chairman and six members. The second, passed only by a majority of 24 to 16, sought the same facilities of the Canadian Government once the first delegation had returned from London. In reply, the Dominions Secretary invited the Convention to send a team to London for discussions opening on 29 April 1947. The Canadian High Commissioner in St John's told the Chairman that his Government would be happy to receive a delegation in Ottawa at a mutually convenient date during the coming summer.

The Dominions Secretary, Lord Addison, held three meetings with the London delegation which had submitted to him in advance a questionnaire covering such matters as the possible cancellation or refunding of the public debt, modification of the leased bases agreement and trade and tariff agreements with Britain. The Secretary of State reported to Parliament on 13 May on these talks.[1] He said that he had made it clear to the delegation that it would always be Britain's desire 'to help Newfoundland within our means'. However, he had been unable to hold out any hope that H.M.G. would take over liability for the public debt, although the British guarantee would continue. Nor could any firm assurances be given that large purchases of frozen fish and iron ore would continue. If, he concluded, the Newfoundland people at the forthcoming referendum voted in favour of the continuation of Commission Government for a further period 'the U.K. Government would continue to be responsible for Newfoundland's financial stability. If, on the other hand, the people decided for responsible government, this would mean that full responsibility for Newfoundland's finances would rest with the Newfoundland Government and people and that the responsibilities undertaken by the U.K. Government in 1934 would cease.' The warning this time was clear and unequivocal. Independence, if chosen, would involve a calculated financial risk. As was later stated in the Government's considered reply to the delegation's questionnaire: 'it would be unusual for the U.K. Government to undertake to make development loans to a country having responsible government'. Government policy, logical though it might seem, was still a long way removed from the current era of golden handshakes, technical aid and Commonwealth assistance loans.

The Secretary of State was equally cold towards another proposal put forward by the delegation, namely that the Convention should debate the record of the Commission of Government. On this he emphasized that he did not regard it as a function of the members to discuss with him 'questions of the policy of the Newfoundland Government in current administrative and other issues. All this was outside the purpose of the delegation. Nor would such a discussion assist the National Convention in arriving at conclusions for their recommendations as to suitable forms of future government in Newfoundland.'[2]

These categorical statements clearly shook the confidence of those who, as good patriots and not solely through personal ambition, wished to see responsible government restored. It brought home to them that in pressing for early independence they would risk once more pitting their country against the vagaries of world trade and commodity fluctuations, this time without the guaranteed financial backing of any powerful friends. The upshot of the London talks was in short to increase the strength within the Convention of the small and hitherto suspect party which called for a

[1] Parliamentary Debates, Lords, vol. 147, 5th ser.

[2] Statement by Secretary of State for Dominion Affairs to National Convention, 1 May 1947.

serious examination of the terms on which Newfoundland might be admitted to the Canadian Confederation.

Disappointed with their delegation's reception in London, the Convention on 22 May adopted a fourth resolution demanding that a further team be sent forthwith to Washington 'for general trade discussions and [*sic*] other relevant matters affecting the future economy of Newfoundland'. But here again disappointment was in store since by reference back to the discussions which a sub-committee of the Convention had held with the Governor in February, the Commission of Government replied that talks of that nature with the U.S. Government were entirely outside the terms of reference and the powers and authority of the Convention. It remained now only to arrange the dispatch of a second delegation to Ottawa. The date for this was finally fixed for 25 June.

There was at this time scant enthusiasm in Canadian circles for the admission of Newfoundland to confederation. Memories of earlier abortive conferences were still live on both sides of the Cabot Strait. The Canadian Government had their own current difficulties in the Dominion–Provincial field. At best Newfoundland looked like a further costly liability to the Federal Exchequer. There was, in addition, a strong current of anti-Canadian feeling in the Island, particularly among the merchant and managerial classes. And in the back of the minds of Canadian Ministers and officials was the fear lest Canada should in some way be suspected of engineering Newfoundland into confederation. However, despite this discouraging atmosphere, the Canadian Prime Minister, Mr Mackenzie King, made a sympathetic statement to the Canadian House of Commons on 24 June, in the course of which he referred to the strong ties uniting Canada with Newfoundland. He announced that he had nominated a committee of eight Ministers, headed by the Minister for External Affairs, Mr St Laurent, to meet with the delegation from Newfoundland. At the first meeting on the following day basic documents were exchanged. The talks were then adjourned for a week for study and to enable the Newfoundlanders to make contact with Canadian departments and to gain an insight into Canadian methods of administration. The thoroughness with which the discussions were conducted throughout July clearly alarmed those members of the Convention in St John's who were opposed to the very thought of confederation. On 17 July, taking as their excuse that delays in Ottawa would set back the date for the eventual referendum, a faction of the Convention purporting to express a majority view telegraphed to their Chairman in Ottawa calling on him to reconvene the Convention immediately. Mr Bradley, unmoved by this tactic, replied that the delegation which he had led to Ottawa was doing no more and no less than the duty imposed on it and that he refused to break off the discussions under pressure from special interests. In the event, the Ottawa talks continued until the end of September, a development which ruled out all prospect of the referendum taking place before the early summer of 1948. At a final joint press conference on 29 September, the eve of the delegation's return to St John's, Mr St Laurent made it clear that there had been no negotiation of any terms of union between Canada and Newfoundland. Both sides had merely been exploring as completely as they could under what conditions union could be made to work. The Canadian Government would report to Parliament as soon as the Cabinet, which had been depleted by the death of the Federal Minister from New Brunswick, was again at full strength in October.

The draft Canadian terms were in the end presented to the National Convention on 6 November 1947. They can be summarized as follows: Newfoundland including Labrador would be a separate province of Canada. The Federal public and welfare services would extend to the Island. Canada would become responsible for the Newfoundland railway, postal, broadcasting, civil aviation, customs, defence and fishery protection services. The Canadian Government would take over the Newfoundland sterling debt, the Island retaining its financial surplus for development needs. In addition Canada would pay the following statutory subsidies: (1) $180,000 and 80 cents per head of the population annually; (2) $1·1 million annually. During the first twelve years of union Canada would also pay Newfoundland a Transitional Grant starting at $3·5 million annually for the first three years, and diminishing annually thereafter. Within eight years of union the Canadian Government would appoint a Royal Commission to review the Island's financial position and to recommend the form and scale of additional assistance. Newfoundland's representation in the Canadian Senate and House of Commons would amount on a population basis to six and seven members respectively.

Clearly the Canadian Government had digested the lesson of earlier failings. Their offer was on any interpretation a generous one. It held out to Newfoundland a real promise of financial security. The prospect of sharing in the full range of Canadian social security benefits—family allowances, unemployment insurance, higher old-age pensions and increased benefits to ex-servicemen could not fail to have a wide popular appeal, particularly in the outports. There was the further point that Canadian goods would enter Newfoundland free of duty; a factor which must lead to a marked lowering of the local cost of living. While this, and the condition that Canadian Federal rates of income tax must apply, would excite violent opposition from the merchant class, the terms as a whole offered unmistakable advantages to the bulk of the population. Indeed, it was soon calculated that the average outport fisherman with say four children would earn more from Canadian family allowances alone than he might hope to make from a normal season's fishing. While comment in the Canadian press was on the whole sympathetic, the reaction in Newfoundland was stormy. The caucus of the Convention favouring a return to responsible government at all costs, now launched a series of violent attacks on Canada in general and on the proposed terms of Union in particular. Its influence was enough to defeat a resolution, tabled in the concluding weeks of deliberation, which sought to include confederation as one of the issues to be put to the people at the referendum.

The Convention ended its labours on 29 January 1948 when it presented its report to the Secretary of State for (now) Commonwealth Relations.[1] Having rehearsed its earlier activities and referred to the work of its various sub-committees, whose reports it annexed, and to the discussions which its two delegations had held in London and Ottawa, the Report set forth in detail the constitutional resolutions which had been put finally to the vote. The first of these, passed unanimously, resolved that

> this Convention recommend to the U.K. Government that the following forms of government be placed before the people at the proposed referendum, namely:
>
> 1. Responsible government as it existed prior to 1934.
> 2. Commission of Government.

A second Resolution had been tabled requesting that there also be put to the people the choice for or against 'confederation with Canada upon the basis submitted to the National Convention on 6 November, 1947, by the Prime Minister of Canada'. But this proposal had been rejected by 29 votes to 16. Finally, the report tabulated the preferences of individual members of the Convention as between one form of Government and another. This, allowing for understandable abstentions, produced the following results:

For responsible government	28 }
For commission government	Nil }
For confederation as against responsible government	12
For confederation as against Commission	12
For responsible government as against confederation	28

[1] Signed Recommendations of the Newfoundland National Convention.

The Canadian Government refused to be dismayed by what must have seemed an ungenerous rejection of generous terms. As soon as the vote on the confederation issue had been taken, Mr St Laurent, soon to be Prime Minister, stated in the Canadian Parliament that his government was 'taking no part whatsoever in presenting [the] terms to the people of Newfoundland, nor would it venture to do or say anything which might be regarded as trying to influence the decision of the free people of Newfoundland'.[1] In answering a supplementary question, he did, however, underline one most important aspect of the Convention's duties, namely that 'it is only an advisory body, and the matter still has to be dealt with by those who have the constitutional responsibility for a decision'. So far as Canada was concerned, he added, the Government's offer was still before the people of Newfoundland. The British Government, all too uncomfortably aware where those 'constitutional responsibilities' lay, made no immediate comment.

Thus ended this strange but proper experiment of democracy functioning without responsibility within the framework of benevolent autocracy. Members of the Convention had been freely and popularly elected. They had been provided with all the data and expert advice on which to frame their recommendations. Their very activities, extending on and off over so many months had, whatever one might think of their conclusions, awakened a real and passionate interest throughout Newfoundland in the Island's political future. If the debates had not always been conducted at a high level of decorum, this was probably due as much to the plain-spokenness of Newfoundlanders as to lack of training in the arts of parliamentary behaviour. If from the deliberations there emerged a sharp cleavage between the 'haves' and 'have-nots', this was only to be expected from the composition of the Convention itself. Whatever the outcome, however unfair it might seem to outsiders that the sizeable minority favouring confederation should have been debarred from bringing this issue to the ballot paper, Mr Herbert had been justified in his foresight in proposing such a body. No one could now say that the Island's future had been settled over the heads of its inhabitants. Indeed, never in the course of Newfoundland's long history had so many words been spoken or written from so many differing viewpoints. And never had Newfoundlanders been granted so much time in which to arrive at what were to prove crucial and irrevocable decisions.

[1] 30 January 1948, Reply to Parliamentary Questions.

17

THE FINAL STEP

Dis-moi qui tu hantes
et je te dirai qui tu es.
Old French-Canadian saying

The British Government now had to weigh their attitude most carefully. While they, like the Canadian Government, were right to insist that the National Convention had been no more than an advisory body, and that the final decision as to what forms of government should be put before Newfoundlanders was theirs alone, they could not afford either to ignore Canadian susceptibilities or wholly to discount the recommendations of the instrument they themselves had forged. They came, however, to be convinced—not unaided by sheaves of telegrams from the confederate interest in Newfoundland—that there was a large body of opinion in the island, greater outside the Convention than within, which would be bitterly disappointed if it were given no opportunity to express a view on the proposed Canadian terms of union. Thus, on 11 March 1948, the Governor, on instructions from the Secretary of State for Commonwealth Relations, now Mr Noel-Baker, released the text of a dispatch in which the British Government made known the conclusions to which they had come.[1] Having referred to the Convention's conclusions and paid tribute to the thoroughness of its work, the dispatch continued:

His Majesty's Government in the United Kingdom appreciate that there has been a feeling amongst some members of the Convention that the entry of Newfoundland into a confederation with Canada should only be arranged after direct negotiations between a local responsible Government and the Canadian Government. The terms offered by the Canadian Government represent, however, the result of long discussion with a body of Newfoundlanders who were elected to the Convention, and the issues involved appear to have been sufficiently clarified to enable the people of Newfoundland to express an opinion as to whether confederation with Canada would commend itself to them. In these circumstances, and having regard to the number of members of the Convention who supported the inclusion of confederation with Canada in the ballot paper, His Majesty's Government have come to the conclusion that it would not be right that the people of Newfoundland should be deprived of an opportunity of considering the issue at the referendum and they have, therefore, decided that confederation with Canada should be included as a third choice on the referendum paper.

[1] Dispatch dated 2 March 1948 from Rt Hon. P. J. Noel-Baker to His Excellency Mr Gordon Macdonald.

The Resolution of the Convention did not indicate any limiting period for the continuance of Commission of Government if this form was found to be favoured by the electorate. Commission of Government was originally established on a temporary basis in view of the difficult financial circumstances of Newfoundland in 1933, and it appears to His Majesty's Government that if it is to be continued there must be some understanding as to the period in which the position would be again reviewed. They have decided, therefore, that the question to be placed on the ballot paper should be limited to the continuation of Commission of Government for a period of five years, on the understanding that before the end of that period arrangements should be made for a further testing of Newfoundland public opinion as to the future form of government at the end of the five year period.

The questions to be put before the people at the National Referendum will, therefore, be—

(*a*) Commission of Government for a further period of five years.
(*b*) Responsible Government as it existed in 1933 prior to the establishment of Commission of Government.
(*c*) Confederation with Canada.

Since on the above basis there will be three questions on the ballot paper, it is intended that there should be provision in the Referendum Act for a second referendum should no one form of government get an absolute majority at the first vote. The form of Government in favour of which the smallest number of votes was cast would in that case be omitted from the ballot paper at the second Poll.

It will be understood that, in the event of a form of government other than Commission of Government being decided upon as a result of the referendum, the Commission of Government will continue in being for the period required to arrange for the establishment of the new form of Government. In the event of the vote being in favour of confederation, means would be provided to enable the full terms and arrangements for the constitution of Newfoundland as a Province of Canada to be discussed and settled between authorised representatives of Newfoundland and Canada.

To this British statement of policy, Mr St Laurent added in the Canadian Lower House on 12 March the reflection that some 50,000 Newfoundlanders had petitioned the National Convention for the right to vote on the Confederation issue and that while the people of Canada would be ready to welcome their Newfoundland neighbours as part of a larger Canada, the latters' decision, which it was for them alone to take, would be received with 'understanding and respect'.

The eliminating ballot, based on the British Government's declaration, was ended on 8 June 1948 when the result of the first island-wide referendum was announced. Some 176,000 voters, over 80 per cent of the electorate, recorded their preferences, which were marked as follows:

For responsible government	69,230
For Confederation	63,110
For Commission government	21,944

Thus, no single choice had predominated. Commission Government must be eliminated and a second referendum held on the straight issue of responsible government versus confederation. It was enough to make both the British and Canadian Governments apprehensive lest the next round of voting should lead to a purely marginal victory for Confederation. In a debate in the Canadian House of Commons on 19 June, Mr St Laurent expressed the hope that there would be a clear-cut majority on the second ballot so as to spare Canada from the 'embarrassing position of having to take in a large group of recalcitrants, or having to renounce the opportunity of completing what the fathers of Confederation originally intended'. He did not think that if the 'constituted authorities came to the Canadian Government and said that the majority in Newfoundland wanted Confederation, Canada could then back away from her offer'.

The situation was an anxious one. It was discussed, with scrupulous regard for the constitutional proprieties, between the British, Canadian and Newfoundland Governments throughout the awkward period between the first and second plebiscites. Whatever personal feelings might be on all sides, it had become clear that, a decision once reached, no delay must ensue either in restoring responsible government or in preparing the way for final negotiations between the Canadian and Newfoundland authorities.

In the event the second referendum campaign proved to be a bitterly contested and close-run thing, with the future provincial Premier, Mr J. R. Smallwood, playing for the Confederate party as dominant and effective a role as Mr Bennett had in years past for the anti-confederates. This time the issue was not whether Newfoundlanders should be conscripted to die in the desert sands of Canada but whether 'baby bonuses' were more important to the average Newfoundlander than the elimination of local stores and industries through closer association with Big Brother across the water. To outside observers it had seemed more than likely that the majority of votes previously cast in favour of continuation of Government by Commission would now be switched in favour of Confederation. But there was a gap of over 6,000 votes to be filled before even the barest majority could emerge. And a resurgence of local patriotism or a tactical card badly played from the pro-Canadian camp could overnight wipe out the latter's prospective slender lead. Much too would depend on the numbers turning out to vote. For all these reasons, the outcome of the second plebiscite, which took place in July, was awaited both in Newfoundland and outside it with the greatest interest and apprehension. It proved to be close indeed. When returns from the outlying districts were received it emerged that no less than 84·7 per cent of registered electors had voted,

78,323 marking their papers in favour of Confederation, and 71,334 for the restoration of responsible government. An analysis of votes cast by districts showed, as foreseen, that the overwhelming support for responsible government came from St John's and the Avalon Peninsula; that is from the professional and commercial classes. Less expectedly, the mining communities voted preponderantly the same way. Fishermen and loggers on the other hand were generally in favour of union with Canada. In all, 18 electoral districts showed majorities for Confederation and 7 for responsible government. All now turned on the reaction of the Canadian Government. Would they consider a majority of a mere 7,000 votes in a poll of close on 150,000 a sufficient mandate to them to enter into final negotiations for Confederation?

Some short delay inevitably occurred while the three Governments exchanged views and the final few hundred votes were being collected from the remoter areas of the Labrador electoral district. On 30 July, however, simultaneous statements were released in London, St John's and Ottawa to the effect that, following consultations, the Canadian Government had expressed itself ready to proceed with arrangements for the entry of Newfoundland into the Canadian Confederation, and that the next step would be for appointed Newfoundland representatives to go to Ottawa 'in order to arrange, in negotiations with representatives of the Canadian Government, the final terms of union. These', the statement continued, 'will later be submitted to the Canadian Parliament, with whom the final decision will rest, for their approval.'[1] The Governor of Newfoundland concurrently announced that he would nominate seven delegates, supported by officials and advisers and led by the Newfoundland Vice-Chairman of the Commission of Government, Mr A. J. Walsh, K.C., to proceed to Ottawa. He added that his selection would be made 'with the object of affording full expression to all Newfoundland interests and it is hoped and confidently expected that all the members, even though some may have been opposed to the decision of the referendum, will bring to the negotiations a spirit of goodwill and the full weight of their wide experience and counsel so that the greatest good to Newfoundland as a whole may result'. For his part the Canadian Prime Minister stated that the result of the second plebiscite had been 'clear and beyond possibility of misunderstanding'. The result had been arrived at without any trace of influence or pressure from Canada. His Government would, therefore, be glad to receive with the least possible delay authorized representatives to discuss the terms of union, which would add strength to 'the two North American democracies in the British Commonwealth of Nations'. The

[1] C.R.O. announcement, 20 July 1948.

Newfoundland delegation nominated to negotiate in Ottawa included the previous Chairman of the National Convention, Mr Bradley; his successor in the concluding weeks of the Convention's labours, Mr John B. McEvoy; Messrs G. A. Crossley, Gordon A. Winter, P. Grouchy, C.B.E. and the untiring propagandist of union, Mr J. R. Smallwood.

While the tripartite statements naturally brought joy to the confederate camp, the large body of opinion opposed to union with Canada was by no means passive. By protest and petition, it now strove to create the suspicion that Britain and Canada had decided at all costs to engineer union in defiance of the wishes of over 70,000 electors. A committee describing itself as the Responsible Government League forcefully though unsuccessfully urged the British and Canadian Governments to receive delegations before any 'irrevocable alteration of the national status of Newfoundland' was decided upon. At the same time it emphasized that responsible government should first be restored and the terms of union submitted to a further plebiscite before Confederation was finally allowed to come about.[1] The League's next desperate throw, when the Newfoundland delegation had already reached Ottawa, was to approach the Speaker of the British House of Commons for the right to present a petition at the Bar of the House. This sought to protest against the decision to submit Newfoundland to the Canadian Confederation other than through a popularly elected Government. But this device was frustrated by the rules of the House itself. As the League and their sympathizers at Westminster discovered, Public Petitions could only be presented to the Commons by one or more Members of a local Legislature. And on this count Newfoundland ironically failed to qualify.

Meanwhile, as might be expected between Governments when detailed financial and constitutional matters were involved, the discussions in Ottawa proved heavy going. By mid-November, however, considerable progress had been made, the size of the provincial subsidies to be paid to Newfoundland remaining as the chief stumbling block. It was at this point that Mr Alan Herbert threw his weight behind the Responsible Government League. With the backing of a number of Members, he tabled a Motion in the British House of Commons on 3 December 1948 referring to the earlier abortive petition to the Speaker. The Motion urged the restoration of self-government to Newfoundland 'so that an election may be held in May 1949, after which the people of the Island, through their own elected Legislature and Government, may decide their future, whether by way of Confederation with Canada or otherwise'.[2] Shortly before this

[1] Petition dated 29 July 1948.
[2] For text of petition see appendix IV below.

development a delegation from the Newfoundland League had arrived in London, heralded by an inspired article in the *Chicago Tribune*, headlined 'Sell-out in Newfoundland'. According to this article,

> England has broken her pledge with us and has actually sold our country to Canada for its debt to that country. The Commission Government here, particularly the Chairman, is using Gestapo methods in a brazen attempt to stifle free speech...steps will be taken shortly to arrange a public demonstration demanding that the British Government remove the King's representative, who has prostituted his position and deliberately created disunity among our people by clever and sectarian tactics.[1]

Such robust language was scarcely designed to enlist the sympathy of British Ministers. Despite the vigorous support of Mr Herbert, who made no secret of his anti-confederate views, the delegation drew no comfort from their visit to London and the Commons Motion lapsed. The Responsible Government movement breathed its penultimate breath at a mass meeting in St John's on 10 December. On the following day agreed terms of Union were signed in Ottawa between the Newfoundland and Canadian delegations.

The Terms of Union[2] proved on close examination to be even more favourable to Newfoundland than those provisionally offered to the delegation from the National Convention in October of the previous year. It was agreed, not unnaturally, that the Labrador as defined in the Privy Council Report of 1927 would remain part and parcel of the new Province of Newfoundland, to which the generality of the British North America Acts 1867–1949 would henceforth apply. Subject to the provisions of these Acts, the Constitution of Newfoundland would again be that which had been in force prior to the suspension of responsible government, save that the Legislative Council would not immediately be revived. The powers and authorities previously exercised by the Governor of Newfoundland would now be vested in the Governor-General of Canada or the Lieutenant-Governor of the Province as the Federal or Provincial constitutions dictated. At the date of union the Provincial Legislature would consist of the same number of members as prior to 1933. Newfoundland would also be represented in the Canadian Senate by six members and in the Lower House by seven.

After making special provision in respect of denominational education and for the continuance of existing statutes, the Terms of Union dealt with the first of a number of problems more closely affecting the livelihood of Newfoundlanders—the fisheries. The sea fishery being under the British North America Acts a federal subject, vested in the Canadian

[1] *Chicago Tribune*, 12 October 1948.

[2] For full text see appendix v.

Minister of Fisheries, Newfoundland's most vital asset had of necessity been a matter of difficult and protracted negotiation. In the end it was agreed to the general satisfaction of both countries that, for a minimum initial period of five years after the date of Union, the fishery laws of Newfoundland would continue in force in the new province, the costs of the Newfoundland Fisheries Board (incidentally one of the more lasting memorials to the Commission of Government itself) and of the administration of the laws being borne by Canada.

Next the Terms of Union dealt with the crucial question of finance. A short bald article at the outset of the financial section—No. 23—stated that 'Canada will assume and provide for the servicing and retirement of the stock issued or to be issued on the security of Newfoundland pursuant to the Loan Act, 1933, of Newfoundland and will take over the Sinking Fund established under the Act'. Next it was agreed that the Island should retain its now considerable financial surplus—estimated at about $30 million—provided first that one-third was set aside during the first eight years of union for expenditure on current account alone, secondly that two-thirds should be available to the Province for the development of resources or the expansion of public services, and thirdly that no part of the surplus should be used to subsidize the production or sale of Newfoundland products in unfair competition with similar products from other Canadian provinces.

In the field of Federal subsidies, grants and taxation, generosity was again the keynote, the outcome being a tribute as much to the wise foresight of the Canadian Government which had learnt from past mistakes as to the enduring obstinacy of the Newfoundland negotiators. It was laid down that the Federal Government would pay to the new Province the following annual subsidies:

(*a*) $180,000;
(*b*) 80 cents per head of population;
(*c*) $1,100,000.

Subsidies (*a*) and (*b*) were defined as being for 'the local purposes of the Province and the support of its Government and Legislature'; subsidy (*c*) being in recognition of the special problems of Newfoundland 'by reason of geography and its sparse and scattered population'. In addition to the subsidies Canada agreed to pay what were described as transitional grants to ease the Island's passage into Confederation and to help her to develop revenue-producing services. These grants, extending over a twelve-year period, would be on a sliding scale, starting at $6·5 million annually for an initial three-year period: descending to $3·95 million in the sixth year and to $0·35 million in the final year.

On taxation the provincial government was to have, in line with other provinces, the option of entering into a tax agreement 'for the rental to the Government of Canada of the income, corporation income and corporation field taxes, and the succession duties tax field'. And finally, in the general financial context, it was agreed that within eight years from the date of Union, the Federal Government would appoint a Royal Commission

> to review the financial position of the Province of Newfoundland and to recommend the form and scale of additional financial assistance, if any, that may be required by the Government of the Province of Newfoundland to enable it to continue public services at the levels and standards reached subsequent to the date of Union, without resorting to taxation more burdensome, having regard to capacity to pay, than that obtaining generally in the region comprising the Maritime Provinces of Nova Scotia, New Brunswick and Prince Edward Island.

The remaining provisions of the Terms of Union set forth the public services, including the railway and steamship services, posts, telecommunications, civil aviation, customs and excise, defence, fishery protection, surveys, lighthouses and the like, which the Federal Government would take over at its own cost. Ex-servicemen—a point of particular concern to the Island in view of the heavy charges previously falling on the Newfoundland exchequer—would henceforth receive the benefits payable from Federal funds to ex-servicemen of other provinces, including pensions liabilities in respect of the First World War and the cost of vocational and educational training. Public servants, whether locally or federally employed, and those retired from the Newfoundland administration would be similarly safeguarded. All Newfoundlanders would become eligible for unemployment insurance benefits, merchant seamen benefits, old age pensions and health grants on the same conditions as already applied throughout the Dominion.

Finally, it was stipulated that

> these Terms are agreed to subject to their being approved by the Parliament of Canada and the Government of Newfoundland, shall take effect notwithstanding the Newfoundland Act, 1933, or any instrument issued pursuant thereto: and shall come into force immediately before the expiration of the thirty first day of March, 1949, if His Majesty has therebefore given His Assent to an Act of the Parliament of the United Kingdom of Great Britain and Ireland confirming the same.

The most significant and encouraging change in the Terms, as compared with those first offered by Canada, was that the twelve-year Transitional Grant was now to amount to a guaranteed minimum of \$42¾ million as against an earlier figure of \$26¼ million. It is pleasing to record that although one Newfoundland delegate absented himself, on the grounds that the agreement was insufficiently generous to the Island, from the brief signing ceremony which took place on 11 December 1948, the same inkwell was then used as for the signature of the original Confederation documents of 1864.

The attitude of the great majority of the Newfoundland delegation—and indeed of a steadily growing number of those on the Island—can best be summarized in the words of the last Chairman of the National Convention, Mr J. B. McEvoy, K.C. Speaking to the Canadian Club in Ottawa early in February 1949 he said:

> As a Newfoundlander who supported the cause of union, and as one who signed the terms of union, which will doubtless result in my eternal glorification, or damnation, depending upon one's point of view, it will be a proud day for me when the union is consummated...The Newfoundlander will then take his proper place in the sun...It means Newfoundland's emancipation from the stranglehold of isolation.

The final stages leading to the enactment of the Terms of Union were complicated both by the fact that the British North America Act had not been wholly 'repatriated' under the provisions of the Statute of Westminster and because of continuing Dominion–Provincial rivalries and suspicions.

The penultimate phase of Newfoundland's long odyssey opened in the Canadian House of Commons on 7 February 1949 when the Prime Minister moved that the House go into Committee to consider the following resolution:

> That it is expedient to present a bill for the approval by parliament of the terms of union of Newfoundland with Canada. The implementation of these terms will involve a charge upon and payment out of moneys in the consolidated revenue fund of Canada.[1]

After rehearsing the history of the struggle for confederation Mr St Laurent, himself a distinguished lawyer, explained what now remained to be done in order to put Union beyond legal or constitutional challenge in the Courts. First, the Terms must be approved by the Canadian Parliament and by the Government of Newfoundland. Then they must also be confirmed by action of Parliament at Westminster. If and when the first two stages were successfully completed, the third would be a mere formality. Anticipating the question why it should prove necessary to have a statute passed by the British Parliament to confirm the entry of Newfoundland into Canada, the Prime Minister returned two answers. In the first

[1] Debates, House of Commons, Dominion of Canada Session 1949, vol. 1, cols. 283 ff.

place, Section 146 of the British North America Act had provided that Newfoundland might be admitted into Confederation following upon joint addresses of the Houses of Parliament of Canada and Newfoundland by order made by [Her] Majesty in Council. But there was now no parliament in Newfoundland. Furthermore, His Majesty no longer, in consequence of the Statute of Westminster, exercised the prerogatives of the Crown over Canada except on the advice of his Canadian Ministers. Secondly, the British Government now had ultimate responsibility for the affairs of Newfoundland. Though, added Mr St Laurent,

it might be thought that Canada, on the decision of its own parliament, should be entitled to add to its territory, and though under the Statute of Westminster the parliament of Canada has the same rights, recognised internationally, to make laws having extra-territorial effect as has the parliament of the United Kingdom, a law of the parliament of Canada would hardly reach out and gather in a territory that was subject to the legislative and administrative jurisdiction of another autonomous nation. And whatever may be the fine points of technical procedure in that regard, the relations between Canada and the United Kingdom are not such that anything which would appear so discourteous would be considered on either side.

The Government had therefore decided to take as a precedent the procedure followed under the British North America Acts when amendments were found necessary in respect of the natural resources of Alberta and Saskatchewan which the Canadian Parliament had decided to hand over to those provinces. In these two cases agreements were made between the Federal Government and the provinces, containing clauses very similar to clause 50 of the proposed Newfoundland–Canadian Terms. These agreements were made subject to the approval of the Canadian Parliament, as well as to confirmation by an Act of Parliament at Westminster. That procedure no one had been 'tempted in any way to test'. It was one requiring short bills—in the case of the Canadian Parliament 'expressing, more or less, only that the terms of agreement of Newfoundland with Canada annexed to the bill as a schedule are ratified and, with respect to the parliament of the United Kingdom, that those terms shall be a schedule to the act which will be introduced before the parliament of the United Kingdom'.

It was clear from the brief debate which followed that all parties in the House were united in their desire to see Newfoundland take her place in the Confederation. The Prime Minister's motion was agreed to unanimously: the bill to approve the Terms of Union was read a first time and on the same evening a further bill 'to amend several statutes to make them applicable to or otherwise conform with the Canadian Confederation as and when Newfoundland becomes a province of Canada' was also given a first reading. There was little at this point to indicate that the Opposition intended to challenge with both ingenuity and persistence the procedures which the Government had chosen to bring union into effect.

The principal debate, during which this challenge was developed, opened on 14 February.[1] The Prime Minister then moved that 'a humble Address be presented to His Majesty the King in the following words:

To the King's Most Excellent Majesty:

Most Gracious Sovereign:

We, Your Majesty's most dutiful and loyal subjects, the House of Commons of Canada in parliament assembled, humbly approach Your Majesty, praying that you may graciously be pleased to cause to be laid before the parliament of the United Kingdom a measure containing the recitals and clauses hereinafter set forth to confirm and give effect to the terms of union agreed between Canada and Newfoundland;

An act to confirm and give effect to the terms of union agreed between Canada and Newfoundland.

Whereas by means of referendum the people of Newfoundland have by a majority signified their wish to enter into confederation with Canada;

And whereas the agreement containing terms of union between Canada and Newfoundland set out in the schedule to this act has been duly approved by the parliament of Canada and by the government of Newfoundland;

And whereas Canada has requested and consented to the enactment of an act of the parliament of the United Kingdom to confirm and give effect to the said agreement and the Senate and House of Commons of Canada in parliament assembled have submitted an address to His Majesty praying that His Majesty may graciously be pleased to cause a bill to be laid before the parliament of the United Kingdom for that purpose.

Be it therefor enacted by the King's Most Excellent Majesty, by and with the advice and consent of the lords spiritual and temporal, and Commons, in this present parliament assembled, and by the authority of the same, as follows:

1. The agreement containing terms of the union between Canada and Newfoundland set out in the schedule to this act is hereby confirmed and shall have the force of law notwithstanding anything in the British North America Acts, 1867 to 1946.

2. This act may be cited as the British North America Act, 1949, and the British North America Act, 1867 to 1946, and this act may be cited together as the British North America Acts, 1867 to 1949.

Mr St Laurent reminded the House that the seemingly anomalous constitutional step now being taken was necessary since, under Section 4 of the Statute of Westminster, action by the British Parliament could not be effective in respect to Canada without joint addresses from the Canadian Houses of Parliament. The addresses could 'go to His Majesty as an

[1] Debates, House of Commons, Dominion of Canada, vol. 1, cols. 493 ff.

expression, through their representatives in parliament, of the will of the people of Canada that union is desired and should take place'.

The then leader of the Opposition, Mr George Drew, now unmasked his constitutional batteries. He yielded to no one, he said, in his desire to see 'the fulfilment of the dream of those who laid the foundation for a great and united nation covering the whole of the northern part of this continent from the Atlantic to the Pacific'. But the constitutional aspects of the resolution now before the House required careful examination in order to ensure that nothing was done to 'fan the flame of discontent, either in Newfoundland or in Canada. That such discontent does exist, we all know.'

Mr Drew went on to emphasize the dangers likely to arise in the future from the fact that the people of Newfoundland, having no legislature of their own, were powerless to express a view on the procedures now under debate. Nor, and this was the real nub of a peculiarly Canadian argument, was any means being offered by the Government for prior consultation with the provinces. No such omission had occurred at the time the provisions of the Statute of Westminster and its applicability to Canada were under consideration. The Government seemed now to be lightly disregarding an important principle: namely, that the provinces had 'a very great interest in the manner in which the British North America Act can be amended'. If Parliament were to agree on this occasion that the Act could be amended by a majority decision, then 'you establish a precedent which tomorrow will lead to the amendment of the constitution, in respect to any aspect of that constitution, by some house of the future which might feel that was a desirable result. The challenge to democracy throughout the world today is the challenge to prevent centralised power in the hands of any government.'

To reinforce his case Mr Drew then moved the adoption of an amendment to the humble Address, the effect of which was that it should be presented only after the Federal Government had consulted with, and had obtained the approval of, the provinces to the proposed terms of union.

So far as the C.C.F. party was concerned, Mr Drew's appeal fell on deaf ears. The motion, as their leader Mr Coldwell said, was a surprising move on the part of the official Opposition. 'None of us were quite prepared for a reversal of the opinion expressed by them last week in the House of Commons.' The matter at issue seemed rather to his party one which brought into bold relief 'the need for the provinces and the dominion coming together as men of goodwill, regardless of party feeling or party affiliation, to see how we can modernise our constitution'. This appeal brought an acid retort from the leader of the Social Credit Party,

Mr Solon E. Low. In his view there was no need for hurry when one was on the wrong road. The question was not what Newfoundland did, but what 'kind of bedfellows' the existing provinces were to find themselves living with. His party would support the Progressive Conservative amendment since, as he put it: 'The provinces of Canada already occupy the Canadian bed. We contend that those Canadian provinces, since they will be very vitally affected by anything that is done about sharing the bed, should be consulted.'

Mr Drew's principal lieutenant, Mr Diefenbaker, marched onwards, the provincial rights banner held aloft. His leader's amendment, he argued, was nothing new. Canadians had stood up, ever since confederation, for provincial rights. Quoting in aid Junius, he warned the House that: 'One precedent creates another. They soon accumulate and constitute law. What yesterday was fact, today is doctrine.' In 1946 the Opposition had tabled a similar amendment when the Government of the day had attempted to circumvent the constitution in order to secure more members. In so doing they had had in mind that, as Macdonald, Cartier, Bennett and Lapointe had said in their day, the pact of confederation should not be amended in whole or in part, save with the consent of the provinces.

To these high principles other backbenchers, particularly from Quebec, added notes of more particular suspicion. Mr Jean François Pouliot for instance took up a remark of the British Lord Chancellor, Viscount Jowitt, to the effect that union would for many years to come impose a great burden on the Canadian people. In his view the Statute of Westminster was 'just bunk'. It changed nothing in the British North America Acts. Britain was glad to get rid of Newfoundland; but this did not mean that Canada should agree to swallow the Island 'in one gulp'. 'Take your time and think about it', he appealed to the House, 'Lord Jowitt has rendered a tremendous service to Canada by warning us against haste.' An even more outspoken case from the Quebec separatist fringe was presented by Mr Maxime Raymond. In his view, the Canadian Government were giving way with unseemly speed to Britain's desire to be rid of Newfoundland. What would be the consequences for Canada? In the first place, increased financial liabilities falling on the wealthiest provinces, Ontario and Quebec; secondly a defence budget still further swollen; thirdly, the involvement of Canada in global war since 'we shall be getting a mortgaged property on which the Imperial Commission has already leased bases to the United States for 99 years'; and fourthly the imperilment of Canadian unity, not least because of the 'imperialist tendencies' of the people of Newfoundland. Front-runner though he might seem to be for the Afro-Asian decade, Mr Raymond revealed his basic fears when he came to quote the *Winnipeg Free Press*. This leading paper, as far back as July 1948, had had the temerity to remark in regard to Union that 'the bargain is not all onesided. Canada also stands to gain. Her population is increased by 350,000 English-speaking stock.'[1] This, as the Member contented himself with saying, 'should give us food for thought'.

But such ultra-nationalist, separatist and States-rights viewpoints did not reflect the sentiments of the majority of the House. As Mr Pearson, then Minister of External Affairs, put it when the debate was continued on 15 February: 'Most of us who came to this Chamber yesterday...came to praise Newfoundland and not, we thought, to bury it in a wrangle over legality and procedure with charges—which I do not think we need take too literally or too seriously—that we who favour union with Newfoundland...are thereby destroying our constitution.' It cannot be said, despite one robust and convoluted backbench intervention at a late stage in the debate to the effect that all who had taken part would find their names added to the scroll of Canadian history, that the remaining speeches added much to what had gone before. The plain facts were that with the exception of a few backbenchers, notably from Quebec, who were suspicious of Newfoundland's entry into confederation on ethnic, religious or financial grounds, the House as a whole welcomed this historic rounding-out of the Canadian nation. The occasion offered the never-to-be missed chance of a provincial dig at the Federal mammoth. But there was no real desire to frustrate the march of history. And so, on 16 February, when the questions were finally put, the Opposition amendment was defeated by 140 votes to 74. Whereupon, as *Hansard* records, 'the members rose and sang "O Canada" and "God Save the King"'.

Immediately thereafter, the House descended from the heights of history to the second reading of the Consequential Provisions Bill to amend the Statute law of Canada. This bread and butter measure, designed to avoid the creation of a legal vacuum while the consequences of Newfoundland's entry into confederation were digested, occupied the detailed attention of the Lower House for ten days and after third reading on 17 February was passed to the Senate.

There the Bill approving the Terms of Union had already been introduced and given a first reading on 14 February. The main debate opened on the following day[2] and by 17 February, to the accompaniment of much echoing argument from the Commons and little by way of novel thought, the Terms of Union and the Address to His Majesty had both received the approbation of the Upper House. It now remained only for His Majesty

[1] *Winnipeg Free Press*, 28 July 1948.
[2] Debates of the Senate, Dominion of Canada, Session 1949, cols. 86 ff.

to approve the petition from His Canadian Parliament and, with His leave, for the British North America (Amendment) Bill to be introduced at Westminster. This was done on 2 March.

As the Commonwealth Secretary, Mr Noel-Baker, said at the outset of the second reading: 'I have a narrowly restricted task in this Debate, I have not to argue the merits of confederation... All that was for Newfoundland and Canada to settle... My task is to present to the House the agreement which [they] have made, to explain how that agreement was arrived at, to justify the action of our Government in the matter, and to ask the House to give the agreement the force of law.' But as he also confessed: 'I know that some hon. Members have some doubts about this Bill, that they regard it with apprehension, and that they view with misgiving the method by which the policy of confederation with Canada is being carried through.'[1]

While, therefore, the Bill, like other amendments to the British North America Acts which still found their way to Westminster, should by tradition have been taken as a formality and as a measure on which the House would not divide or inject a note of controversy, political feelings on this occasion still pulsed strongly, giving the debate a far more controversial character than would normally be the case. After all, Parliament was being asked not merely to set its seal on something which the sister Parliament of Canada had requested, but to sign away for all time the independent or quasi-independent existence of a fellow Commonwealth partner. However logical the decision, however properly arrived at, it was hardly likely to gain unanimous support.

Mr Noel-Baker anticipated some of the criticisms likely to be made of the Bill: that no means had been found of first restoring to the people of Newfoundland their own Legislature; that an appeal from certain interests in Newfoundland to the Judicial Committee of the Privy Council against the very aims of the legislation was pending and could not be heard before the date now fixed for Union; or that, as had already been argued in the Canadian Parliament, the Address to His Majesty had been founded on the wrong section of the British North America Act. In answer to the first point the Minister rehearsed the now familiar arguments. To the second he replied that, whatever the advice of the Privy Council, it would not affect the sovereign right of Parliament to legislate as it saw fit. On the third, he contented himself by repeating the legal explanations already given by Mr St Laurent to the Canadian House of Commons.

The democratic dilemma with which all Members, tacitly or otherwise, felt themselves to be faced, was admirably exposed by Mr Oliver Stanley. Foreshadowing the amendment shortly to be moved by (now) Sir Alan

[1] House of Commons, Parliamentary Debates, cols. 371 ff. (2 March 1949).

Herbert, he emphasized that what the House had to decide was whether the British Government had indeed ascertained 'objectively and in a judicial fashion' the will of the people of Newfoundland. He appreciated the strong feelings of the Responsible Government League which had led them to petition Parliament at Westminster. And he realized the dangers of deciding the future of a whole country on so narrow a majority. But there were weighty arguments on the other side. Why for instance were the complaints from the petitioners against the whole method of ascertaining the people's wishes withheld until the second, or at least the first referendum, had been completed? And what about the feelings of the Canadian Government and people? If the British Parliament rejected the Bill, might not this lead Canada to withdraw altogether from her proposals to Newfoundland? And would not their action mean that the House had decided to accept the view of the minority in Newfoundland rather than of the majority? The greater worry, as Mr Stanley saw it, was that the House should reach a decision without allowing proper time to the Privy Council to hear the pending appeal from the Supreme Court of Newfoundland. Even though there might be no more than a thousand to one chance of that appeal succeeding, he urged the Government on moral grounds to have the operative date of federation postponed until the hearing had been completed.

Now, and for the last time, Sir Alan Herbert broke his lance in support of the Responsible Government cause. The essence of the Amendment which he moved was that the Bill should not be proceeded with 'until it has been considered and approved in the Legislature of Newfoundland'. In a speech charged more with emotion than with logic he listed the errors of the British Government and the grievances of the Responsible Government League. The basis of their appeal to the Privy Council could, he said, be summarized under the following heads:

(*a*) Confederation can be brought about only in accordance with a law which is binding on the people of Newfoundland.

(*b*) Section 146 of the British North America Act, 1867, is such a law. But Confederation is not to take place under the provisions of that Section. That is for the reason that under that Section Confederation could come about only upon an Address from the Houses of the Legislature of Newfoundland, and no such Address can be presented while the provisions of the Old Letters Patent are suspended.

(*c*) Therefore it is proposed to establish Confederation under a new Imperial Act, which in effect repeals Section 146 of the 1867 Act. It provides that the Agreement 'shall have the force of law notwithstanding anything in the British North America Acts, 1867 to 1946'.

(*d*) But the Imperial Act will not be binding on the people of Newfoundland because (*a*) the Imperial Parliament has no power to make a law binding the people of Newfoundland except at the request and with the consent of a Parliament of that Dominion, and there has been no request and consent of such a Parliament, alternatively (*b*) if the request and consent can be given by the people upon a referendum, the referendum must be held under a valid law, and the Referendum Act was invalid.

All too conscious of the fact that it was he himself who had first proposed the establishment of the National Convention, Sir Alan now tried to throw doubt on the results of the subsequent referenda by arguing not only that the Legislature of Newfoundland should have been re-established to ratify their findings but that the British Government should have made it a condition precedent that any change in Newfoundland's constitutional status could only result from a two-thirds majority of the peoples' votes. Even the American constitution and the rules of the M.C.C. provided at least this latter safeguard. What now were the facts? So far as Newfoundland was concerned, the Terms of Union had been approved by the Government of Newfoundland, consisting of 'seven people appointed by the Crown, four of whom are Englishmen. There is not even a majority of Newfoundlanders in the Government of Newfoundland which approved of the terms by which that Dominion loses its sovereignty. Is that democracy? Is that what we understand by the traditional practices of this country and Commonwealth?' There followed much in Herbertian vein about the robust and independent spirit of the Newfoundlanders and regarding the dubiety of Canada's financial offer which, according 'to a man rather experienced in these matters' would present the Island with a deficit of $70 million after twelve years of confederation—'A hell of a way', as he added, 'to run a railway.' And, in conclusion, 'I have done my best for these people, and I can do no more, but I do say this: if the policy of this Bill prevails, I for one shall not be sorry to go out from a Parliament which can so affront a proud, British, loyal, white people, and the good name and honour of my own beloved country'.[1]

Leaving aside his seconder, Sir Patrick Hannon, Sir Alan's eloquent pleas found little support in the House. One former Parliamentary Under Secretary for Commonwealth Relations, Mr Parker, veered rather to the other extreme by maintaining that the majority of Newfoundlanders had cast their votes against a repetition of sectarian strife, jobbery, corruption and the return to power of the Water Street merchants. While the difficulty of proceeding with the Bill with an appeal to the Privy Council still pending was what seemed most to worry the House, the overall perplexity was

[1] The Government had already announced their decision to abolish the University seats.

perhaps best illustrated by a backbencher, Mr Gammans. The Government, he said,

> have landed the House in an absolutely impossible and unenviable position. If we support the Bill we are laying ourselves open to a charge of offending, and mortally offending nearly 50% of the people of this loyal and ancient colony. If we oppose the Bill, we appear to be unfriendly, not only to the remainder of the people of Newfoundland, but also to Canada as well...I am sure that the end in view is desirable and probably inevitable. But could not this have been done more cleverly and more tactfully? As it is, the Bill will leave a very nasty taste behind it...

No such misgivings assailed the Under Secretary of State for Commonwealth Relations. Mr Gordon Walker began his speech in reply to the debate with the words: 'Practically without exception, the issue in this debate has been one of method and not of objective.' He could find no validity in the legal objections which had been raised and, while appreciating the moral issue of the pending appeal to the Privy Council, said flatly that the House was in essence dealing with a political, not a judicial matter. The responsibility lay with Parliament and could not be dodged. The Government could therefore hold out no hope that the legislation would be delayed until the Privy Council had tendered its advice. It had to be borne in mind that this appeal, which had been entered only at the eleventh hour, sought to challenge acts done as long ago as 1947. Moreover, even if the passage of the Bill was now delayed, what was to stop some other case being started as soon as the first appeal was resolved? The Government had been fully justified in putting Confederation as one of the issues on the ballot paper. To have done otherwise would have meant depriving large numbers of Newfoundlanders of their right to express an opinion. As to the size of the eventual majority 'democratic organisations...depend upon clear and simple majorities on clear and simple issues...whether the vote was sufficient for Confederation was really a question for Canada to settle'.

There had been a tendency, concluded Mr Gordon Walker, to talk

> as if Newfoundland were being cast away and sold into slavery by confederating with Canada...I think the right way of looking at this is to regard it as an ampler and fuller life which is being opened out for Newfoundland in the Commonwealth. Newfoundland has decided between two sorts of self-government. It has decided to be a self-governing province within the Confederation of Canada rather than to be a self-governing nation, and a very small one, in a dangerous and difficult world. It is not choosing between slavery and self-government but between one sort of self-government and another, both of them within the Commonwealth.

On which Sir Alan Herbert's amendment was defeated by 217 votes to 15 and the Bill was read a second time.

The concluding stages in the Lower House were taken on 9 March.[1] Sir Alan Herbert then moved a series of amendments clause by clause, the effect of which was again to propose that the Bill should not have force of law until its contents had first been approved by the Parliament of Newfoundland. The Attorney-General, Sir Hartley (later Lord) Shawcross, rose to demolish this and other contentions. It may be useful for the last time to summarize the views of the then British Government. Taking first the suggestion that Confederation could only be effected under Section 146 of the British North America Act, 1867, Sir Hartley pointed out that this was in a sense an enabling Section. Under it Newfoundland might be admitted into Confederation by Order-in-Council and without the necessity of any further statute or legislation by Parliament at Westminster. But it could not properly be suggested that this was the only and exclusive means by which union could thereafter have been effected. All that the 1867 Statute did was to provide a method, short of legislation by the Parliament at Westminster, by which union could be brought about. But there was no doubt at all that actual legislation would have produced exactly the same result. Thus, given that the British Parliament at that date enjoyed complete and unfettered sovereignty over all the Dominions, they could at that time have passed another Act which would have effected total union between Canada and Newfoundland without regard to the provision of the Statute of 1867. Indeed, Parliament had in 1915 passed another amendment to the British North America Acts which in theory materially altered the representation which Newfoundland would have enjoyed in the Canadian Senate, had union been brought about at that time.

Turning next to the contention that the present Bill involved an infringement of the Statute of Westminster, the Attorney-General emphasized that this Statute was 'an adoptive Act'; that is, it was brought into operation in relation to particular Commonwealth countries if and when the legislatures of those countries chose to adopt it. But Newfoundland never did take this step; furthermore, Section 7 of the Statute expressly excluded the alteration or amendment of the British North America Acts from its scope. Thus, there was clearly nothing contrary to the Statute of Westminster in the Bill now before Parliament.

Thirdly, Sir Hartley dealt with the contention that what was now proposed to be done should only be done on a request from a Legislative Assembly in Newfoundland. On this he pointed out that after the passage of the Newfoundland Act, 1933, the United Kingdom Parliament enjoyed

[1] House of Commons, Parliamentary Debates, vol. 462, cols. 1259 ff.

unfettered sovereignty over Newfoundland which, although in name a Dominion, in fact became a colony. Since that date Parliament at Westminster had passed a number of Statutes applicable to Newfoundland and no one had at any time doubted the capacity of Parliament to do so. In the circumstances, the people of Newfoundland had made their request to the British Government in the only way open to them.

Finally, the Attorney-General countered the criticisms already voiced about the pending appeal to the Privy Council. As he pointed out, there were precedents for Parliament proceeding with legislation while relevant appeals were pending to the Court of Appeal or to the House of Lords in Britain. Parliament on those occasions had made the law which it thought ought to be made and this was clearly its sovereign right. Most of the arguments raised under this head were of little more than academic and historical interest. To suggest at this late stage that there was no power in law to hold the National Convention or referenda in Newfoundland reminded him of the story of the steward on the cross-channel steamer who said to the green-faced passenger 'You cannot be sick here'; to which the latter promptly retorted that he had just been sick and was indeed sick again on the spot. Thus the local position could not overcome the facts of the case. The referendum was a fact and a fact at least as important as the petition from the Responsible Government League with which Sir Alan Herbert had made such play.

These weighty arguments clearly influenced the House and deflected it finally from any lingering desire to upset the constitutional applecart. The Commons were undoubtedly further swayed by a last-minute plea from the Commonwealth Secretary, Mr Noel-Baker, who suggested that since Sir Alan Herbert had helped to prolong the unhappy bitterness in Newfoundland, he should now help to secure the acceptance of Confederation. A Labour backbencher gave the final *coup de grace* to the Responsible Government faction by adding that 'if half the slop we have heard from the Opposition tonight had been converted into real effort to do something for our oldest Dominion in the intervening years this Bill would not have been necessary'. Instead of being 'a bad debt to the British dominions' the island would henceforth become an asset of which all might be proud. It was left to Mr Noel-Baker, before the Bill was read a third time and passed, to point out that both the Coalition and present Labour Governments had been engaged for over five years on a consistent plan for the future of Newfoundland. Governments, as he emphasized, could not carry forward such a policy for so long a period and at the last moment switch their operation. Thus, it was to be hoped that all acrimony would be forgotten and that Confederation would end in good for the people of Newfoundland.

The Bill reached the Upper House on 15 March, where the second reading was moved by the Leader of the 1943 Goodwill Parliamentary Mission, Lord Ammon.[1] His speech was remarkable only for its reference to the fact that before the appeal from Newfoundland had reached the Privy Council it had been dismissed in the Court of first instance in Newfoundland by the Judge in these terms: 'The action is based on fundamental errors of law and logic which are apparent on the face of the papers and which are fatal to it...logically, legally and practically it seems to me to be nonsense.' Furthermore, the full Supreme Court Bench in Newfoundland, when the case came before it on appeal, had dismissed the action without the Attorney-General even being called upon to speak. In such circumstances to put the clock back at this late stage would not only cause great embarrassment in Britain's relations with Canada; it would bring consternation to the majority—a growing majority—of the people of Newfoundland who favoured confederation.

For the rest, and with minor variants, the debate followed the same pattern as in the Lower House, though, as might be expected, on a less emotional note. Lord Semphill moved an amendment in the same terms as those tabled by Sir Alan Herbert. Viscount Swinton spoke forcefully in support of the action proposed. Viscount Simon, with the weight of a previous Lord Chancellorship to support him, cast further interesting light on the much debated appeal to the Privy Council. As he pointed out after studying the judgement handed down in the Lower Court in Newfoundland, each of the contentions advanced by the petitioners had been examined with great care and he personally had much admiration for the way in which the Judges had applied the constitutional law. It was significant that the judgement, apart from referring to the fact that the claim was legally and otherwise nonsense, also made the point forcefully that it was a dead horse and that flogging would not bring it to life or make any difference to the petitioners. The upshot of all this in Lord Simon's view was that should the appeal ever come before the Privy Council—and as he emphasized no case had yet been deposited there—the Privy Council would not be called on to decide its merits. They would merely have the question before them of whether it was not 'manifestly a frivolous and vexatious proceeding'. Never, concluded Lord Simon, had there been 'a more astounding effort to get a political question decided by a court of law than exists for this particular litigation'.

In the upshot, Lord Semphill did not press his amendment to a Division and the Bill was read a second time on the same day. The Third Reading was briefly disposed of on 22 March when the Commonwealth Secretary,

[1] House of Lords, Parliamentary Debates, vol. 161, cols. 309 ff.

Viscount Addison, brought the long marathon to its conclusion with the words:

This Bill marks the fact that by their own wish, and with the good will of others, the citizens of Newfoundland are to join with the other Provinces of this great Federation, with all the rights of a great Province. It is, I think, a farseeing and wise decision that will fortify the strength of Newfoundland, that will extend the bounds of benefit and opportunity for all its citizens, and that will assure the liberties that are enshrined in this Bill for the people of Newfoundland in a wider and stronger association.[1]

Immediately thereafter the Bill was read a third time and passed. On the following day it received the Royal Assent.[2]

On 23 March the Canadian Prime Minister was thus able to inform the Commons that simple ceremonies to celebrate the act of union would take place in Ottawa and St John's on 31 March or 1 April. In the upshot, and despite some consequent ribaldry, the latter date was preferred. In Newfoundland itself a few Union flags were half-masted or draped in black. But these were the sole outward signs of continuing opposition to Confederation. The inner thoughts of irredeemable patriots, of merchants or what one could now almost describe as 'Little Newfoundlanders' were expressed only privately. The local newspaper with the largest circulation in the Island, the *Evening Telegram*, was more forthright. Its leading editorial roundly asserted that

before our island home lies, if we as citizens of Canada choose to play our part, not begrudgingly or sullenly, but wholeheartedly and cheerfully, a brighter and greater future...There are without a doubt few Newfoundlanders who do not experience feelings of regret in closing the chapter which records nearly a century of history since the Oldest Colony was granted self-government...with those regrets are also entertained the hope that the new era means the broadening of the horizon of Newfoundland: the acquiring in union of enhanced strength...assurance, too, that the dread of want in the minds of the widow, the aged and the infirm has been materially lightened. United in a common allegiance to the Crown, holding the same religious beliefs, practising the same code of ethics in our every day life...we the people of Newfoundland should find little difficulty in forming with our new fellow-countrymen close bonds of fellowship.[3]

On Confederation day similar sentiments were expressed on Parliament Hill in Ottawa and at Government House, St John's, where simultaneous ceremonies took place. In the provincial capital the Chief Justice and Leader of the negotiating delegation to Canada, Sir Albert Walsh, K.C.,

[1] House of Lords, Parliamentary Debates, vol. 161, col. 586.

[2] Geo. VI, c. 1.

[3] St John's, *Evening Telegram*, 1 April 1949.

was sworn in as first Lieutenant-Governor of the Province—an act accompanied by the presentation to him from the Canadian Minister of Mines and Resources, Mr Gibson, of a certificate of Canadian citizenship. In Ottawa, while the official Canadian carilloneur played in the peace tower of Parliament the well-known Newfoundland folksong 'Squid Jigging Ground', Mr St Laurent and Mr Bradley—on that same day sworn in as the first Newfoundlander to take office in the Federal Cabinet—exchanged appropriate speeches.[1] As the latter summed up the historic occasion: 'In fancy we can see them now—Macdonald, Brown, Cartier in Canada and Carter and Shea in Newfoundland—bending over this scene in silent and profound approval.' What better words to conclude with than his—'We are all Canadians now.'

[1] For a full record of the official ceremonies in Ottawa and St John's, see Debates, House of Commons, Dominion of Canada, Session 1949, vol. III, cols. 2276–82.

EPILOGUE

> I venture in this concluding chapter upon a series of prophecies regarding Newfoundland...I...set the time limit at twenty five years, which would bring us down to the year 1955...There will be...a large university in St. John's, education will be free and compulsory. Illiteracy will be abolished...The population of Newfoundland will be half as great again as it is now.
>
> J. R. SMALLWOOD, 1930

Close on twenty years have passed since the Act of Union. Tomorrow's Newfoundland leaders were born Canadian citizens. To them 1933 can be no more than an old man's tale and the era of Commission Government an anachronism. Even a Newfoundlander looking back from the peaks of war-time prosperity in 1945 might have been hard put to it to recall how his country had come to surrender its Dominion Status.

Yet this would have been to render the Commissioners less than justice. They had come in 1933 on an appalling heritage. They laboured against great odds. A number of them, Newfoundlanders and British alike, have since passed on, among them such outstanding personalities as Sir Wilfred Woods, Sir Harold Puddester, and the lovable, respected, penultimate Governor of the Island, Admiral Sir Humphrey Walwyn. But *si vis monumentum*...Gander Airport, so vital to the allied cause in the Second World War, was a tribute to their foresight and pertinacity. There is today in the Island a well-organized, properly recruited, permanent civil service cadre. The Fisheries Board has become a model for other provinces; the financial system placed on a sound basis. Hospitals and schools are accepted facts of life. No more do vital statistics record, as they did in 1935, an infant mortality rate of 103 per 1,000; or reports emphasize the absence of children from school 'due to lack of clothing, and particularly of footwear'.[1] Certainly the Commissioners benefited from the fortuitous prosperity that came with war. Admittedly they carried through no grandiose development plan. But they had laid the groundwork for recovery long before prosperity returned. It was no fault of theirs that deficit financing, pump-priming, Commonwealth Assistance Loans, Keynsian philosophies were things as yet undreamt of. Nor could they be blamed for the framework of rigid Treasury control and benevolent autocracy which had been fashioned for them. Within the limitations imposed they 'builded better than they knew'. Few Newfoundlanders, living today with the monuments they left behind them, would fail to give credit to their labours.

1 'Newfoundland, Annual Report of the Commission of Government for the year 1936', Cmd. 5425, p. 11.

Nor could one conceivably apportion blame to the Commissioners for the way in which Confederation came about. They merely held the ring as agents for the British and to some degree Canadian Governments. If the point is raised at all, it is solely because suspicions have been voiced that, in deciding the fate of Newfoundland, democratic processes were in part at least suppressed: that Confederation, to put it bluntly, had been 'engineered'.

Nothing could have been further from the truth. Although in 1945 the idea of union with Canada as a final solution to the Island's perennial problems was a still alien concept, its attractions grew rapidly from the moment steps were taken to establish the National Convention. Even the narrow majority achieved at the second referendum failed to reflect true feeling in the Island by the time Confederation came about. The Responsible Government League had fought hard. But its petitions and appeals, and the emotional support which they attracted at the eleventh hour at Westminster, no longer reflected the considered views of the majority of Newfoundlanders. The League represented above all merchant opinion. It was a self-protection society rather than a broadly based patriotic movement. And, like all pressure groups, its protests and propaganda gave a false impression of its underlying support and strength.

Robust patriotism did of course play its part. There are still Newfoundlanders living who for understandable reasons continue to regret the passing of their national identity. But, when Confederation came, bitterness was by no means as widespread as the League and its supporters in the British Parliament had prophesied.

It is no part of this book to review the fortunes of Newfoundland since that time, nor, at less than twenty years' remove, to attempt a final judgement on the consequences, good or otherwise, of union.

Facts, however, can scarcely be denied and a few of them, taken at random, will show how the Island has fared since 1949.

At that date, the population of Newfoundland was in the region of 350,000. Today it is over half a million. In 1949 the energetic promoter of the Confederation cause, Mr J. R. Smallwood, was elected as leader and Premier of Newfoundland's first provincial government. He has held office uninterruptedly since that date; in the process surviving five elections in the Liberal cause. Prior to Confederation, statements of net ordinary revenue and expenditure showed a tendency, even in palmy wartime years, to balance out an annual average of $30 million. For the financial year 1964/5, leaving aside capital account, revenue was estimated at $116 million and expenditure at $111 million.[1] Even in 1949 little positive had

[1] Province of Newfoundland, Estimates of Revenue and Expenditure 1964/5.

been done to attract fresh investment to Newfoundland or to open up the Labrador. Yet in 1963 a leading British Sunday newspaper could devote the greater part of its colour supplement to 'Newfoundland's place in the Sun'.[1] Even allowing for the passing euphoria of such promotions, it is worth noting such phrases as: 'Half of Newfoundland's annual 550 million lb fish production runs through modern fresh frozen filleting plants', 'Capital investment has tripled Newfoundland's mineral production (currently £35 million a year) in ten years...', 'Newfoundland this year and next will open major new iron ore mines and copper and gold mines. One of the world's top producers of iron and fluorspar, it will soon rank among the top world producers of asbestos fibre.'

Above all, in the aftermath of the legal battle for possession of the Labrador, the development of the vast iron ore deposits in the Wabush and Knob Lake areas has been of great significance. Hundreds of miles of railway have been driven inland from Seven Islands on the St Lawrence River through desolate country. Towns have sprung up in areas where previously even the hardiest trapper had barely penetrated; and the water potential of the giant Hamilton (or as they have since been renamed Churchill) Falls has now been made accessible. Not that these assets are without their accompanying drawbacks. The development of the iron ore regions and the influx of workers from Quebec have re-awakened the interest of the provincial government in the Labrador boundary question. And the use to which the Churchill Falls' immense reservoir of cheap hydro-electric power should be put has given rise to a dispute—as yet unresolved—between Quebec and Newfoundland. Yet despite these difficulties and disputes it is clear that the wealth of Newfoundland Labrador is now firmly within man's grasp.

In truth, earlier illusions have now become profitable realities. It is possible that the continuous increase of population may bring fresh unemployment problems in its wake. But the accent is still on economic diversification and growth. Although the material drawbacks of the denominational system have not yet been fully overcome, more and more government money is being poured into health and education, and the Premier has recently launched a bounty scheme to eliminate isolated outports, which he describes with justification as the 'curse of Newfoundland'.

Already some attempts had been made to persuade people from the offshore islets to migrate to the Island itself. The latest scheme is, however, more far-reaching. It is designed to bring in the remote and the virtually inaccessible to more populous centres where they can benefit from social and municipal services hitherto denied them. Fishermen themselves would

[1] *The Sunday Times*, Colour Magazine, 3 March 1963.

also profit from this programme since it would offer a far better opportunity for selling their catch to central processing plants. The scheme involves families receiving a bounty of $2,000 apiece, 75 per cent to be borne by the Federal Government and the remainder by the Province provided—and this must still be a big 'if'—all members of a particular community agree to move.

The economic advantages of the project are self-evident. But, given Newfoundland's history and the tough individualism of those born and bred in the remoter outports the concept, however logical, amounts to a social revolution. If successful, it could well be concluded that Newfoundland has finally turned her back on the past.

But however long the experiment takes to mature and whatever the immediate opposition, there is no doubt that economic and social developments such as those briefly described above would, even twenty years ago, have seemed mere opium dreams.

Above all, the visitor who knew Newfoundland in pre-union days, and, who returns there now, cannot fail to be impressed by the human and material changes effected in so short a time. Education has advanced by leaps and bounds: the health and prosperity of the people have grown and with these improvements the size of the population itself. The completion of the trans-island highway has opened up Newfoundland to itself and to tourism as never before. And each year brings new industrial and economic growth.

From the most casual reading of Newfoundland's history it must remain doubtful whether, even with the unparalleled prosperity generated by a second world war, the Island could have achieved today's stability by 'going it alone'. Modernization of the fisheries; a greater diversification of the economy would undoubtedly have come about, if only through bitter experience. But the massive investment and industrial development which have taken place since 1949 rest on the fact that, as the tenth province, Newfoundland is now part of a great and growing nation. If Newfoundlanders have, many of them with reluctance, sacrificed a praiseworthy patriotism, they have in return gained the assurance and confidence which membership of a vaster community imparts.

From the struggle for settlement, the autocratic and haphazard rule of the Fishing Admirals, the despairing battles with Imperial mercantile interests, through representative to responsible government, and on from one financial crisis to another, the people of Newfoundland have run the whole gamut of imperial experiment. Plunged from prosperity to poverty, from autonomy to quasi-dictatorship, they have at last, through the freely expressed will of the majority, found haven in a greater port. The Island may have surrendered her Dominion Status but, through a mightier partner, her welfare and her membership of the Commonwealth remain assured. The Newfoundlander of today is at last reaping the harvest which his forebears sowed with so much sweat and bitterness and toil.

A Canadian Senator who knows and well loves Newfoundland said to me recently, 'Its no longer the same. The old character has gone. The people have been Canadianized.' He was not meaning to disparage his own country. But I knew what he felt. It reminded me of the changes that have overtaken my own English village. Until the end of the war it was small, inward looking, quaint. Visitors from London, less than 50 miles away, were referred to in the pub as 'foreigners'. There was the manor house and a few large properties: scattered around them three or four dozen farm labourers' cottages. Merchants' homes and fishermen's shacks. Comfort on the one hand: picturesque poverty on the other. Today all is changed. The 'foreigners' and refugees from bombed-out areas have taken over. 'Desirable villas' and council houses have risen mushroom-like at every corner. The old character has gone: the farm hands almost vanished. Walking down the village street, which now boasts its service station and three shops, I share the Senator's regrets. And yet, we do now have a bus service and the septic tank at the bottom of the garden is a mere uneasy memory. No more in Newfoundland than in our village can one turn back the page. For the prosperous, the privileged, the past still holds its charms. But today's farm labourer, like the fisherman, is surely happier with his stomach full, his children dry-shod and his roof intact. Local patriotisms may suffer: the modern way of life create a dulling sameness. But from new-found prosperity a fresh and more vigorous sense of regional identity may spring. Despite the mainland invasion of the Island, despite political absorption, Newfoundland has too much of history, of rugged obstinacy, of native character ever to lose her true identity.

SELECT BIBLIOGRAPHY

Ammon, Charles George (1st Baron). *Newfoundland: the Forgotten Island* (Fabian Research Series, no. 86). Fabian Publications Ltd. and Victor Gollancz, 1944. 28 pp.

Anspach, Rev. Lewis Amadeus. *History of the Island of Newfoundland*, 2nd ed. Sherwood Gilbert and Piper, 1827. 512 pp.

Bennet, Charles Fox. *Four Letters on the Subject of Confederation.* St John's, Newfoundland, *Morning Chronicle*, 1870. 32 pp.

Birkenhead, 1st Lord, *see* Smith, F. E.

Cormack, W. E. *Narrative of a Journey across the Island of Newfoundland.* St John's, Newfoundland, *Morning Post*, 1856. 68 pp. (2nd ed. edited by F. A. Bruton, Longmans Green, 1928).

Dominion Office. *Report on the Financial and Economic Position of Newfoundland.* H.M.S.O. 1946. 46 pp. (Cmd. 6849.)

Great Britain, Privy Council. *Labrador.* In the matter of the boundary between the Dominion of Canada and the Colony of Newfoundland in the Labrador Peninsula, 1926–7, 12 vols.

Grenfell, Wilfred Thomason *et al. Labrador: the Country and the People*, new ed. New York, Macmillan and Co., 1910. 497 pp.

Grenfell, Wilfred Thomason. *Labrador Doctor*, 3rd ed. Hodder and Stoughton, 1921. 307 pp.

Harvey, Rev. Moses. *Across Newfoundland with the Governor.* St John's, Newfoundland, *Morning Chronicle*, 1879. 71 pp.

Harvey, Rev. Moses. *Newfoundland as it is in 1894: a Handbook and Tourists' Guide.* Kegan Paul, Trench, Trubner and Co., 1894. 298 pp.

Harvey, Rev. Moses. *Newfoundland in 1900.* New York, South Publishing Co., 1900. 187 pp.

Hatton, Joseph and Harvey, Rev. Moses. *Newfoundland: the Oldest British Colony.* Boston. Doyle and Whittle, 1888. 489 pp.

Innis, H. *The Cod Fisheries.* Toronto, 1954.

Keith, Dr Arthur Berriedale. *Constitutional History of the First British Empire.* Oxford, Clarendon Press, 1930. 443 pp.

Lodge, Thomas. *Dictatorship in Newfoundland.* Cassells, 1939. 273 pp.

MacKay, Robert Alexander (ed.). *Newfoundland: Economic, Diplomatic and Strategic Studies.* Oxford University Press, 1946. 577 pp.

McLintock, A. H. *The Establishment of Constitutional Government in Newfoundland 1783–1832.* Longmans Green, 1941. 246 pp.

Morris, Edward Patrick (1st Baron). 'Genesis of the "French Shore" question', in *Newfoundland Magazine*, July 1900, pp. 69–83.

Morris, Edward Patrick (1st Baron). 'Newfoundland', in *The British Empire, a survey, edited by Hugh Gunn*, vol. 1, pp. 1–27. W. Collins, Sons and Co. Ltd., 1924.

Morton, W. L. *The Critical Years: The Union of British North America 1857–1873.*

Mosdell, H. M. *Newfoundland: its manifold attractions for the capitalist, the settler and the tourist.* St Johns, Newfoundland, Government Printer, 1920. 94 pp.

Newfoundland. House of Assembly. Documents relating to the proceedings of the Conference at Ottawa upon the subject of Confederation with Canada. St John's, Newfoundland, Government Printer, 1895. 47 pp.

Newfoundland Royal Commission. Report. H.M.S.O., 1933. 283 pp. (Cmd. 4480. *Chairman*, Lord Amulree).

Prowse, D. W. *History of Newfoundland from the English, Colonial and French Records*. Macmillan and Co., 1895. 742 pp.

Responsible Government League. *The Case for Responsible Government*. The League, 1948. 16 pp.

Rose, Dr J. Holland *et al. The Cambridge History of the British Empire*, vol. VI, *Canada and Newfoundland*. Cambridge University Press, 1930.

Smallwood, Joseph Roberts. *The New Newfoundland*. New York, Macmillan and Co., 1931. 277 pp.

Smallwood, Joseph Roberts (ed.). *The Book of Newfoundland*. St John's, Newfoundland. Newfoundland Book Publishers Ltd., 1937, 2 vols.

Smith, Frederick Edwin (1st Earl of Birkenhead). *The Story of Newfoundland*. Horace Marshall and Son, 1920. 192 pp. London.

Tanner, Vaine. *Outlines of the Geography, Life and Customs of Newfoundland–Labrador* (Acta Geographica T. 8, no. 1). Helsinki, Societas Geographica Fenniae, 1944. 909 pp. (Reprinted Cambridge University Press, 1947, 2 vols.)

Willson, Beckles. *Tenth Island*. Grant Richards, 1897. 208 pp.

APPENDIX I

THE EARL OF ROSEBERY TO MR WADDINGTON

Enclosure 1 in No. 106 in North America No. 122

Foreign Office, July 24, 1886

M. L'Ambassadeur,

Her Majesty's Government have read with attention the note which Your Excellency did me the honour to address to me on the 21st ultimo respecting the Newfoundland fishery question, and in which you inform me that, in view of the attitude taken up by the Legislature of Newfoundland towards the Fishery Arrangement signed at Paris in November last, the Government of the Republic have felt themselves compelled to issue new instructions to their naval officers to secure to French fishermen the exercise of their Treaty rights. Under those instructions the French Commanders are enjoined:–

1. To seize and confiscate the gear belonging to 'foreigners', resident or non-resident, fishing on that part of the Newfoundland coast stated by the French Government to be reserved to the French;

2. To protest against all building or working of mines on that part of the coast which they designate as 'the French Shore', an appellation derived from the enjoyment by French citizens of certain fishery rights during the fishing season;

3. To disregard the jurisdiction of the local magistrates on British territory;

4. To modify the attitude of toleration recently observed by them in regard to the salmon fisheries, and to protect French citizens in the pursuit of the lobster fishing as well as in that of cod.

In describing the above measures, your Excellency states that the French Government are resolved to exercise in the fullest and most rigorous manner the rights conferred upon France by the Treaties.

I cannot conceal from your Excellency the concern with which Her Majesty's Government have received such a communication from your Government.

It is in no way the wish of Her Majesty's Government to contest the right of the French Government to demand that French fishermen shall be secured in the due exercise of their Treaty privileges. But they must emphatically protest against the interpretation of those privileges which is put forward in your Excellency's note under reply and is implied in the measures to which that note refers.

They have repeatedly affirmed in the course of numerous negotiations that such claims are not supported by the Treaties concluded between the two countries, and it would be a matter of great regret if the instructions which have been sent out to the French naval officers to enforce these claims should lead to complications which the patience and moderation of both Governments, and the good sense and forbearance of their respective naval commanders on that coast, have succeeded in averting during a long period of years.

I have no desire to reopen the discussion on the numerous points in dispute, but I cannot refrain from deprecating more particularly the claim put forward by your Government to ignore during the fishing season the territorial jurisdiction flowing from the sovereign rights of the British Crown over the whole of the Island of Newfoundland, expressly conferred by the terms of the XIIIth Article of the Treaty of Utrecht; nor can I pass in silence the reiterated assertion in your note of an exclusive right of fishing on the part of the coast on which the French Treaty rights exist. There can be no doubt that the inhabitants of the coast must not 'interrupt by their competition' the French fishermen, but Her Majesty's Government can hardly believe that the French Government could intend to apply to them the term 'foreigners', or to question the right of the Colonists to procure the means of subsistence by fishing on their own coast, so long as they do not interfere with the Treaty rights of the French fishermen. Such a claim has no precedent in history, and would be not only repugnant to reason, but opposed to the practice of years, and to the actual terms of the Declaration of Versailles, which provides that the old methods of fishery 'shall not be deviated from by either party', showing conclusively that the French right to the fishery is not an exclusive one.

Her Majesty's Government accepted provisionally the recent arrangement signed at Paris with satisfaction, as offering, on the whole, a reasonable compromise, but it is unnecessary to state that, during the whole of the negotiations, it was perfectly well understood that its ratification by Her Majesty's Government must be subject to its acceptance by the Legislature of Newfoundland. Her Majesty's Government are still in communication with the Colonial authorities, and have not abandoned the hope that the arrangement may yet bear good fruit.

In the meanwhile, the two Governments have during the last two years practically carried it out as far as circumstances have permitted. It will be a matter for very serious regret on the part of Her Majesty's Government if the French Government, ignoring that amicable arrangement, should now by any aggressive action unnecessarily provoke a recurrence of the grave difficulties of which both nations have had so long and regrettable an experience.

I have thought it well to lose no time in taking exception on the part of Her Majesty's Government to some of the positions taken up in your Excellency's note to which it would be impossible for them to assent. I have not, therefore, waited to include in this Despatch the answer of Her Majesty's Government to the proposal of a modus vivendi made verbally by your Excellency to me on the 22nd ultimo, and repeated in your Excellency's aide-memoire of the 23rd. With that I will deal in a separate communication; but in the meantime, I should be glad to learn that the new instructions to the French naval officers have been suspended, as they would offer a serious obstacle to the friendly conclusion of such an arrangement.

I have etc.

(*Signed*) ROSEBERY

APPENDIX II

Convention between Great Britain and France, respecting Newfoundland, and West and Central Africa.—Signed at London, April 8, 1904.[1]

[Ratifications exchanged at London, December 8, 1904.]

His Majesty the King of the United Kingdom of Great Britain and Ireland and of the British Dominions beyond the Seas, Emperor of India, and the President of the French Republic, having resolved to put an end, by a friendly Arrangement, to the difficulties which have arisen in Newfoundland, have decided to conclude a Convention to that effect, and have named as their respective Plenipotentiaries:

His Majesty the King of the United Kingdom of Great Britain and Ireland and of the British Dominions beyond the Seas, Emperor of India, the Most Honourable Henry Charles Keith Petty-Fitzmaurice, Marquess of Lansdowne, His Majesty's Principal Secretary of State for Foreign Affairs; and

The President of the French Republic, his Excellency M. Paul Cambon, Ambassador of the French Republic at the Court of His Majesty the King of the United Kingdom of Great Britain and Ireland and of the British Dominions beyond the Seas, Emperor of India;

Who, after having communicated to each other their full powers, found in good and due form, have agreed as follows, subject to the approval of their respective Parliaments:–

ART. I. France renounces the privileges established to her advantage by Article XIII of the Treaty of Utrecht, and confirmed or modified by subsequent provisions.

II. France retains for her citizens, on a footing of equality with British subjects, the right of fishing in the territorial waters on that portion of the coast of Newfoundland comprised between Cape St. John and Cape Ray, passing by the north; this right shall be exercised during the usual fishing season closing for all persons on the 20th October of each year.

The French may therefore fish there for every kind of fish, including bait, and also shell fish. They may enter any port or harbour on the said coast, and may there obtain supplies of bait and shelter on the same conditions as the inhabitants of Newfoundland, but they will remain subject to the local Regulations in force; they may also fish at the mouths of the rivers, but without going beyond a straight line drawn between the two extremities of the banks, where the river enters the sea.

They shall not make use of stake-nets or fixed engines without permission of the local authorities.

On the above-mentioned portion of the coast, British subjects and French citizens shall be subject alike to the laws and regulations now in force, or which

[1] Signed also in the French language.

may hereafter be passed for the establishment of a close time in regard to any particular kind of fish, or for the improvement of the fisheries. Notice of any fresh laws or regulations shall be given to the Government of the French Republic three months before they come into operation.

The policing of the fishing on the above-mentioned portion of the coast, and for prevention of illicit liquor traffic and smuggling of spirits, shall form the subject of regulations drawn up in agreement by the two Governments.

III. A pecuniary indemnity shall be awarded by His Britannic Majesty's Government to the French citizens engaged in fishing or the preparation of fish on the Treaty Shore, who are obliged either to abandon the establishments they possess there, or to give up their occupation, in consequence of the modification introduced by the present Convention into the existing state of affairs.

This indemnity cannot be claimed by the parties interested unless they have been engaged in their business prior to the closing of the fishing season of 1903.

Claims for indemnity shall be submitted to an Arbitral Tribunal composed of an officer of each nation, and, in the event of disagreement, of an Umpire appointed in accordance with the procedure laid down by Article XXXII of The Hague Convention. The details regulating the constitution of the Tribunal and the conditions of the inquiries to be instituted for the purpose of substantiating the claims, shall form the subject of a special Agreement between the two Governments.

IV. His Britannic Majesty's Government, recognizing that, in addition to the indemnity referred to in the preceding Article, some territorial compensation is due to France in return for the surrender of her privilege in that part of the Island of Newfoundland referred to in Article II, agree with the Government of the French Republic to the provisions embodied in the following Articles:–

V. The present frontier between Senegambia and the English Colony of Gambia shall be modified so as to give to France Yarbutenda and the lands and landing-places belonging to that locality...

VI. The group known as the Iles de Los, and situated opposite Konakry, is ceded by His Britannic Majesty to France.

VII. Persons born in the territories ceded to France by Articles V and VI of the present Convention may retain British nationality by means of an individual declaration to that effect...

VIII To the east of the Niger the following line shall be substituted for the boundary fixed between French and British possessions by the Convention of the 14th June, 1898, subject to the modifications which may result from the stipulations introduced in the sixth and seventh paragraphs of the present Article...

[Here follow detailed provisions]

...It is further agreed that on Lake Chad, the frontier line shall, if necessary, be modified so as to assure to France a communication through open water at all seasons between her possessions on the north-west and those on the south-east of the Lake, and a portion of the surface of the open waters of the Lake at least proportionate to that assigned to her by the map forming Annex 2 of the Convention of the 14th June, 1898.

APPENDIX III

THE GOOSE BAY AGREEMENT

Signed at St John's, Newfoundland, October 10, 1944
(Canada, Treaty Series, 1944, No. 30)
Memorandum of Agreement

Made this tenth day of October Anno Domini one thousand nine hundred and forty-four BETWEEN The Government of Canada represented herein by the High Commissioner for Canada in Newfoundland of the first part AND The Government of Newfoundland represented herein by the Commissioner for Public Utilities and Supply of the second part.

WHEREAS the development of a strategic air base for the defence of Canada, Newfoundland and Labrador, within the general scheme of hemisphere defence and as a basis of operations in the Atlantic area, is considered by the Governments of Canada and Newfoundland to be of the utmost importance:

Therefore the undersigned, duly authorized to that effect, have agreed as follows:–

1. (1) The Government of Newfoundland will lease to His Majesty the King in right of Canada ALL THAT certain piece or parcel of land situated at Goose Bay in Labrador described as follows: Beginning at a concrete post marked 'A' at the most northerly point of Terrington Basin at ordinary high water mark, the said point being North Latitude 53 degrees 22 minutes 24·6 seconds and West Longitude 60 degrees 24 minutes 21·5 seconds; thence North astronomically 305 chains; thence West astronomically 640 chains; thence South astronomically 920 chains more or less to the northern shore of the Hamilton River at ordinary high water mark; thence easterly along the northern shore of the Hamilton River at ordinary high water mark to Goose Bay; thence northerly and westerly along the shore of Goose Bay at ordinary high water mark to Terrington Basin; thence westerly and northerly along the shore of Terrington Basin at ordinary high water mark to the point of beginning; containing 120 square miles more or less; hereinafter referred to as the Air Base; reserving nevertheless from the Air Base all mines and minerals; TO HOLD the same unto His Majesty the King in right of Canada for a period of ninety-nine years from the first day of September Anno Domini one thousand nine hundred and forty-one for the purposes of the construction, operation and maintenance of an air base thereon for operations by land or water for the purposes set forth in the recital hereto.

(2) Such lease shall be authorized or ratified in such manner as may be agreed upon by the Governments of Canada and Newfoundland.

2. During the period of the lease the Government of Canada shall have the right to construct, maintain, operate, manage and control an air base at the Air Base and without restricting the generality of the foregoing shall have as incidental thereto the following rights, namely:

(*a*) to build and maintain a roadway approximately 22 miles in length from the Air Base to Northwest River and such other roads outside the Air Base as may be agreed with the Government of Newfoundland from time to time. All roads built hereunder outside the Air Base shall become public highways. Where the Air Base separates two roads or two parts of the same road, passage through the Air Base will be permitted, subject to such reasonable limitations as are necessary for the protection of the Air Base and its operations;

(*b*) to take from the neighbouring streams and rivers such water as may be necessary for the purposes of the Air Base;

(*c*) to develop, construct and operate power plants for the use of the Air Base and for such purposes to use such water storage and power sites as may be agreed and upon such conditions as may be imposed by the Government of Newfoundland;

(*d*) to construct radio stations and transmission lines and operate communications by radio, telephone and telegraph for the purposes of the Air Base, subject to agreement with the Secretary for Posts and Telegraphs of the Government of Newfoundland as to frequencies and power output in the case of radio communications;

(*e*) to construct docks, wharves, slipways, piers and anchorages for ships and aircraft at such places as may from time to time be agreed with the Government of Newfoundland.

3. For the duration of the war and for such time thereafter as the Governments agree to be necessary or advisable in the interests of common defence:

(*a*) the management and control of the Air Base shall be under the direction of the Royal Canadian Air Force, wireless and meteorological services being supplied by the Department of Transport of the Government of Canada;

(*b*) use of the Air Base will be made available to United Kingdom military aircraft and to aircraft of the United States Navy and Army Air Forces. The Government of Canada may permit the Governments of the United Kingdom and the United States to erect buildings at the Air Base for the accommodation of aircraft and military personnel, and may permit such Governments to station Naval and Air Force military personnel at the Air Base;

(*c*) the use of the Air Base by civil aircraft shall be permitted insofar as such use is a necessary part of the war effort, and the Air Base shall be available for such other civilian use as may be mutually agreed upon;

(*d*) in addition to any arrangements for the co-ordination of the wireless and meteorological services with other operating air bases and stations, such services at the Air Base may be co-ordinated with those operated by the Government of the United States in Canadian territory adjacent to Labrador and by the Royal Air Force.

4. The Government of Canada may from time to time erect within the Air Base such works, buildings and fortifications as it may deem to be necessary for the maintenance of the Air Base as an operational air base and for its defence, and may station at the Air Base such military personnel as may be required for the defence thereof.

5. Civil and military aircraft owned by the Government of Newfoundland shall have the right to use the Air Base on terms not less favourable than those of the Government of Canada.

6. The right of the United Kingdom to use the Air Base for military aircraft shall be the subject of consultation and agreement between the Governments of Canada, the United Kingdom and Newfoundland after the war, and, in the meantime, the rights of the United Kingdom under Article 3 of this Agreement shall continue unimpaired.

7. The Government of Canada will employ Newfoundland labour as far as practicable at the Air Base.

8. Duly authorized officers of the Government of Newfoundland shall have access at all reasonable times to the Air Base in the course of the carrying out of their duties.

9. The Government of Canada shall transfer free of cost to the Government of Newfoundland any land within the Air Base reasonably required by the Government of Newfoundland for the erection of buildings for the accommodation of its officials or for any other Government purposes.

10. In order to avoid doubt it is hereby declared that the laws of Newfoundland shall be applicable throughout the Air Base and to all persons therein or thereon.

11. The development of the Air Base being primarily for defence, the air base and its facilities shall not during the war be used for civil or for commercial operations, except as provided in clause (*c*) of Article 3 hereof. The question of its or their use for civil and commercial operations after the war, and all matters incidental thereto, will form the subject of discussion between the Governments of Canada, the United Kingdom and Newfoundland, and this discussion will take place not later than twelve months after the war.

12. The Government of Canada agrees that it will not, without the consent of the Government of Newfoundland, transfer to any third party in whole or in part the rights, powers and authority herein granted to the Government of Canada.

Signed at St John's, Newfoundland, in duplicate, this tenth day of October, A.D. 1944.

On behalf of the Government of Canada:

J. S. MACDONALD

On behalf of the Government of Newfoundland:

W. W. WOODS

APPENDIX IV

PETITION FROM NEWFOUNDLAND TO BRITISH HOUSE OF COMMONS

Extract from Parliamentary Debates, House of Commons, Volume 462

TO THE HONOURABLE THE COMMONS OF THE UNITED KINGDOM OF GREAT BRITAIN AND NORTHERN IRELAND IN PARLIAMENT ASSEMBLED:

The HUMBLE PETITION of the undersigned people of Newfoundland SHOWETH as follows:–

1. Your Petitioners are loyal British subjects and qualified electors of the Dominion of Newfoundland.

2. In 1933 upon the request of the Legislative Council and Assembly of Newfoundland, the Letters Patent of 1876 and 1905 were suspended and new Letters Patent were issued bearing date January 30th, 1934, which provided for the administration of the Island until such time as it became self-supporting again.

3. The arrangements made for the administration of Newfoundland, during the period of the suspension of Letters Patent 1876 and 1905 clearly indicated that:–

'It would be understood that as soon as the Island's difficulties are overcome and the country is again self-supporting Responsible Government, on request from the people of Newfoundland would be restored.'

4. In 1948 the Newfoundland National Convention unanimously agreed that Newfoundland was and had been for several years self-supporting and recommended that the people of Newfoundland be given the opportunity of requesting the restoration of Responsible Government or the retention of Commission of Government. But, contrary to this recommendation, plebiscites were held in 1948 in which an issue was made of the question of Confederation with Canada.

5. In the referendum of July 22nd, 1948, less than 43 per cent. of the total electorate voted for Confederation with Canada which percentage Your Petitioners hold is insufficient to justify any change in the Newfoundland constitution as it existed under Letters Patent 1876 and 1905.

6. Moreover Your Petitioners protest any official recognition of the results of the said referendum on the grounds that

(*a*) the said referendum was contrary to the letter and spirit of the Letters Patent 1934;

(*b*) it was a denial of the majority vote of the National Convention;

(*c*) it did not take into account Section 146 of the British North America Act, 1867, wherein provision was made as to the procedure to be followed in the event of union between Canada and Newfoundland;

(*d*) it asked the electorate to commit their country to Confederation with Canada without any negotiation of terms;

(*e*) it circumvented the pledge given Newfoundland in 1933, relating to the restoration of Responsible Government.

YOUR PETITIONERS THEREFORE humbly pray

(*a*) that immediate provision may be made for the restoration to Newfoundland of Responsible Government as under Letters Patent 1876 and 1905 and in accordance with Letters Patent 1934;

(*b*) that no negotiations be undertaken or concluded for Union of Newfoundland with Canada, other than by representatives of a duly elected Government of the people of Newfoundland.

And as in duty bound Your Petitioners will ever pray etc.

APPENDIX V

TERMS OF UNION OF NEWFOUNDLAND WITH CANADA

MEMORANDUM OF AGREEMENT ENTERED INTO ON THE ELEVENTH DAY OF DECEMBER, 1948, BETWEEN CANADA AND NEWFOUNDLAND.

WHEREAS a delegation appointed from its members by the National Convention of Newfoundland, a body elected by the people of Newfoundland, consulted in 1947 with the Government of Canada to ascertain what fair and equitable basis might exist for the union of Newfoundland with Canada;

WHEREAS, following discussions with the delegation, the Government of Canada sent to His Excellency the Governor of Newfoundland for submission to the National Convention a statement of terms which the Government of Canada would be prepared to recommend to the Parliament of Canada as a fair and equitable basis for union, should the people of Newfoundland desire to enter into confederation;

WHEREAS the proposed terms were debated in the National Convention in Newfoundland and were before the people of Newfoundland when, by a majority at a referendum held on the twenty-second day of July, 1948, they expressed their desire to enter into confederation with Canada;

WHEREAS the Governments of the United Kingdom, Canada and Newfoundland agreed after the referendum that representatives of Canada and Newfoundland should meet and settle the final terms and arrangements for the union of Newfoundland with Canada;

AND WHEREAS authorized representatives of Canada and authorized representatives of Newfoundland have settled the terms hereinafter set forth as the Terms of Union of Newfoundland with Canada;

It is therefore agreed as follows:

TERMS OF UNION

UNION

1. On, from, and after the coming into force of these Terms (hereinafter referred to as the date of Union), Newfoundland shall form part of Canada and shall be a province thereof to be called and known as the Province of Newfoundland.

2. The Province of Newfoundland shall comprise the same territory as at the date of Union, that is to say, the island of Newfoundland and the islands adjacent thereto, the Coast of Labrador as delimited in the report delivered by the Judicial Committee of His Majesty's Privy Council on the first day of March, 1927, and approved by His Majesty in His Privy Council on the twenty-second day of March, 1927, and the islands adjacent to the said Coast of Labrador.

APPLICATION OF THE BRITISH NORTH AMERICA ACTS

3. The British North America Acts, 1867 to 1946, shall apply to the Province of Newfoundland in the same way and to the like extent as they apply to the provinces heretofore comprised in Canada, as if the Province of Newfoundland had been one of the provinces originally united, except insofar as varied by these Terms and except such provisions as are in terms made or by reasonable intendment may be held to be specially applicable to or only to affect one or more and not all of the provinces originally united.

REPRESENTATION IN PARLIAMENT

4. The Province of Newfoundland shall be entitled to be represented in the Senate by six members, and in the House of Commons by seven members out of a total membership of two hundred and sixty-two.

5. Representation in the Senate and in the House of Commons shall from time to time be altered or readjusted in acccordance with the British North America Acts, 1867 to 1946.

6. (1) Until the Parliament of Canada otherwise provides, the Province of Newfoundland shall for the purposes of the election of members to serve in the House of Commons, be divided into the electoral divisions named and delimited in the Schedule to these Terms, and each such division shall be entitled to return one member.

(2) For the first election of members to serve in the House of Commons, if held otherwise than as part of a general election, the Governor General in Council may cause writs to be issued and may fix the day upon which the polls shall be held, and, subject to the foregoing, the laws of Canada relating to by-elections shall apply to an election held pursuant to any writ issued under this Term.

(3) The Chief Electoral Officer shall have authority to adapt the provisions of The Dominion Elections Act, 1938, to conditions existing in the Province of Newfoundland so as to conduct effectually the first election of members to serve in the House of Commons.

PROVINCIAL CONSTITUTION

7. The Constitution of Newfoundland as it existed immediately prior to the sixteenth day of February, 1934, is revived at the date of Union and shall, subject to these Terms and the British North America Acts, 1867 to 1946, continue as the Constitution of the Province of Newfoundland from and after the date of Union, until altered under the authority of the said Acts.

Executive

8. (1) For the Province of Newfoundland there shall be an officer styled the Lieutenant-Governor, appointed by the Governor General in Council by instrument under the Great Seal of Canada.

(2) Pending the first appointment of a Lieutenant-Governor for the Province of Newfoundland and the assumption of his duties as such, the Chief Justice, or if the office of Chief Justice is vacant, the senior judge, of the Supreme Court of Newfoundland, shall execute the office and functions of Lieutenant-Governor under his oath of office as such Chief Justice or senior judge.

9. The Constitution of the Executive Authority of Newfoundland as it existed immediately prior to the sixteenth day of February, 1934, shall, subject to these Terms and the British North America Acts, 1867 to 1946, continue as the Constitution of the Executive Authority of the Province of Newfoundland from and after the date of Union, until altered under the authority of the said Acts.

10. The Lieutenant-Governor in Council shall as soon as may be after the date of Union adopt and provide a Great Seal of the Province of Newfoundland and may from time to time change such seal.

11. All powers, authorities, and functions that under any statute were at or immediately prior to the date of Union vested in or exercisable by the Governor of Newfoundland, individually, or in Council, or in Commission,

(*a*) as far as they are capable of being exercised after the date of Union in relation to the Government of Canada, shall be vested in and shall or may be exercised by the Governor General, with the advice, or with the advice and consent, or in conjunction with, the King's Privy Council for Canada or any member or members thereof, or by the Governor General individually, as the case requires, subject nevertheless to be abolished or altered by the Parliament of Canada under the authority of the British North America Acts, 1867 to 1946; and

(*b*) as far as they are capable of being exercised after the date of Union in relation to the Government of the Province of Newfoundland, shall be vested in and shall or may be exercised by the Lieutenant-Governor of the Province of Newfoundland, with the advice, or with the advice and consent, or in conjunction with, the Executive Council of the Province of Newfoundland or any member or members thereof, or by the Lieutenant-Governor individually, as the case requires, subject nevertheless to be abolished or altered by the Legislature of the Province of Newfoundland under the authority of the British North America Acts, 1867 to 1946.

12. Until the Parliament of Canada otherwise provides, the powers, authorities, and functions vested in or imposed on any member of the Commission of Government of Newfoundland, as such member or as a Commissioner charged with the administration of a Department of the Government of Newfoundland, at or immediately prior to the date of Union in relation to matters other than those coming within the classes of subjects by the British North America Acts, 1867 to 1946, assigned exclusively to the Legislature of a province, shall in the Province of Newfoundland be vested in or imposed on such person or persons as the Governor General in Council may appoint or designate.

13. Until the Legislature of the Province of Newfoundland otherwise provides, the powers, authorities, and functions vested in or imposed on any member of the Commission of Government of Newfoundland, as such member or as a Commissioner charged with the administration of a Department of the

Government of Newfoundland, at or immediately prior to the date of Union in relation to matters coming within the classes of subjects by the British North America Acts, 1867 to 1946, assigned exclusively to the Legislature of a province, shall in the Province of Newfoundland be vested in or imposed on such person or persons as the Lieutenant-Governor in Council may appoint or designate.

Legislature

14. (1) Subject to paragraph two of this Term, the Constitution of the Legislature of Newfoundland as it existed immediately prior to the sixteenth day of February, 1934, shall, subject to these Terms and the British North America Acts, 1867 to 1946, continue as the Constitution of the Legislature of the Province of Newfoundland from and after the date of Union, until altered under the authority of the said Acts.

(2) The Constitution of the Legislature of Newfoundland insofar as it relates to the Legislative Council shall not continue, but the Legislature of the Province of Newfoundland may at any time re-establish the Legislative Council or establish a new Legislative Council.

15. (1) Until the Legislature of the Province of Newfoundland otherwise provides, the powers, authorities, and functions vested in or imposed on a Minister or other public officer or functionary under any statute of Newfoundland relating to the Constitution of the Legislature of Newfoundland as it existed immediately prior to the sixteenth day of February, 1934, shall, subject to these Terms and the British North America Acts, 1867 to 1946, be vested in or imposed on such person or persons as the Lieutenant-Governor in Council may appoint or designate.

(2) Until the Legislature of the Province of Newfoundland otherwise provides,

(*a*) the list of electors prepared pursuant to The List of Electors Act, 1957, shall be deemed to be the list of electors for the purposes of The Election Act, 1913, subject to the provisions of The Election Act, 1913, respecting supplementary lists of electors;

(*b*) the franchise shall be extended to female British subjects who have attained the full age of twenty-one years and are otherwise qualified as electors;

(*c*) the Coast of Labrador together with the islands adjacent thereto shall constitute an additional electoral district to be known as Labrador and to be represented by one member, and residents of the said district who are otherwise qualified as electors shall be entitled to vote; and

(*d*) the Lieutenant-Governor in Council may by proclamation defer any election in the electoral district of Labrador for such period as may be specified in the proclamation.

16. The Legislature of the Province of Newfoundland shall be called together not later than four months after the date of Union.

EDUCATION

17. In lieu of section ninety-three of the British North America Act, 1867, the following Term shall apply in respect of the Province of Newfoundland:

In and for the Province of Newfoundland the Legislature shall have exclusive authority to make laws in relation to education, but the Legislature will not have authority to make laws prejudicially affecting any right or privilege with respect to denominational schools, common (amalgamated) schools, or denominational colleges, that any class or classes of persons have by law in Newfoundland at the date of Union, and out of public funds of the Province of Newfoundland provided for education,

(*a*) all such schools shall receive their share of such funds in accordance with scales determined on a non-discriminatory basis from time to time by the Legislature for all schools then being conducted under authority of the Legislature; and

(*b*) all such colleges shall receive their share of any grant from time to time voted for all colleges then being conducted under authority of the Legislature, such grant being distributed on a non-discriminatory basis.

CONTINUATION OF LAWS

General

18. (1) Subject to these Terms, all laws in force in Newfoundland at or immediately prior to the date of Union shall continue therein as if the Union had not been made, subject nevertheless to be repealed, abolished, or altered by the Parliament of Canada or by the Legislature of the Province of Newfoundland according to the authority of the Parliament or of the Legislature under the British North America Acts, 1867 to 1946, and all orders, rules, and regulations made under any such laws shall likewise continue, subject to be revoked or amended by the body or person that made such orders, rules, or regulations or the body or person that has power to make such orders, rules, or regulations after the date of Union, according to their respective authority under the British North America Acts, 1867 to 1946.

(2) Statues of the Parliament of Canada in force at the date of Union, or any part thereof, shall come into force in the Province of Newfoundland on a day or days to be fixed by Act of the Parliament of Canada or by proclamation of the Governor General in Council issued from time to time, and any such proclamation may provide for the repeal of any of the laws of Newfoundland that

(*a*) are of general application;

(*b*) relate to the same subject matter as the statute or part thereof so proclaimed; and

(*c*) could be repealed by the Parliament of Canada under paragraph one of this Term.

(3) Notwithstanding anything in these Terms, the Parliament of Canada may with the consent of the Legislature of the Province of Newfoundland repeal any law in force in Newfoundland at the date of Union.

(4) Except as otherwise provided by these Terms, all courts of civil and criminal jurisdiction and all legal commissions, powers, authorities, and functions, and all officers and functionaries, judicial, administrative, and ministerial, existing in Newfoundland at or immediately prior to the date of Union, shall continue in the Province of Newfoundland as if the Union had not been made, until altered, abolished, revoked, terminated, or dismissed by the appropriate authority under the British North America Acts, 1867 to 1946.

Supply

19. Any statute of Newfoundland enacted prior to the date of Union for granting to His Majesty sums of money for defraying expenses of, and for other purposes relating to, the public service of Newfoundland, for the financial year ending the thirty-first day of March, one thousand nine hundred and fifty, shall have effect after the date of Union according to its terms, until otherwise provided by the Legislature of the Province of Newfoundland.

Patents

20. (1) Subject to this Term, Canada will provide that letters patent for inventions issued under the laws of Newfoundland prior to the date of Union shall be deemed to have been issued under the laws of Canada, as of the date and for the term thereof.

(2) Canada will provide further that in the event of conflict between letters patent for an invention issued under the laws of Newfoundland prior to the date of Union and letters patent for an invention issued under the laws of Canada prior to the date of Union

(*a*) the letters patent issued under the laws of Newfoundland shall have the same force and effect in the Province of Newfoundland as if the Union had not been made, and all rights and privileges acquired under or by virtue thereof may continue to be exercised or enjoyed in the Province of Newfoundland as if the Union had not been made; and

(*b*) the letters patent issued under the laws of Canada shall have the same force and effect in any part of Canada other than the Province of Newfoundland as if the Union had not been made, and all rights and privileges acquired under or by virtue thereof may continue to be exercised or enjoyed in any part of Canada other than the Province of Newfoundland as if the Union had not been made.

(3) The laws of Newfoundland existing at the date of Union shall continue to apply in respect of applications for the grant of letters patent for inventions under the laws of Newfoundland pending at the date of Union, and any letters patent for inventions issued upon such applications shall, for the purposes of this Term, be deemed to have been issued under the laws of Newfoundland prior to the date of Union; and letters patent for inventions issued under the laws of Canada upon applications pending at the date of Union shall, for the purposes of this Term, be deemed to have been issued under the laws of Canada prior to the date of Union.

(4) Nothing in this Term shall be construed to prevent the Parliament of Canada from providing that no claims for infringement of a paten issued in

Canada prior to the date of Union shall be entertained by any court against any person for anything done in Newfoundland prior to the date of Union in respect of the invention protected by such patent, and that no claims for infringement of a patent issued in Newfoundland prior to the date of Union shall be entertained by any court against any person for anything done in Canada prior to the date of Union in respect of the invention protected by such patent.

Trade Marks

21. (1) Canada will provide that the registration of a trade mark under the laws of Newfoundland prior to the date of Union shall have the same force and effect in the Province of Newfoundland as if the Union had not been made, and all rights and privileges acquired under or by virtue thereof may continue to be exercised or enjoyed in the Province of Newfoundland as if the Union had not been made.

(2) The laws of Newfoundland existing at the date of Union shall continue to apply in respect of applications for the registration of trade marks under the laws of Newfoundland pending at the date of Union and any trade marks registered upon such applications shall, for the purposes of this Term, be deemed to have been registered under the laws of Newfoundland prior to the date of Union.

Fisheries

22. (1) In this Term, the expression 'Fisheries Laws' means the Act No. 11 of 1936, entitled 'An Act for the creation of the Newfoundland Fisheries Board', the Act No. 14 of 1936, entitled 'An Act to Prevent the Export of Fish Without Licence', the Act No. 32 of 1936, entitled 'An Act to Amend the Newfoundland Fisheries Board Act (No. 11 of 1936)', the Act No. 37 of 1938, entitled 'An Act further to Amend the Newfoundland Fisheries Board Act, 1936', the Act No. 10 of 1942, entitled 'An Act Respecting Permits for the Exportation of Salt Fish', the Act No. 39 of 1943, entitled 'An Act Further to Amend the Newfoundland Fisheries Board Act, 1936', the Act No. 16 of 1944, entitled 'An Act Further to Amend the Newfoundland Fisheries Board Acts, 1936–38', and the Act No. 42 of 1944, entitled 'An Act Further to Amend the Newfoundland Fisheries Board Act, 1936', insofar as they relate to the export marketing of salted fish from Newfoundland to other countries or to any provinces of Canada.

(2) Subject to this Term, all Fisheries Laws and all orders, rules, and regulations made thereunder shall continue in force in the Province of Newfoundland as if the Union had not been made, for a period of five years from the date of Union and thereafter until the Parliament of Canada otherwise provides, and shall continue to be administered by the Newfoundland Fisheries Board; and the costs involved in the maintenance of the Board and the administration of the Fisheries Laws shall be borne by the Government of Canada.

(3) The powers, authorities, and functions vested in or imposed on the Governor in Commission or the Commissioner for Natural Resources under any of the Fisheries Laws shall after the date of Union respectively be vested in or imposed on the Governor General in Council and the Minister of Fisheries of Canada or such other Minister as the Governor General in Council may designate.

(4) Any of the Fisheries Laws may be repealed or altered at any time within the period of five years from the date of Union by the Parliament of Canada with the consent of the Lieutenant-Governor in Council of the Province of Newfoundland and all orders, rules, and regulations made under the authority of any Fisheries Laws may be revoked or altered by the body or person that made them or, in relation to matters to which paragraph three of this Term applies, by the body or person that under the said paragraph three has power to make such orders, rules, or regulations under the Fisheries Laws after the date of Union.

(5) The Chairman of the Newfoundland Fisheries Board or such other member of the Newfoundland Fisheries Board as the Governor General in Council may designate shall perform in the Province of Newfoundland the duties of Chief Supervisor and Chief Inspector of the Department of Fisheries of the Government of Canada, and employees of the Newfoundland Fisheries Board shall become employees in that Department in positions comparable to those of the employees in that Department in other parts of Canada.

(6) Terms eleven, twelve, thirteen and eighteen are subject to this Term.

FINANCIAL TERMS

Debt

23. Canada will assume and provide for the servicing and retirement of the stock issued or to be issued on the security of Newfoundland pursuant to The Loan Act, 1933, of Newfoundland and will take over the Sinking Fund established under that Act.

Financial Surplus

24. (1) In this Term the expression 'financial surplus' means the balances standing to the credit of the Newfoundland Exchequer at the date of Union (less such sums as may be required to discharge accounts payable at the date of Union in respect of appropriations for the public services) and any public moneys or public revenue (including loans and advances referred to in Term twenty-five) in respect of any matter, thing, or period prior to the date of Union recovered by the Government of the Province of Newfoundland subsequent to the date of Union.

(2) Newfoundland will retain its financial surplus subject to the following conditions:

(*a*) one-third of the surplus shall be set aside during the first eight years from the date of Union, on deposit with the Government of Canada, to be withdrawn by the Government of the Province of Newfoundland only for expenditures on current account to facilitate the maintenance and improvement of Newfoundland public services, and any portion of this one-third of the surplus remaining unspent at the end of the eight-year period shall become available to the Province of Newfoundland without the foregoing restriction;

(*b*) the remaining two-thirds of the surplus shall be available to the Government of the Province of Newfoundland for the development of resources and for the establishment or extension of public services within the Province of Newfoundland; and (*c*) no part of the surplus shall be used to subsidize the production or sale of products of the Province of Newfoundland in unfair competition with similar products of other provinces of Canada, but nothing in this paragraph shall preclude the Province of Newfoundland from assisting industry by developmental loans on reasonable conditions or by ordinary provincial administrative services.

(3) The Government of the Province of Newfoundland will have the right within one year from the date of Union to deposit with the Government of Canada all or any part of its financial surplus held in dollars and on the thirty-first day of March and the thirtieth day of September in each year to receive with respect thereto interest at the rate of two and five-eighths per centum per annum during a maximum period of ten years from the date of Union on the minimum balance outstanding at any time during the six-month period preceding payment of interest.

Loans

25. (1) The Province of Newfoundland will retain its interest in, and any securities arising from or attaching to, any loans or advances of public funds made by the Government of Newfoundland prior to the date of Union.

(2) Unless otherwise agreed by the Government of Canada, paragraph one of this Term shall not apply to any loans or advances relating to any works, property, or services taken over by Canada pursuant to Term thirty-one or Term thirty-three.

Subsidies

26. Canada will pay to the Province of Newfoundland the following subsidies:

(*a*) an annual subsidy of $180,000 and an annual subsidy equal to 80 cents per head of the population of the Province of Newfoundland (being taken at 325,000 until the first decennial census after the date of Union), subject to be increased to conform to the scale of grants authorized by the British North America Act, 1907, for the local purposes of the Province and the support of its Government and Legislature, but in no year shall sums payable under this paragraph be less than those payable in the first year after the date of Union; and

(*b*) an additional annual subsidy of $1,100,000 payable for the like purposes as the various fixed annual allowances and subsidies provided by statutes of the Parliament of Canada from time to time for the Provinces of Nova Scotia, New Brunswick, and Prince Edward Island or any of them and in recognition of the special problems of the Province of Newfoundland by reason of geography and its sparse and scattered population.

Tax Agreement

27. (1) The Government of Canada will forthwith after the date of Union make an offer to the Government of the Province of Newfoundland to enter into a tax agreement for the rental to the Government of Canada of the income, corporation income, and corporation tax fields, and the succession duties tax field.

(2) The offer to be made under this Term will be similar to the offers to enter into tax agreements made to other provinces, necessary changes being made to

adapt the offer to circumstances arising out of the Union, except that the offer will provide that the agreement may be entered into either for a number of fiscal years expiring at the end of the fiscal year in 1952, as in the case of other provinces, or for a number of fiscal years expiring at the end of the fiscal year in 1957, at the option of the Government of the Province of Newfoundland, but if the Government of the Province of Newfoundland accepts the latter option the agreement will provide that the subsequent entry into a tax agreement by the Government of Canada with any other province will not entitle the Government of the Province of Newfoundland to any alteration in the terms of its agreement.

(3) The offer of the Government of Canada to be made under this Term may be accepted by the Government of the Province of Newfoundland within nine months after the date of the offer but if it is not so accepted will thereupon expire.

(4) The Government of the Province of Newfoundland shall not by any agreement entered into pursuant to this Term be required to impose on any person or corporation taxation repugnant to the provisions of any contract entered into with such person or corporation before the date of the agreement and subsisting at the date of the agreement.

(5) If the Province of Newfoundland enters into a tax agreement pursuant to this Term the subsidies payable under Term twenty-six will, as in the case of similar subsidies to other provinces, be included in the computation of tax agreements payments.

Transitional Grants

28. (1) In order to facilitate the adjustment of Newfoundland to the status of a province of Canada and the development by the Province of Newfoundland of revenue-producing services, Canada will pay to the Province of Newfoundland each year during the first twelve years after the date of Union a transitional grant as follows, payment in each year to be made in equal quarterly instalments commencing on the first day of April, namely,

First year	$6,500,000
Second year	6,500,000
Third year	6,500,000
Fourth year	5,650,000
Fifth year	4,800,000
Sixth year	3,950,000
Seventh year	3,100,000
Eighth year	2,250,000
Ninth year	1,400,000
Tenth year	1,050,000
Eleventh year	700,000
Twelfth year	350,000

(2) The Government of the Province of Newfoundland will have the right to leave on deposit with the Government of Canada any portion of the transitional grant for the first eight years with the right to withdraw all or any portion thereof in any subsequent year and on the thirty-first day of March and the

thirtieth day of September in each year to receive in respect of any amounts so left on deposit interest at the rate of two and five-eighths per centum per annum up to a maximum period of ten years from the date of Union on the minimum balance outstanding at any time during the six-month period preceding payment of interest.

Review of Financial Position

29. In view of the difficulty of predicting with sufficient accuracy the financial consequences to Newfoundland of becoming a province of Canada, the Government of Canada will appoint a Royal Commission within eight years from the date of Union to review the financial position of the Province of Newfoundland and to recommend the form and scale of additional financial assistance, if any, that may be required by the Government of the Province of Newfoundland to enable it to continue public services at the levels and standards reached subsequent to the date of Union, without resorting to taxation more burdensome, having regard to capacity to pay, than that obtaining generally in the region comprising the Maritime Provinces of Nova Scotia, New Brunswick, and Prince Edward Island.

MISCELLANEOUS PROVISIONS

Salaries of Lieutenant-Governor and Judges

30. The salary of the Lieutenant-Governor and the salaries, allowances, and pensions of the judges of such superior, district, and county courts as are now or may hereafter be constituted in the Province of Newfoundland shall be fixed and provided by the Parliament of Canada.

Public Services, Works and Property

31. At the date of Union, or as soon thereafter as practicable, Canada will take over the following services and will as from the date of Union relieve the Province of Newfoundland of the public costs incurred in respect of each service taken over, namely,

(*a*) the Newfoundland Railway, including steamship and other marine services;

(*b*) the Newfoundland Hotel, if requested by the Government of the Province of Newfoundland within six months from the date of Union;

(*c*) postal and publicly-owned telecommunication services;

(*d*) civil aviation, including Gander Airport;

(*e*) customs and excise;

(*f*) defence;

(*g*) protection and encouragement of fisheries and operation of bait services;

(*h*) geographical, topographical, geodetic, and hydrographic surveys;

(*i*) lighthouses, fog alarms, buoys, beacons, and other public works and services in aid of navigation and shipping;

(*j*) marine hospitals, quarantine, and the care of ship-wrecked crews;

(*k*) the public radio broadcasting system; and

(*l*) other public services similar in kind to those provided at the date of Union for the people of Canada generally.

32. (1) Canada will maintain in accordance with the traffic offering a freight and passenger steamship service between North Sydney and Port aux Basques, which, on completion of a motor highway between Corner Brook and Port aux Basques, will include suitable provision for the carriage of motor vehicles.

(2) For the purpose of railway rate regulation the Island of Newfoundland will be included in the Maritime region of Canada, and through-traffic moving between North Sydney and Port aux Basques will be treated as all-rail traffic.

(3) All legislation of the Parliament of Canada providing for special rates on traffic moving within, into, or out of, the Maritime region will, as far as appropriate, be made applicable to the Island of Newfoundland.

33. The following public works and property of Newfoundland shall become the property of Canada when the service concerned is taken over by Canada, subject to any trusts existing in respect thereof, and to any interest other than that of Newfoundland in the same, namely,

(*a*) the Newfoundland Railway, including rights of way, wharves, drydocks, and other real property, rolling stock, equipment, ships, and other personal property;

(*b*) the Newfoundland Airport at Gander, including buildings and equipment, together with any other property used for the operation of the Airport;

(*c*) the Newfoundland Hotel and equipment;

(*d*) public harbours, wharves, break-waters, and aids to navigation;

(*e*) bait depots and the motor vessel Malakoff;

(*f*) military and naval property, stores, and equipment;

(*g*) public dredges and vessels except those used for services that remain the responsibility of Newfoundland and except the nine motor vessels known as the Clarenville boats;

(*h*) the public telecommunication system, including rights of way, land lines, cables, telephones, radio stations, and other real and personal property;

(*i*) real and personal property of the Broadcasting Corporation of Newfoundland; and

(*j*) subject to the provisions of Term thirty-four, customs houses, and post-offices and generally all public works and property, real and personal, used primarily for services taken over by Canada.

34. Where at the date of Union any public buildings of Newfoundland included in paragraph (*j*) of Term thirty-three are used partly for services taken over by Canada and partly for services of the Province of Newfoundland the following provisions shall apply:

(*a*) where more than half the floor space of a building is used for services taken over by Canada the building shall become the property of Canada and where more than half the floor space of a building is used for services of the Province of Newfoundland the building shall remain the property of the Province of Newfoundland;

(*b*) Canada shall be entitled to rent from the Province of Newfoundland on terms to be mutually agreed such space in the buildings owned by the Province of Newfoundland as is used for the services taken over by Canada, and the Province of Newfoundland shall be entitled to rent from Canada on terms to be mutually agreed such space in the buildings owned by Canada as is used for the services of the Province of Newfoundland;

(*c*) the division of buildings for the purposes of this Term shall be made by agreement between the Government of Canada and the Government of the Province of Newfoundland as soon as practicable after the date of Union; and

(*d*) if the division in accordance with the foregoing provisions results in either Canada or the Province of Newfoundland having a total ownership that is substantially out of proportion to the total floor space used for its services an adjustment of the division will be made by mutual agreement between the two Governments.

35. Newfoundland public works and property not transferred to Canada by or under these Terms will remain the property of the Province of Newfoundland.

36. Without prejudice to the legislative authority of the Parliament of Canada under the British North America Acts, 1867 to 1946, any works, property, or services taken over by Canada pursuant to these Terms shall thereupon be subject to the legislative authority of the Parliament of Canada.

Natural Resources

37. All lands, mines, minerals, and royalties belonging to Newfoundland at the date of Union, and all sums then due or payable for such lands, mines, minerals, or royalties, shall belong to the Province of Newfoundland, subject to any trusts existing in respect thereof, and to any interest other than that of the Province in the same.

Veterans

38. Canada will make available to Newfoundland veterans the following benefits, on the same basis as they are from time to time available to Canadian veterans, as if the Newfoundland veterans had served in His Majesty's Canadian forces, namely,

(*a*) The War Veterans' Allowance Act, 1946, free hospitalization and treatment, and civil service preference will be extended to Newfoundland veterans who served in the First World War or the Second World War or both;

(*b*) Canada will assume as from the date of Union the Newfoundland pension liability in respect of the First World War, and in respect of the Second World War Canada will assume as from the date of Union the cost of supplementing disability and dependants' pensions paid by the Government of the United Kingdom or an Allied country to Newfoundland veterans up to the level of the Canadian rates of pensions, and, in addition, Canada will pay pensions arising from disabilities that are pensionable under Canadian law but not pensionable either under the laws of the United Kingdom or under the laws of an Allied country;

(*c*) The Veterans' Land Act, 1942, Part IV of the Unemployment Insurance Act, 1940, The Veterans' Business and Professional Loans Act, and The Veterans' Insurance Act will be extended to Newfoundland veterans who served in the Second World War;

(*d*) a re-establishment credit will be made available to Newfoundland veterans who served in the Second World War equal to the reestablishment credit that might have been made available to them under The War Service Grants Act, 1944, if their service in the Second World War had been service in the Canadian forces, less the amount of any pecuniary benefits of the same nature granted or paid by the Government of any country other than Canada;

(*e*) Canada will assume, as from the date of Union, the cost of vocational and educational training of Newfoundland veterans of the Second World War on the same basis as if they had served in His Majesty's Canadian forces; and

(*f*) sections six, seven, and eight of The Veterans' Rehabilitation Act will be extended to Newfoundland veterans of the Second World War who have not received similar benefits from the Government of any country other than Canada.

Public Servants

39. (1) Employees of the Government of Newfoundland in the services taken over by Canada pursuant to these Terms will be offered employment in these services or in similar Canadian services under the terms and conditions from time to time governing employment in those services, but without reduction in salary or loss of pension rights acquired by reason of service in Newfoundland.

(2) Canada will provide the pensions for such employees so that the employees will not be prejudiced, and the Government of the Province of Newfoundland will reimburse Canada for the pensions for, or at its option make to Canada contributions in respect of, the service of these employees with the Government of Newfoundland prior to the date of Union, but these payments or contributions will be such that the burden on the Government of the Province of Newfoundland in respect of pension rights acquired by reason of service in Newfoundland will not be increased by reason of the transfer.

(3) Pensions of employees of the Government of Newfoundland who were retired on pension before the service concerned is taken over by Canada will remain the responsibility of the Province of Newfoundland.

Welfare and Other Public Services

40. Subject to these Terms, Canada will extend to the Province of Newfoundland, on the same basis and subject to the same terms and conditions as in the case of other provinces of Canada, the welfare and other public services provided from time to time by Canada for the people of Canada generally, which, in addition to the veterans' benefits, unemployment insurance benefits, and merchant seamen benefits set out in Terms thirty-eight, forty-one, and forty-two respectively, include family allowances under The Family Allowances Act, 1944, unemployment insurance under The Unemployment Insurance Act, 1940, sick mariners' benefits for merchant seamen and fishermen under the Canada Shipping Act, 1934, assistance for housing under The National Housing Act, 1944, and, subject to the Province of Newfoundland entering into the necessary agreements or making the necessary contributions, financial assistance under The National Physical Fitness Act for carrying out plans of physical fitness, health grants, and contributions under the Old Age Pensions Act for old age pensions and pensions for the blind.

Unemployment Insurance

41. (1) Subject to this Term, Canada will provide that residents of the Province of Newfoundland in insurable employment who lose their employment within six months prior to the date of Union and are still unemployed at that date, or who lose their employment within a two-year period after that date, will be entitled for a period of six months from the date of Union or six months from the date of unemployment, whichever is the later, to assistance on the same scale and under the same conditions as unemployment insurance benefits.

(2) The rates of payment will be based on the individual's wage record for the three months preceding his loss of employment, and to qualify for assistance a person must have been employed in insurable employment for at least thirty per centum of the working days within the period of three months preceding his loss of employment or thirty per centum of the working days within the period since the date of Union, whichever period is the longer.

Merchant Seamen

42. (1) Canada will make available to Newfoundland merchant seamen who served in the Second World War on British ships or on ships of Allied countries employed in service essential to the prosecution of the war, the following benefits, on the same basis as they are from time to time available to Canadian merchant seamen, as if they had served on Canadian ships, namely,

(*a*) disability and dependants' pensions will be paid, if disability occurred as a result of enemy action or counter-action, including extraordinary marine hazards occasioned by the war, and a Newfoundland merchant seaman in receipt of a pension from the Government of the United Kingdom or an Allied country will be entitled, during residence in Canada, to have his pension raised to the Canadian level; and

(*b*) free hospitalization and treatment, vocational training, The Veterans' Land Act, 1942, and The Veterans' Insurance Act will be extended to disability pensioners.

(2) Vocational training, Part IV of The Unemployment Insurance Act, 1940, and The Veterans' Insurance Act will be extended to Newfoundland merchant seamen who were eligible for a Special Bonus or a War Service Bonus, on the same basis as if they were Canadian merchant seamen.

(3) The Unemployment Insurance Act, 1940, and The Merchant Seamen Compensation Act will be applied to Newfoundland merchant seamen as they are applied to other Canadian merchant seamen.

Citizenship

43. Suitable provision will be made for the extension of the Canadian citizenship laws to the Province of Newfoundland.

Defence Establishments

44. Canada will provide for the maintenance in the Province of Newfoundland of appropriate reserve units of the Canadian defence forces, which will include the Newfoundland Regiment.

Economic Survey

45. (1) Should the Government of the Province of Newfoundland institute an economic survey of the Province of Newfoundland with a view to determining what resources may profitably be developed and what new industries may be established or existing industries expanded, the Government of Canada will make available the services of its technical employees and agencies to assist in the work.

(2) As soon as may be practicable after the date of Union, the Government of Canada will make a special effort to collect and make available statistical and scientific data about the natural resources and economy of the Province of Newfoundland, in order to bring such information up to the standard attained for the other provinces of Canada.

Oleomargarine

46. (1) Oleomargarine or margarine may be manufactured or sold in the Province of Newfoundland after the date of the Union and the Parliament of Canada shall not prohibit or restrict such manufacture or sale except at the request of the Legislature of the Province of Newfoundland, but nothing in this Term shall affect the power of the Parliament of Canada to require compliance with standards of quality applicable throughout Canada.

(2) Unless the Parliament of Canada otherwise provides or unless the sale and manufacture in, and the interprovincial movement between, all provinces of Canada other than Newfoundland, of oleomargarine and margarine, is lawful under the laws of Canada, oleomargarine or margarine shall not be sent, shipped, brought, or carried from the Province of Newfoundland into any other province of Canada.

Income Taxes

47. In order to assist in the transition to payment of income tax on a current basis Canada will provide in respect of persons (including corporations) resident in Newfoundland at the date of Union, who were not resident in Canada in 1949 prior to the date of Union, and in respect of income that under the laws of Canada in force immediately prior to the date of Union was not liable to taxation, as follows:

(*a*) that prior to the first day of July, 1949, no payment will be required or deduction made from such income on account of income tax;

(*b*) that for income tax purposes no person shall be required to report such income for any period prior to the date of Union;

(*c*) that no person shall be liable to Canada for income tax in respect of such income for any period prior to the date of Union; and

(*d*) that for individuals an amount of income tax for the 1949 taxation year on income for the period after the date of Union shall be forgiven so that the tax on all earned income and on investment income of not more than $2,250 will be reduced to one-half the tax that would have been payable for the whole year if the income for the period prior to the date of Union were at the same rate as that subsequent to such date.

Statute of Westminster

48. From and after the date of Union the Statute of Westminster, 1931, shall apply to the Province of Newfoundland as it applies to the other Provinces of Canada.

Saving

49. Nothing in these Terms shall be construed as relieving any person from any obligation with respect to the employment of Newfoundland labour incurred or assumed in return for any concession or privilege granted or conferred by the Government of Newfoundland prior to the date of Union.

Coming into Force

50. These Terms are agreed to subject to their being approved by the Parliament of Canada and the Government of Newfoundland; shall take effect notwithstanding the Newfoundland Act, 1933, or any instrument issued pursuant thereto; and shall come into force immediately before the expiration of the thirty-first day of March, 1949, if His Majesty has theretofore given His Assent to an Act of the Parliament of the United Kingdom of Great Britain and Northern Ireland confirming the same.

Signed in duplicate at Ottawa this eleventh day of December, 1948.

On behalf of Canada:

LOUIS S. ST LAURENT
BROOKE CLAXTON

On behalf of Newfoundland:

ALBERT J. WALSH
F. GORDON BRADLEY
PHILIP GRUCHY
JOHN B. MCEVOY
JOSEPH R. SMALLWOOD
G. A. WINTER

SCHEDULE

In this Schedule the expression 'District' means District as named and delimited in the Act 22 George V Chapter 7 entitled 'An Act to amend Chapter 2 of the Consolidated Statutes of Newfoundland (Third Series) entitled "Of the House of Assembly".'

Grand Falls–White Bay shall consist of the Districts of White Bay, Green Bay and Grand Falls, and all the territory within a radius of five miles of the Railway Station at Gander, together with the Coast of Labrador and the Islands adjacent thereto.

Bonavista–Twillingate shall consist of the Districts of Twillingate, Fogo, Bonavista North, and Bonavista South, but shall not include any part of the territory within a radius of five miles from the Railway Station at Gander.

Trinity–Conception shall consist of the Districts of Trinity North, Trinity South, Carbonear–Bay de Verde, Harbour Grace, and Port de Grave.

St John's East shall consist of the District of Harbour Main–Bell Island and that part of the Province bounded as follows, that is to say: By a line commencing at a point where the centre line of Beck's Cove Hill intersects the North shore of the Harbour of St John's, thence following the centre line of Beck's Cove Hill to the centre of Duckworth Street, thence westerly along the centre line of Duckworth Street to the centre of Theatre Hill, thence following the centre line of Theatre Hill to the centre of Carter's Hill, thence following the centre line of Carter's Hill and Carter's Street to the centre of Freshwater Road, thence following the centre line of Freshwater Road to its intersection with the centre of Kenmount Road, and thence along the centre line of Kenmount Road to its intersection with the North Eastern boundary of the District of Harbour Main–Bell Island, thence along the said North Eastern boundary of the District of Harbour Main–Bell Island to the shore of Conception Bay and thence following the coastline around Cape St Francis and on to the Narrows of St John's Harbour and continuing along by the North Shore of St John's Harbour to a point on the North Shore of the said Harbour intersected by the centre line of Beck's Cove Hill, the point of commencement.

St John's West shall consist of the Districts of Placentia–St Mary's and Ferryland, and that part of the Province bounded as follows, that is to say: By a line commencing at the Motion Head of Petty Harbour and running in a straight line to the Northern Goulds Bridge (locally known as Doyle's Bridge) thence following the centre line of Doyle's Road to Short's Road, thence in a straight line to a point one mile west of Quigley's, thence in a straight line to the point where the North Eastern boundary of the District of Harbour Main–Bell Island intersects Kenmount Road, thence along the centre line of Kenmount Road and Freshwater Road to Carter's Street, thence down the centre line of Carter's Street and Carter's Hill to Theatre Hill and thence along the centre line of said Theatre Hill to the centre line of Duckworth Street and thence easterly along the centre line of Duckworth Street to the top of Beck's Cove Hill, thence from the centre line of said Beck's Cove Hill, to the shore of St John's Harbour and thence following the shore of St John's Harbour and, passing through the Narrows by the North of Fort Amherst and thence following the coastline Southerly to the Motion Head of Petty Harbour, the point of commencement.

Burin–Burgeo shall consist of the Districts of Placentia West, Burin, Fortune Bay–Hermitage, and Burgeo and LaPoile and all the unorganized territory bounded on the North and West by the Districts of Grand Falls, on the South by the Districts of Burgeo and LaPoile and Fortune Bay–Hermitage, on the East by the Districts of Trinity North, Bonavista South and Bonavista North.

Humber–St George's shall consist of the Districts of St George's–Port au Port, Humber, and St Barbe, and all the unorganized territory bounded on the North by the District of Humber, on the East by the District of Grand Falls, on the South by the District of Burgeo and LaPoile, and on the West by the District of St George's-Port au Port.

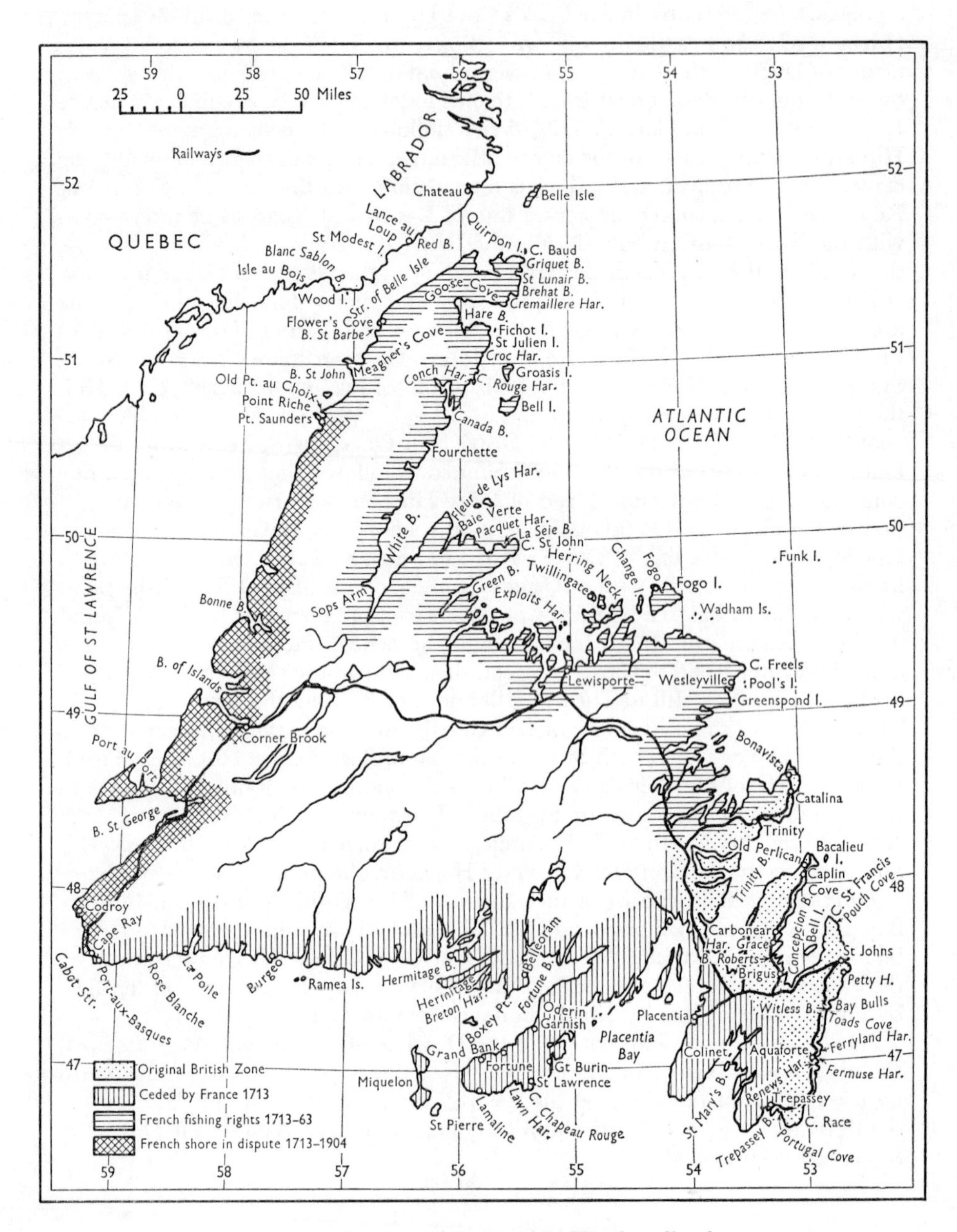

Map 1. France and England in Newfoundland.

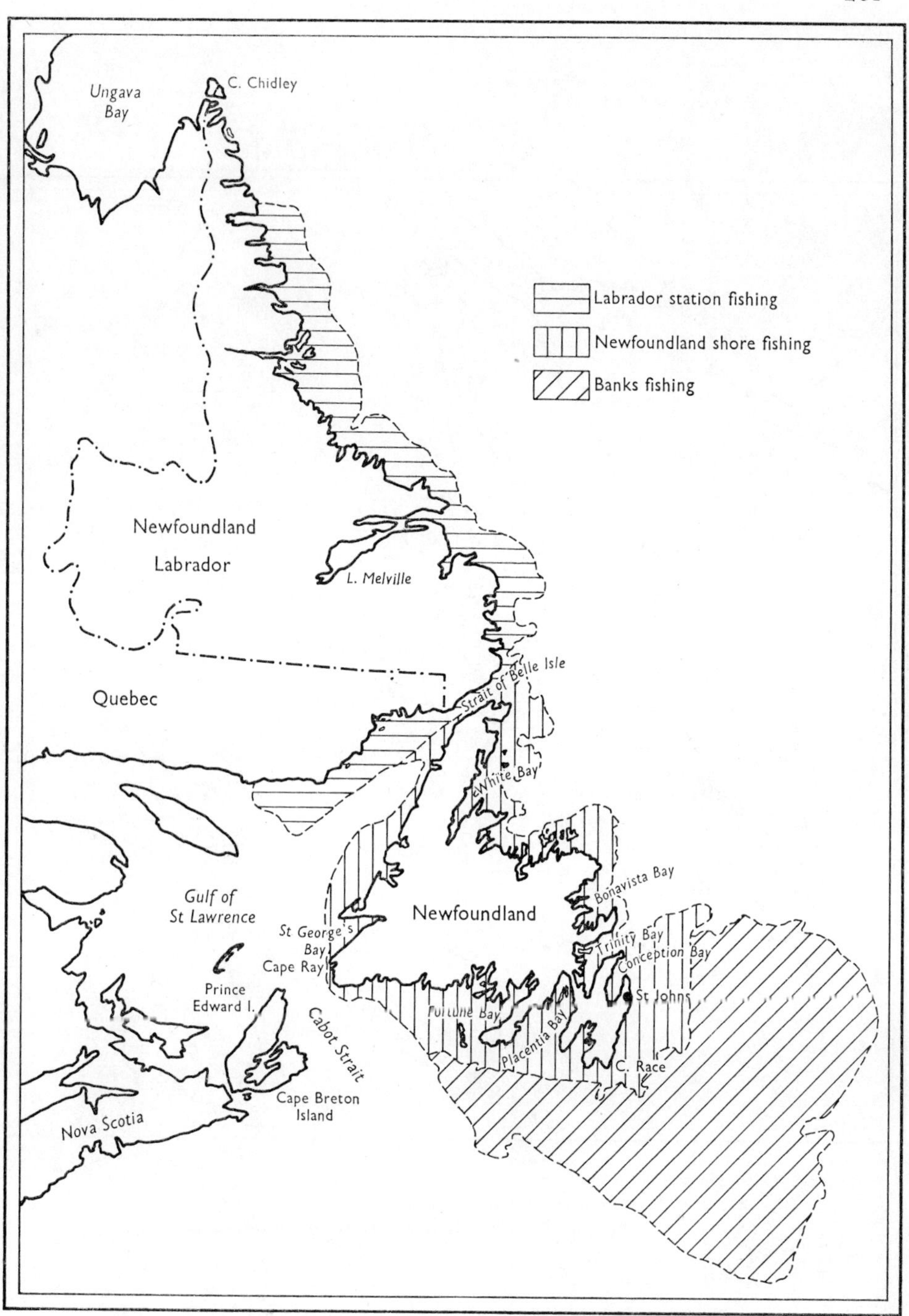

Map 2. Newfoundland and Labrador. Fishing areas.

Map 3. Newfoundland. Main railway routes.

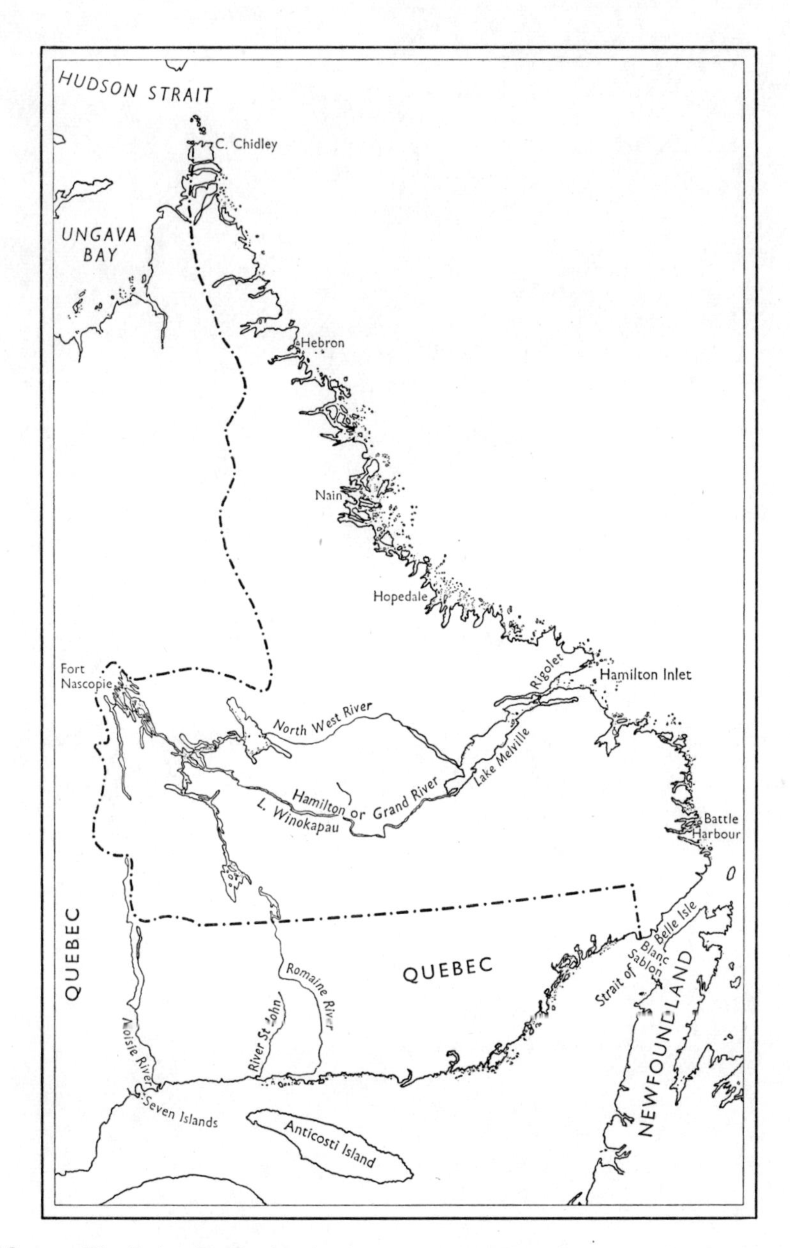

Map 4. The Labrador Peninsula showing the Newfoundland-Quebec boundary as defined by the Privy Council in 1926.

INDEX